IMAGES
of America

BILL TAGUE'S BERKSHIRES
VOLUME II

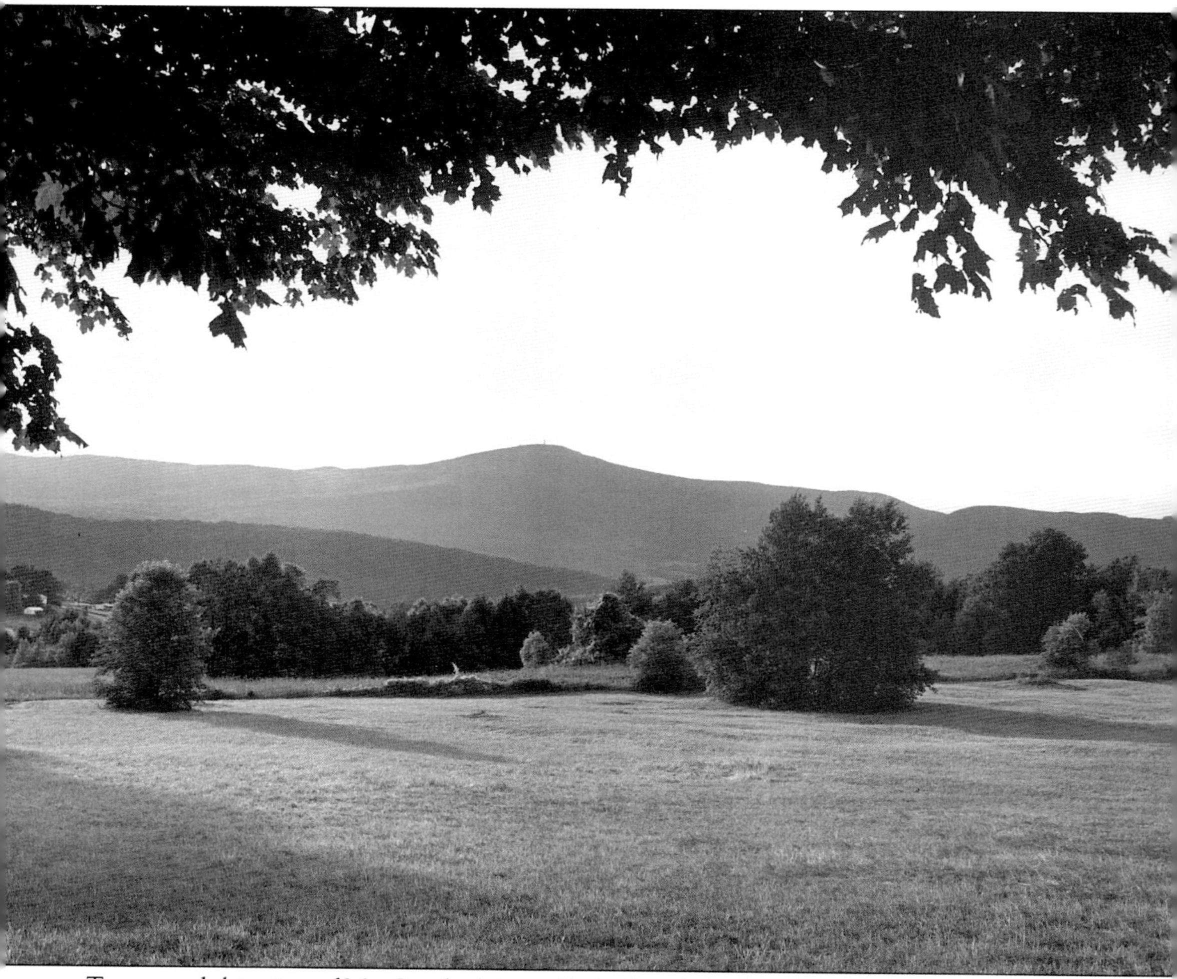

Tague used this view of Mt. Greylock in an Eagle Eye photo layout December 29, 1979, to sum up the decade of the 1970s with the caption: "Upheavals and changes in the economy, human behavior, relations among nations, came and went during the decade of the 1970s but the landscape and quality of life in the Berkshires remained essentially stable, as suggested by a 1976 view of Greylock from Wells Road in Cheshire . . . "

ON THE COVER: Photographer Bill Tague's son Timothy, age one, appears in a 1955 photograph taken in the dandelion-carpeted Tyringham Valley of the southern Berkshires. Said Bill's Eagle Eye caption: "Timothy Tague is not trying to pick them all. He wants only a few to eat."

IMAGES
of America

BILL TAGUE'S BERKSHIRES VOLUME II

Tyler Resch

ARCADIA
PUBLISHING

ISBN 978-0-7385-6386-2

Published by Arcadia Publishing
Charleston, South Carolina

Printed in the United States of America

For all general information contact Arcadia Publishing at:
Telephone 843-853-2070
Fax 843-853-0044
E-mail sales@arcadiapublishing.com
For customer service and orders:
Toll-Free 1-888-313-2665

Visit us on the Internet at www.arcadiapublishing.com

When caption material in this book appears in quotation marks, it is quoting directly from the photo's caption in one of Tague's original weekly "Eagle Eye" layouts in *The Berkshire Eagle*.

Dedicated to the children of Bill and Irene Tague:
Timothy, Peter, and Susan.

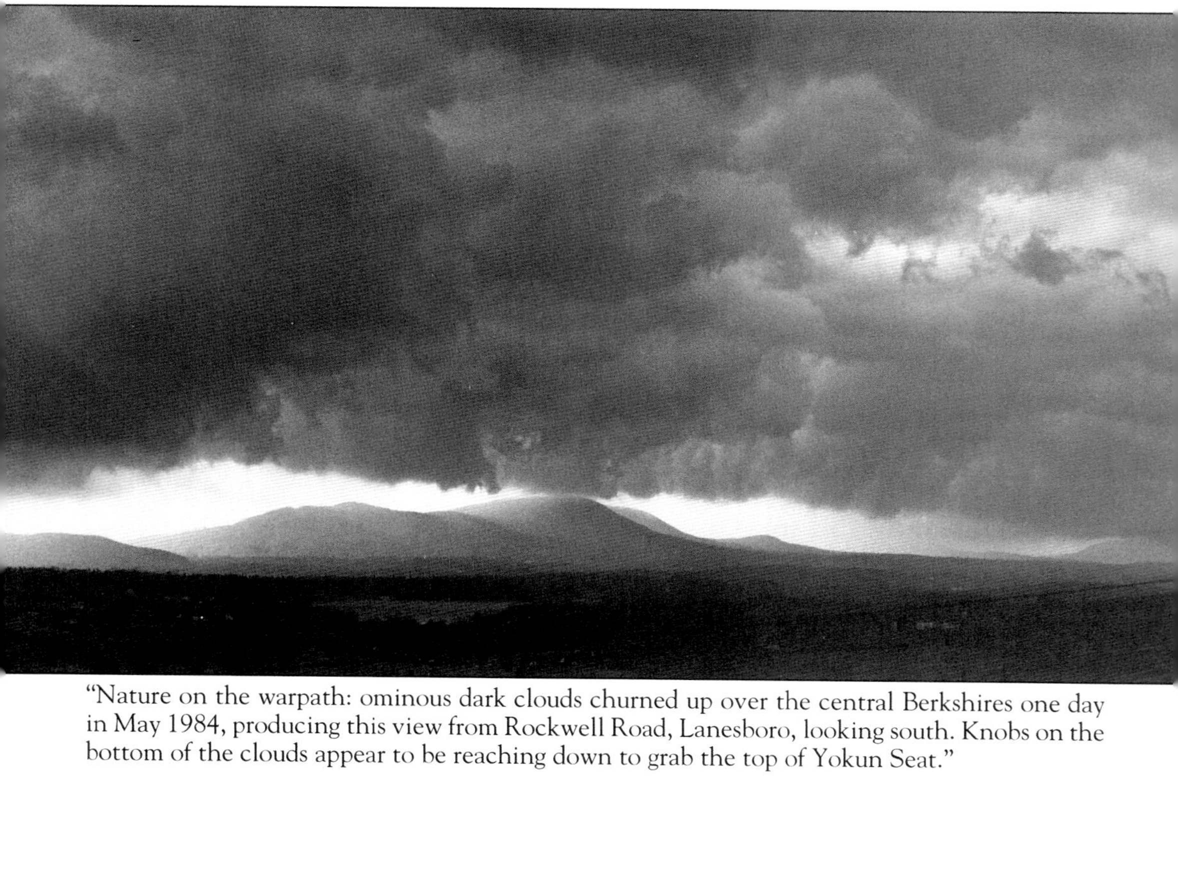

"Nature on the warpath: ominous dark clouds churned up over the central Berkshires one day in May 1984, producing this view from Rockwell Road, Lanesboro, looking south. Knobs on the bottom of the clouds appear to be reaching down to grab the top of Yokun Seat."

Contents

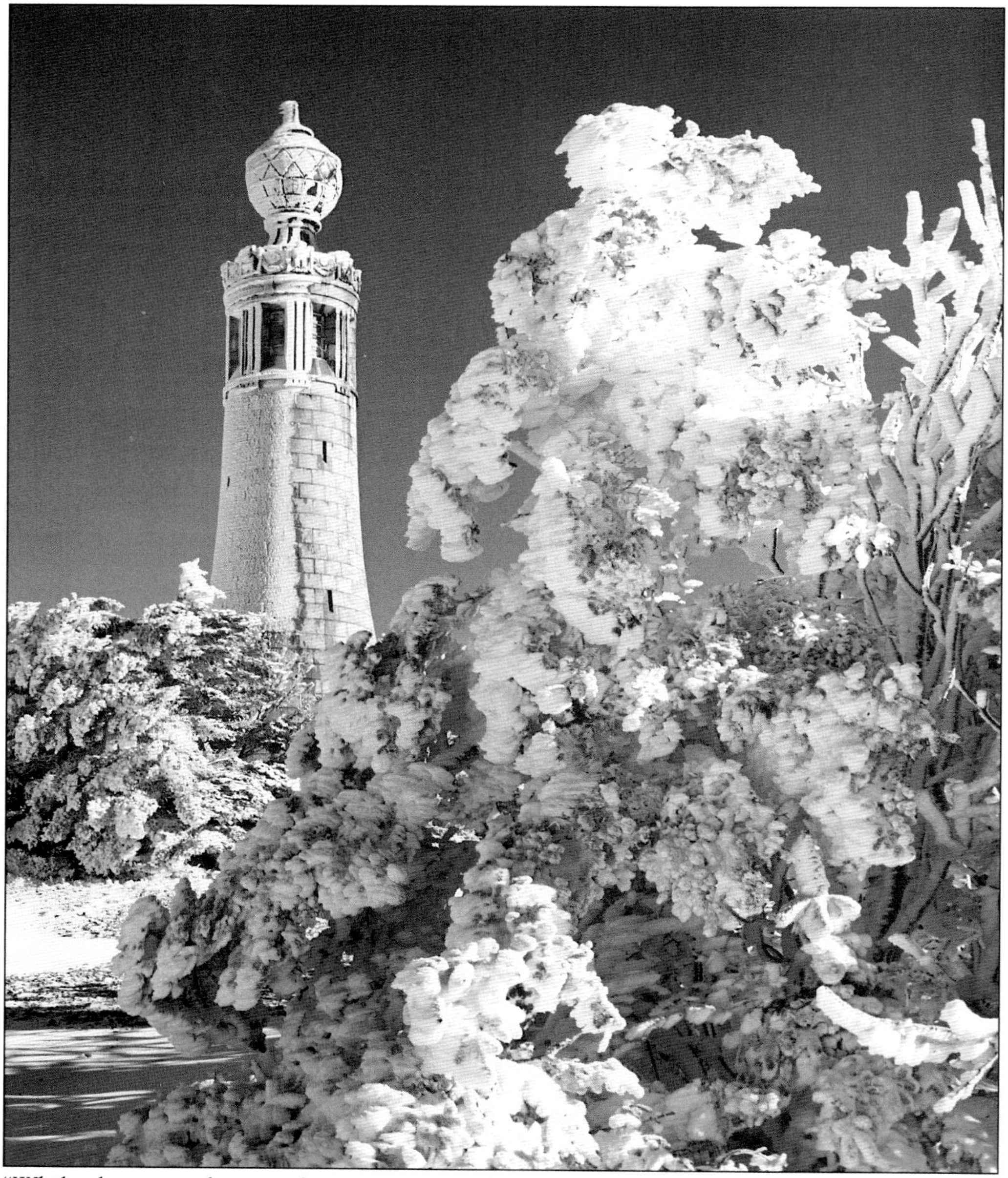

"While the warm fingers of spring were gradually caressing the lower Berkshires this week, the summit of Mount Greylock was still flamboyantly frozen in the grip of winter" —April 2, 1983.

Bill Tague's Legacy

People who knew Bill Tague well weren't surprised when he chose a site at the foothills of Mount Greylock to build his new home. Bill not only loved the mountain dearly but fought vigorously to preserve its dignity when it was threatened by what he and many others considered undesirable commercial development.

Fortunately for Bill, his beloved wife, Irene, was in full agreement, and it was here that they raised their family, two sons and a daughter, and where in the darkroom studio he built himself, including the plumbing, he turned out many of his Eagle Eye photos which grace the pages of this second volume of his works.

Works? Yes, although this self-taught photographer greatly enjoyed finding appealing and unusual subjects for his lens, creating his weekly Eagle Eye for *The Berkshire Eagle* wasn't an easy task. Unlike regular staff photographers on that newspaper, he had other daily duties to perform, mostly as a news reporter. For many years he covered the police and fire stations and daily sessions of the district court, establishing a reputation with court officials, lawyers, and others for the accuracy and documentation of his reports.

In 1982 he won a New England award from United Press International for a series of articles on teen drinking.

Bill wrote the captions for his Eagle Eye pictures, captions that were almost as eye-catching as the photos themselves. Thomas O. Morton, a retired managing editor of *The Eagle*, praised the captions, saying they were so effective that "we adopted Bill's style for all of our pictures."

Snow Country magazine, considered tops in its field nationally, devoted six pages in its December 1997 issue of 223 pages to a feature on Tague by David Rothman, illustrated with 13 Eagle Eye snow pictures.

Rothman, of Crested Butte, Colorado, who knew Tague from skiing in the Berkshires, said that Bill "lived with a camera in his hands. His photographic work touches on every aspect of life in the Berkshires, from the towns to the mountains, from childhood to old age. His pictures portray an American past that is simultaneously real and idyllic. In fact, Tague's work is often likened to the paintings of another Berkshire artist, Norman Rockwell."

Some people said that Bill could be gruff and called him a curmudgeon. So what? One thing is for sure—he wasn't a hypocrite. Like an umpire, he called them as he saw them. He said what he thought, not necessarily what he thought others would like to hear. He never would have qualified for the U.S. Diplomatic Corps.

But there was a gentle side of this man, reflected in his love of beauty as evident in so many of his pictures. This is Bill Tague's legacy. Need more be said?

—Ted Giddings
(retired city editor, *The Berkshire Eagle*)

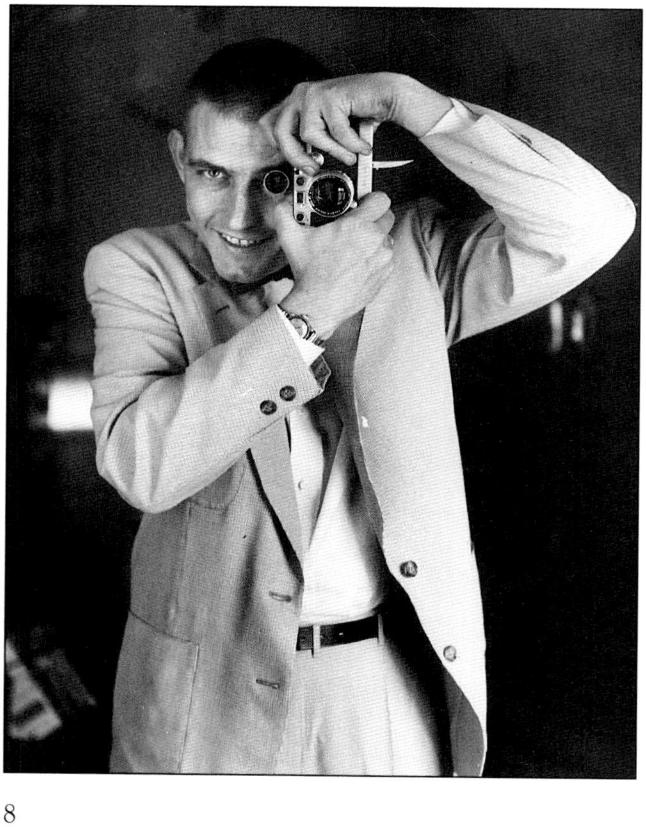

Photographer William H. Tague when Eagle Eye began, January 26, 1952. Tague published the weekly picture page in the daily *Berkshire Eagle* of Pittsfield, Massachusetts, until his death in November 1990.

One

Mountainous Backgrounds

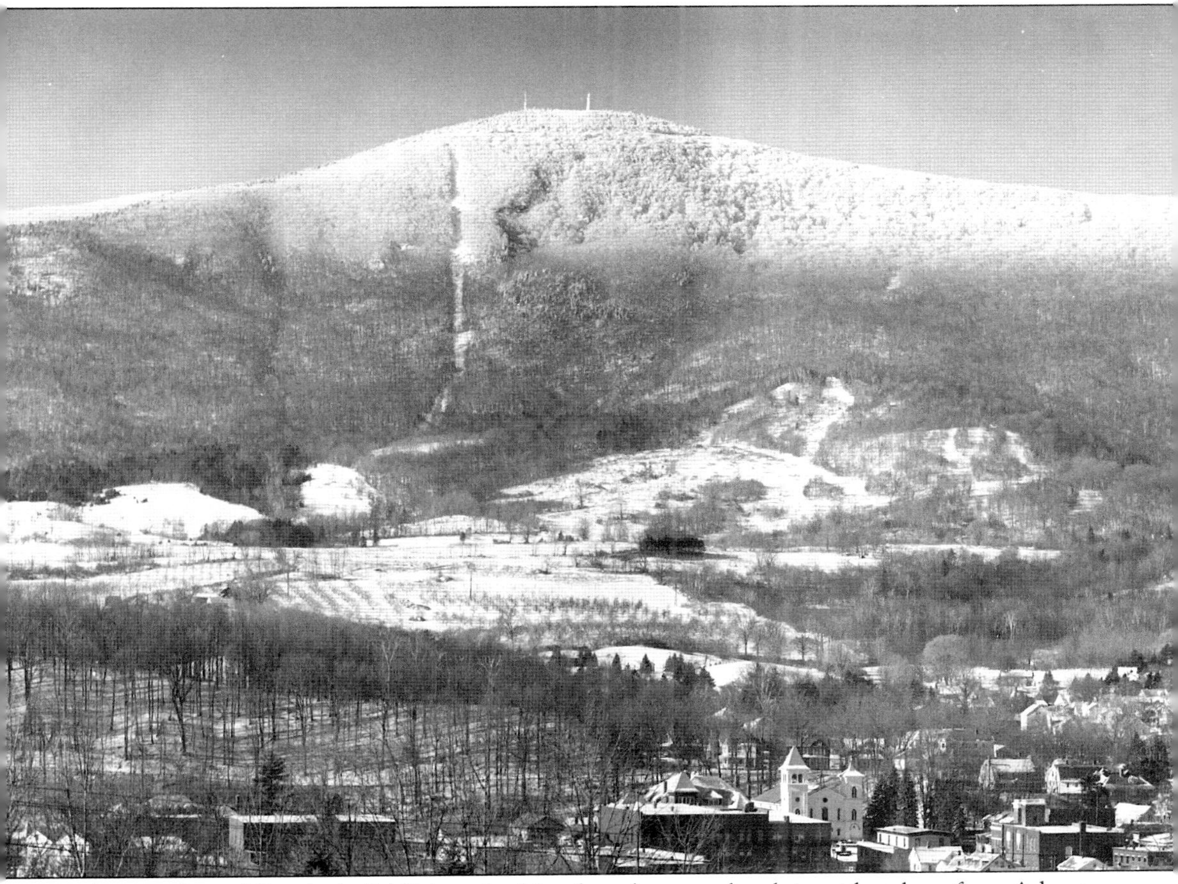

The grandeur of Greylock, 3,491 breathtaking feet above sea level, is evident here from Adams. "There are many higher mountains in the States, but none has the graceful, softly rolling, uniquely undulating, almost sensuous curves of our lovely hills."

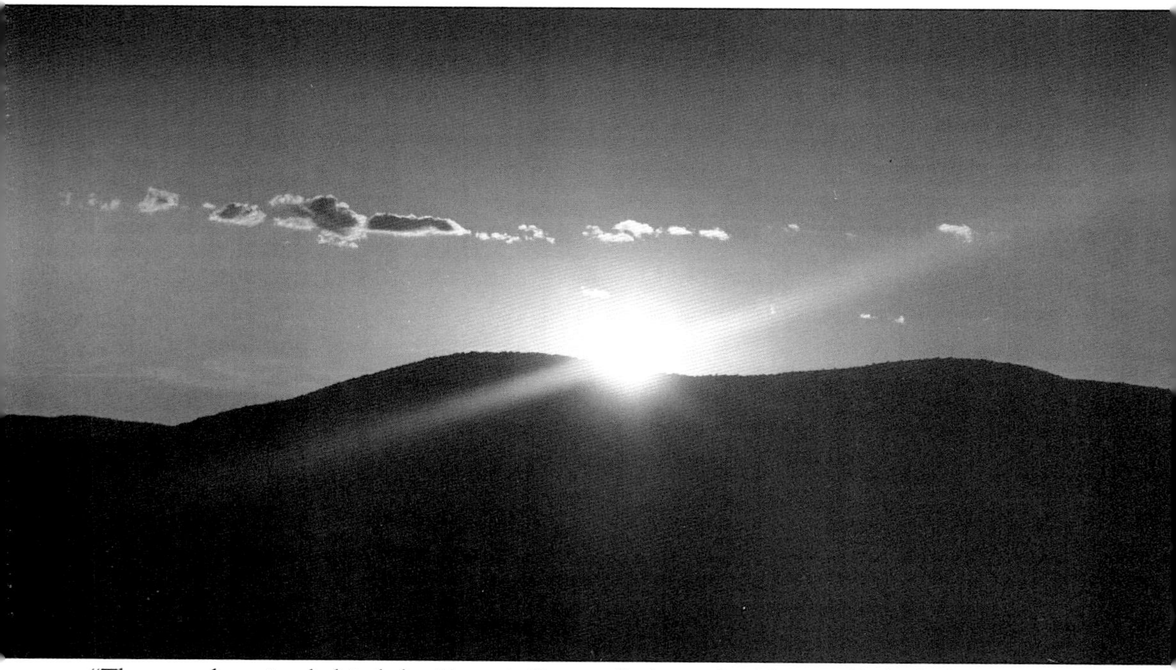

"The sun, dropping behind the Taconic Range, flashes a final burst of light before retiring for the night."

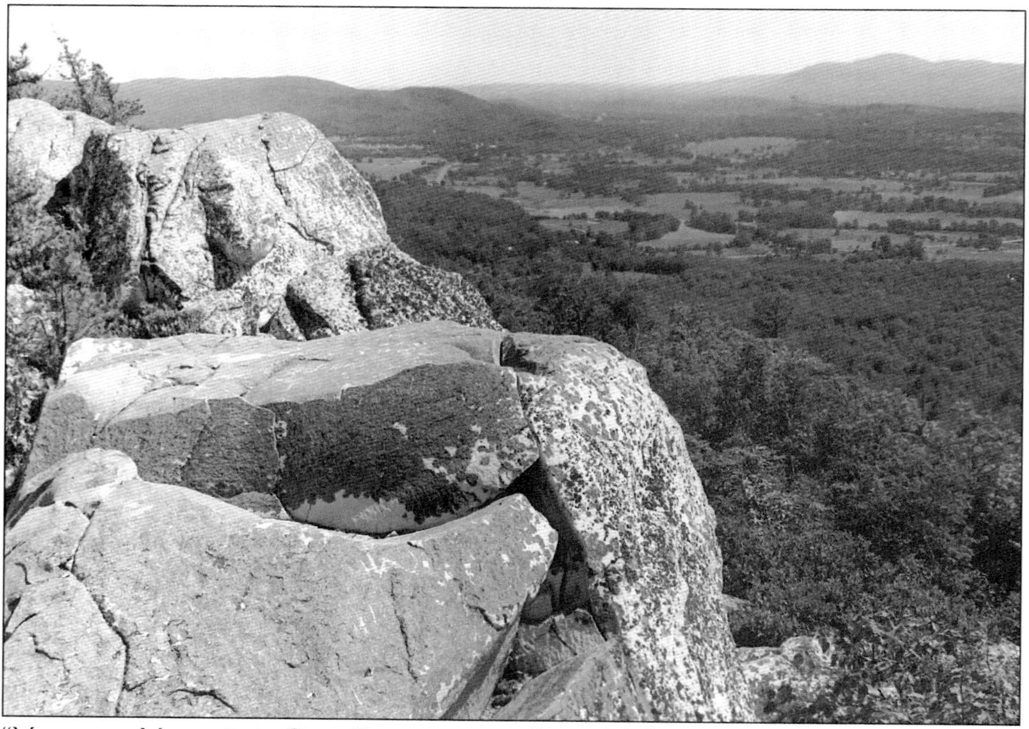

"Monument Mountain in Great Barrington, popular with hikers, inspired a poem by that name by William Cullen Bryant, who practiced law and was married there."

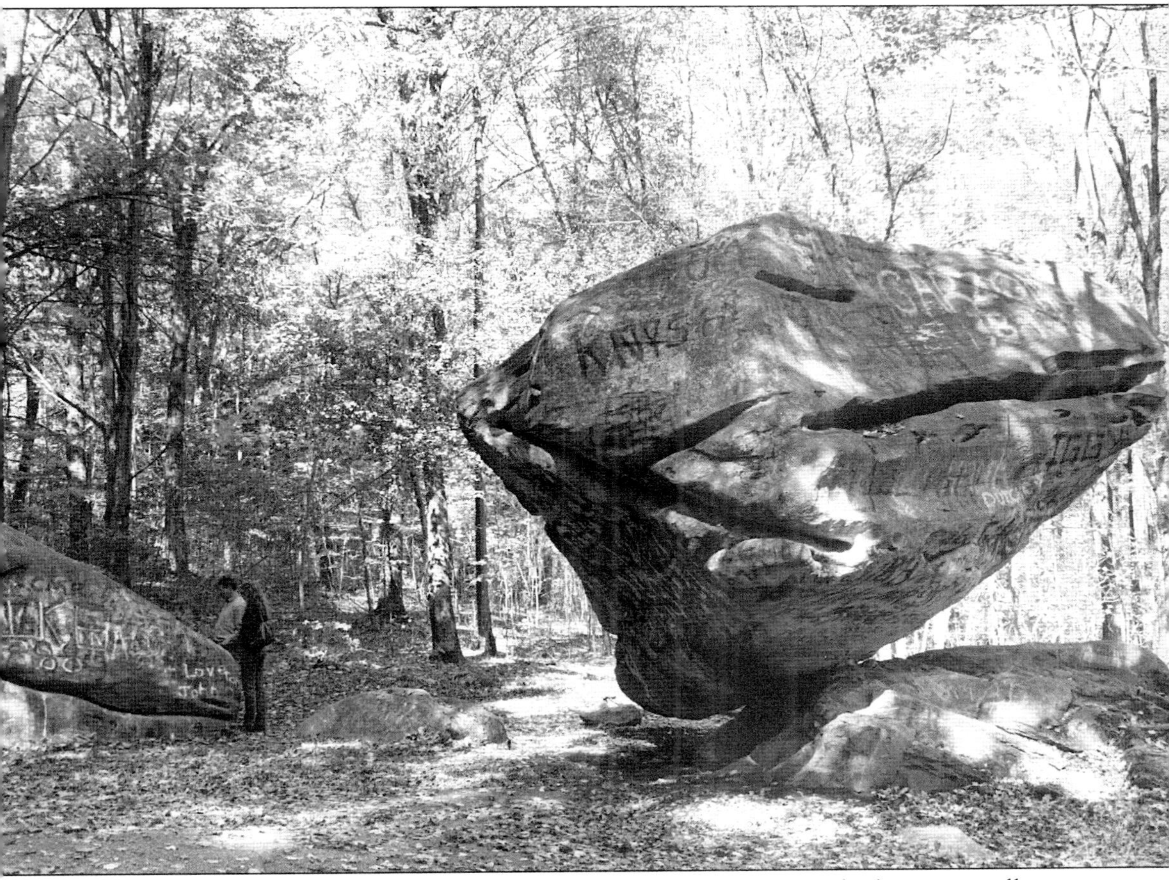

Balance Rock in the town of Lanesboro has long been a trysting spot for lovers as well as an attraction for graffiti carvers and vandals. But the behemoth has defied the efforts of most everyone to upend this famous chunk of mountain, which weighs thousands of tons.

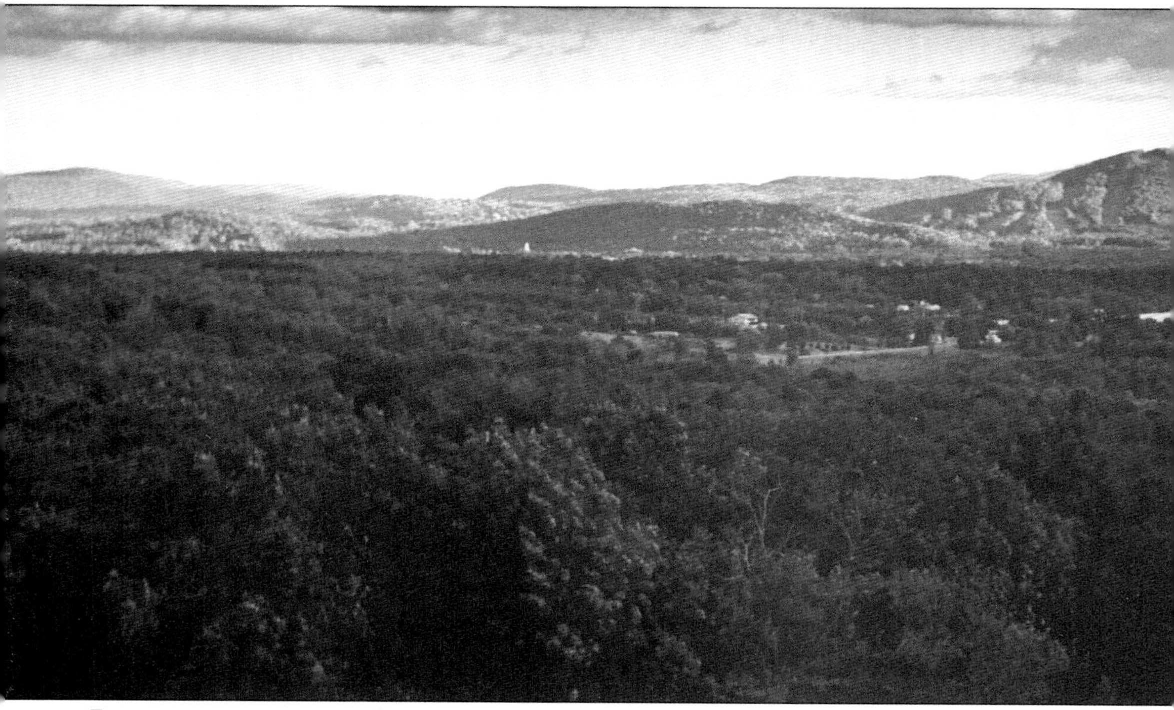

From two vantage points, the mountain splendors of the Berkshires are captured on film: above, from Lanesboro looking south; below, from the high point of Partridge Road in Pittsfield looking

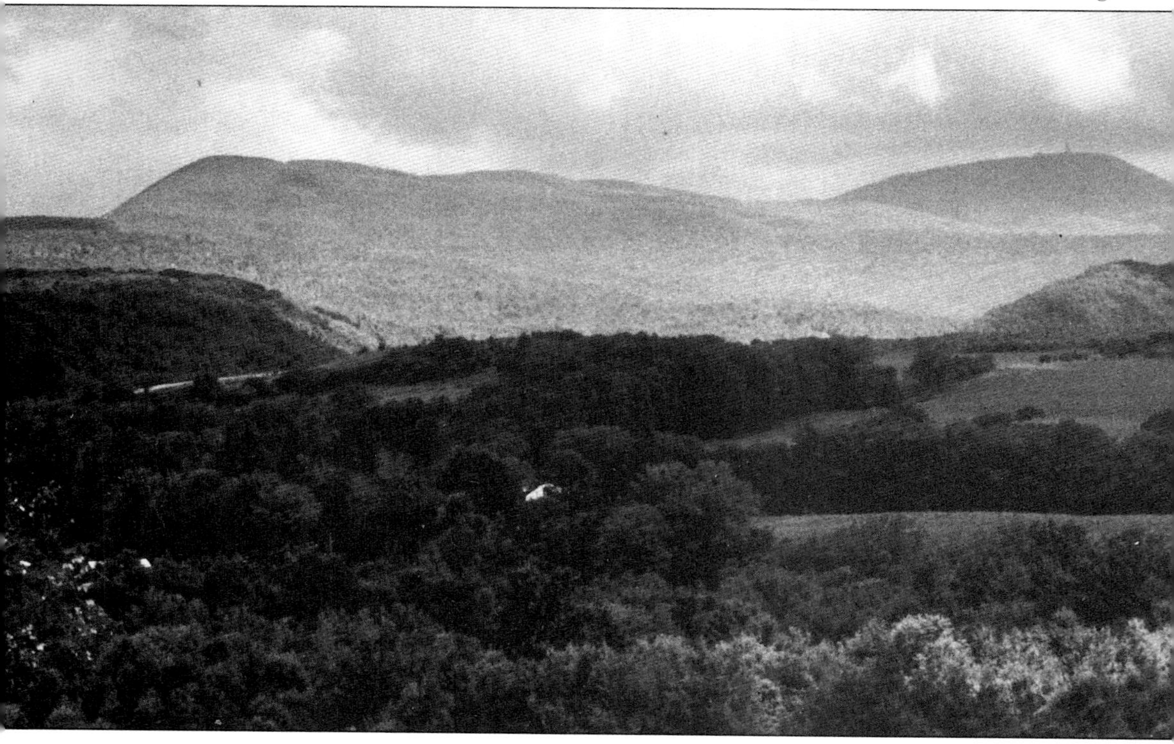

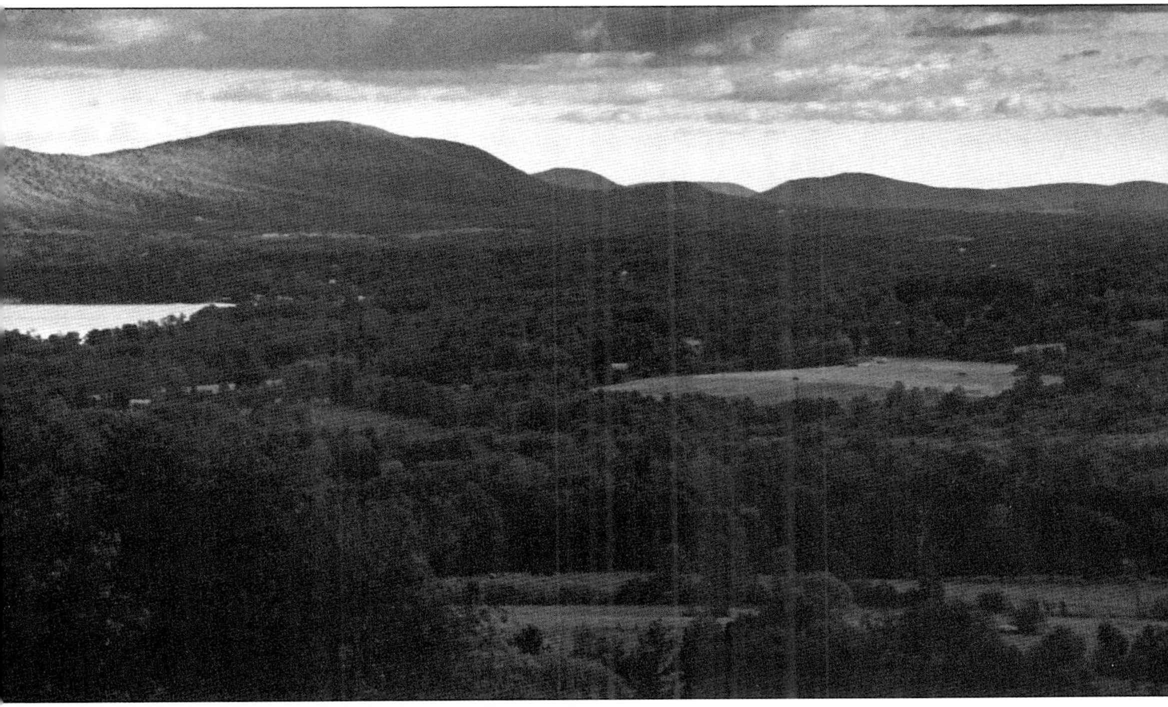

north.

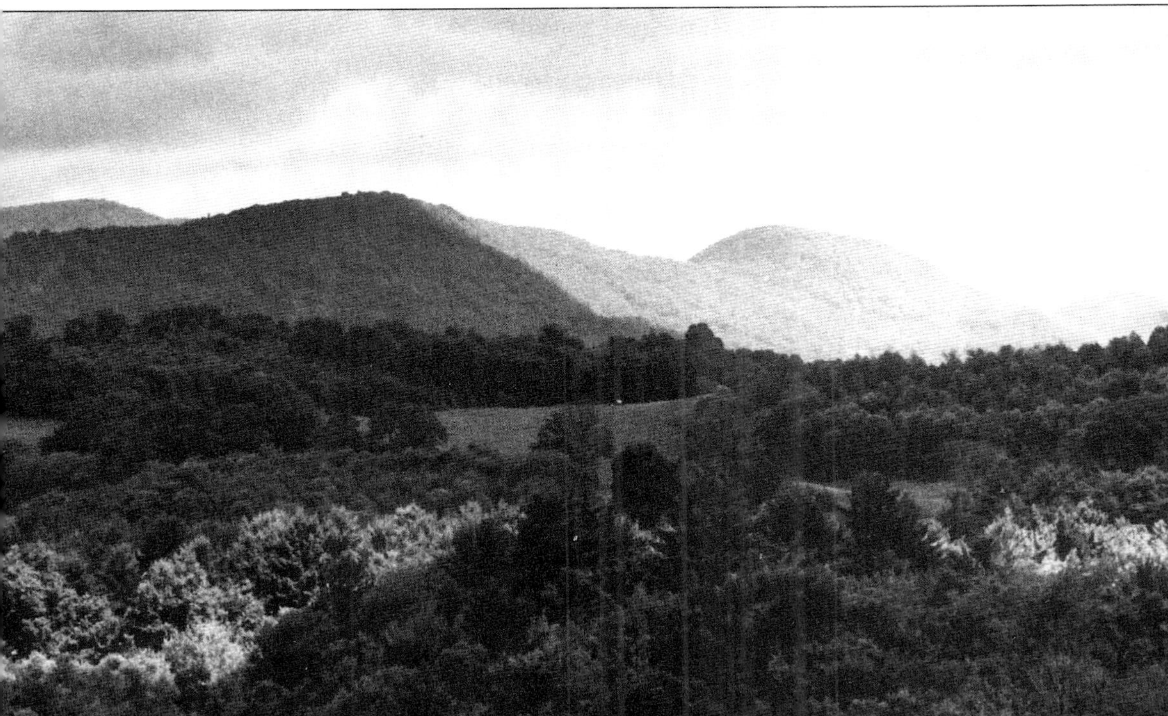

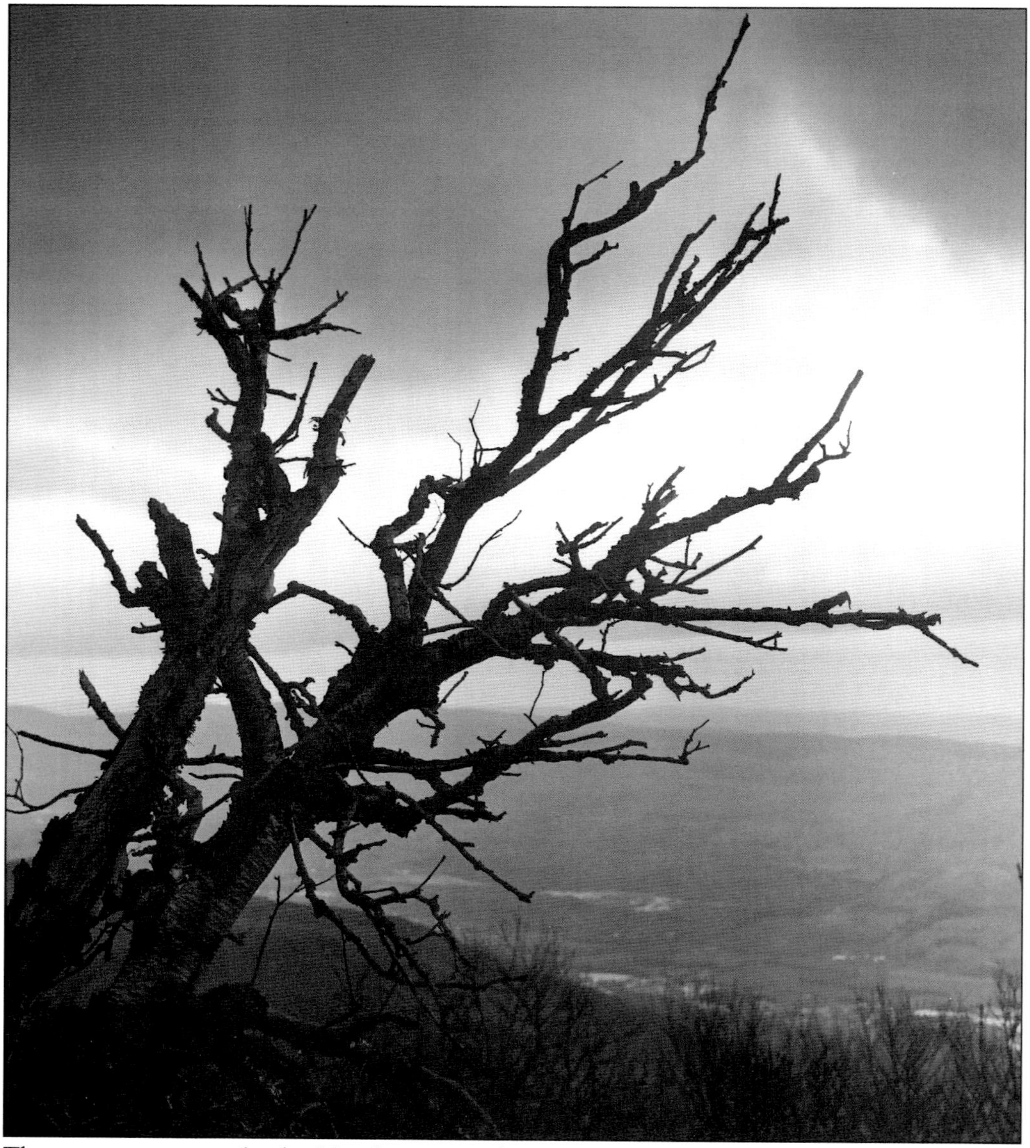

The craggy remains of a dead birch create a dramatic scene near the top of Greylock looking south.

Two

The Way We Were: Mostly 1950s and 1960s

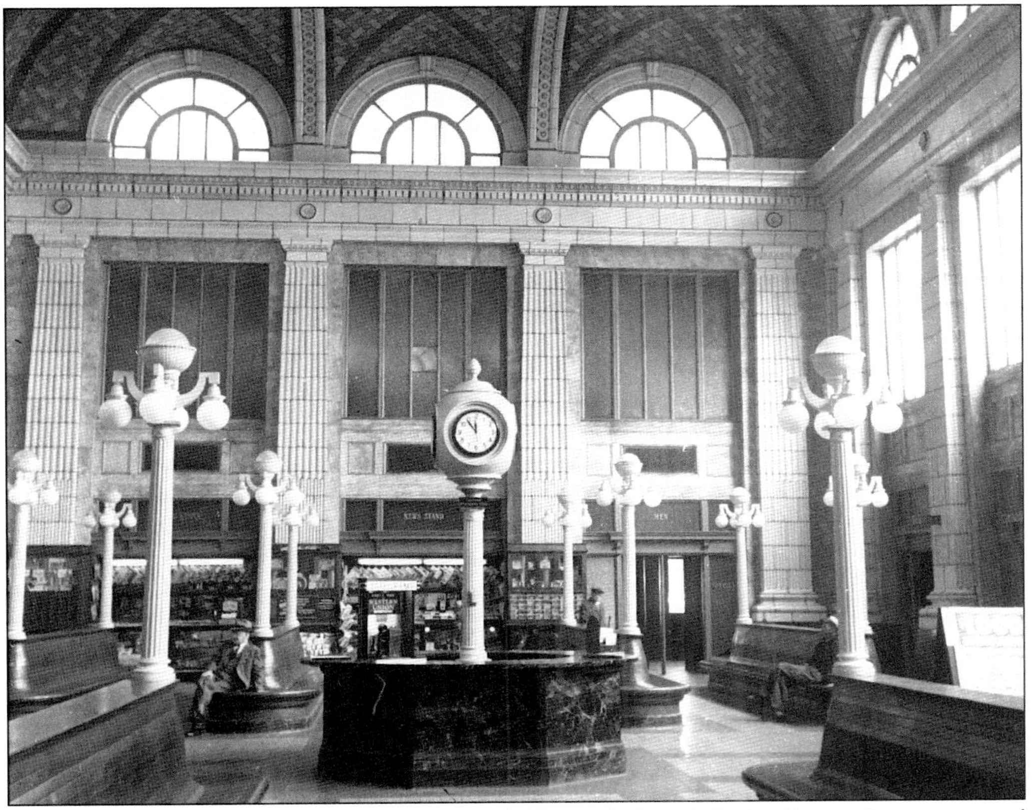

The fact that this elegant railroad station was deliberately demolished still provokes sorrow and sadness in all Berkshirites who value heritage, history, and the dignity of the built environment. This architectural treasure, Pittsfield's Union Station, photographed here in 1954, was dedicated in August 1914 and demolished in August 1968 in the cause of "urban renewal." Waiting-room walls were of green-veined marble. The wonder of its day was the fact that it was entirely lit by electricity.

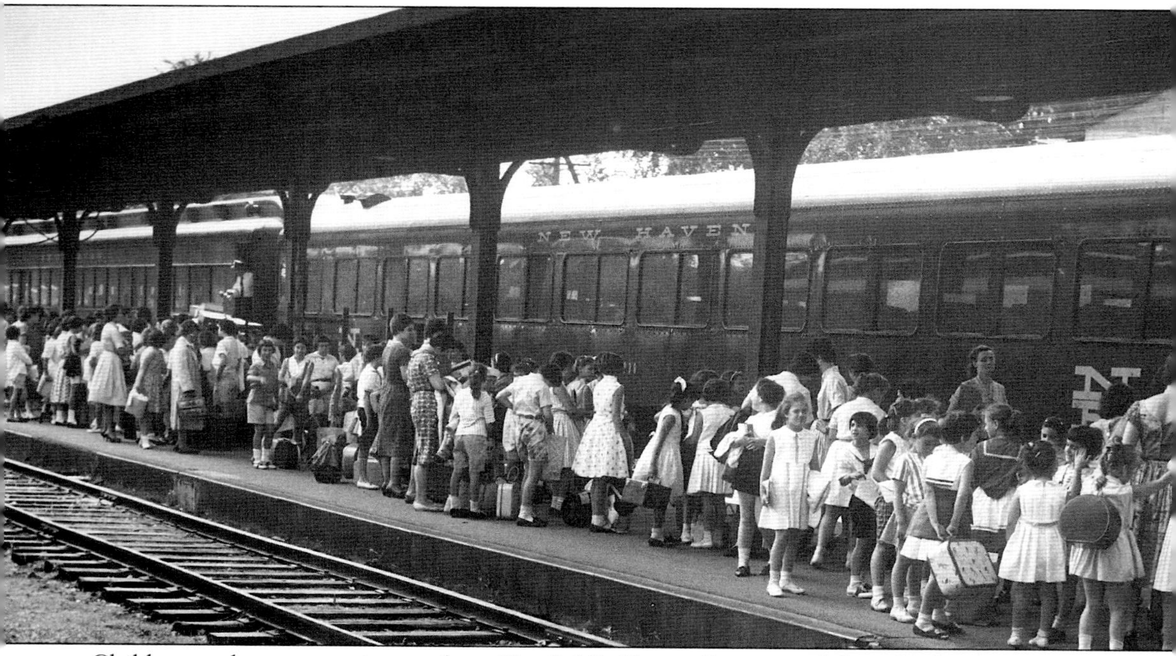

Children and parents wait eagerly at Pittsfield's Union Station in July 1959 for the arrival of Fresh Air children from New York City.

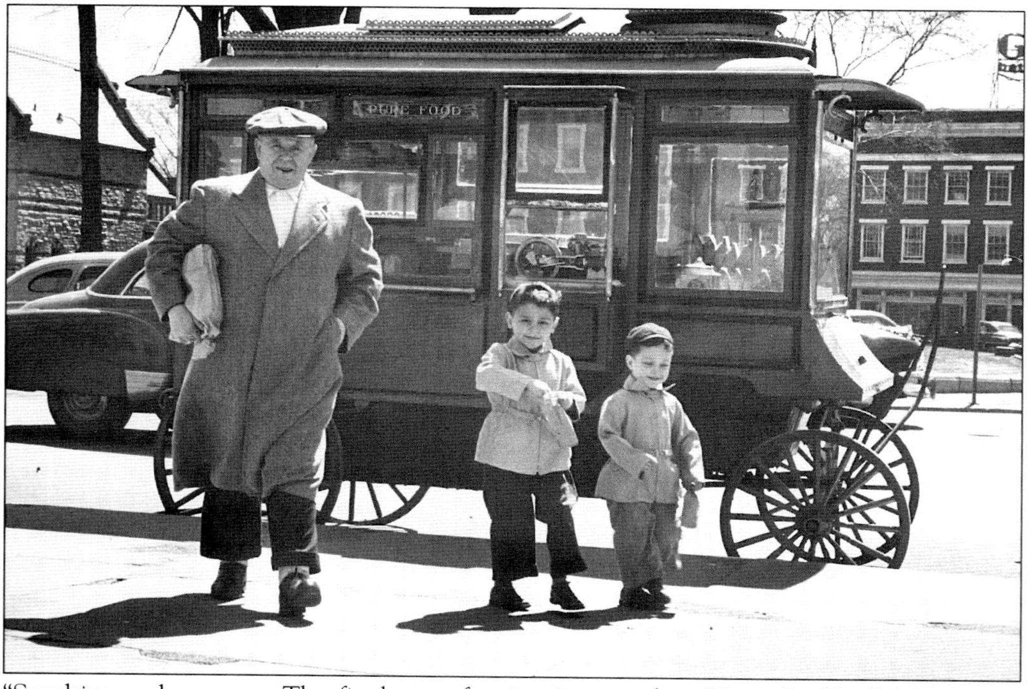

"Sunshine and popcorn: The final test of spring is met when Harry C. (Stuffy) McGinnis rolls out his popcorn wagon to the corner of Park Square and North Street. Among the first customers were Joseph Izzo of 581 East Street and his sons, Phillip, 5, and little brother David, 3 1/2" —April 19, 1952. The popcorn wagon had been a popular fixture here since 1909.

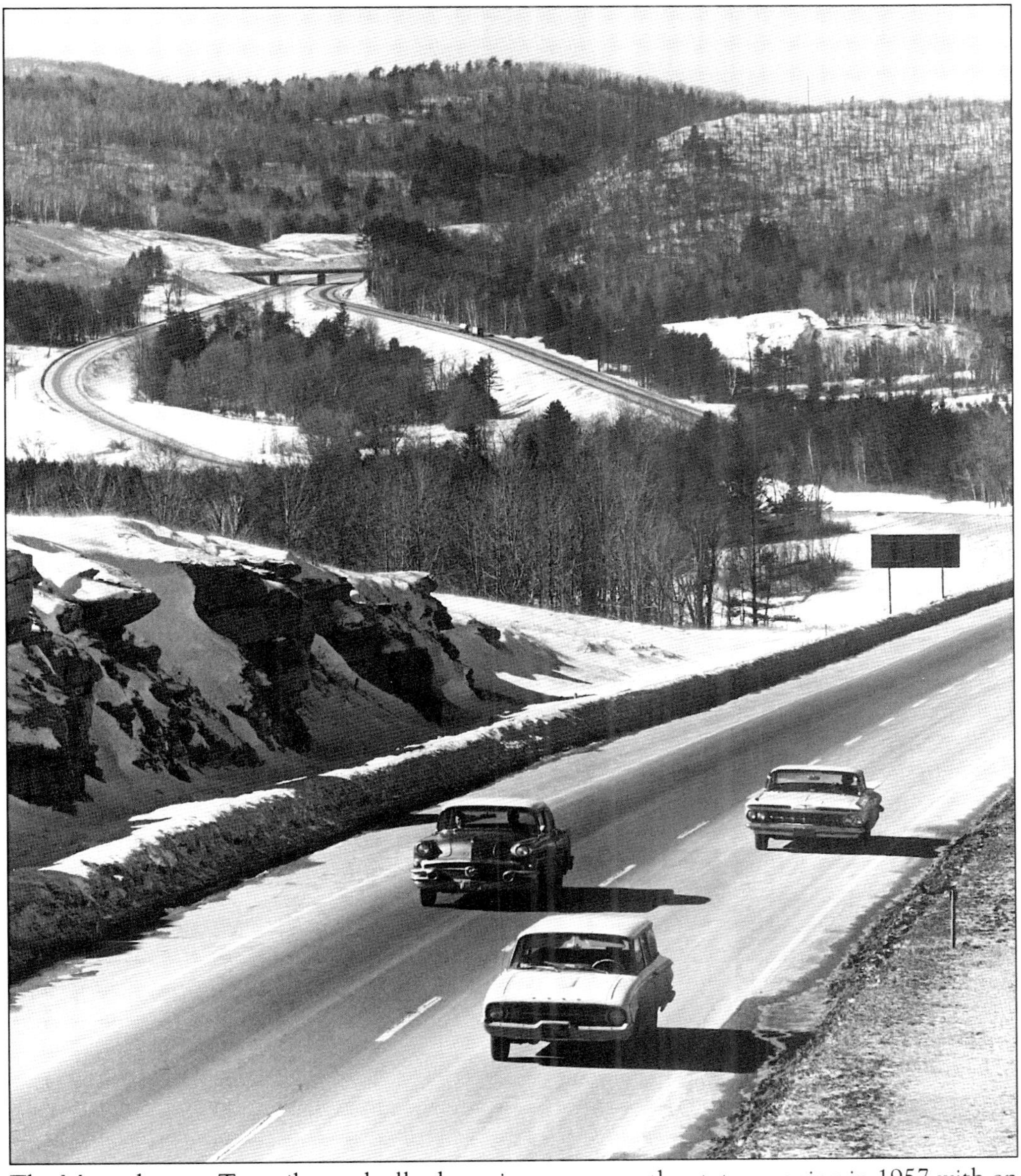

The Massachusetts Turnpike gradually thrust its way across the state, opening in 1957 with an interchange serving the Berkshires at Lee. Here Tague pictured it rolling through the hills in February 1963. The cars—a Buick, Ford Falcon, and Chevy—seem like vintage classics in the late 1990s.

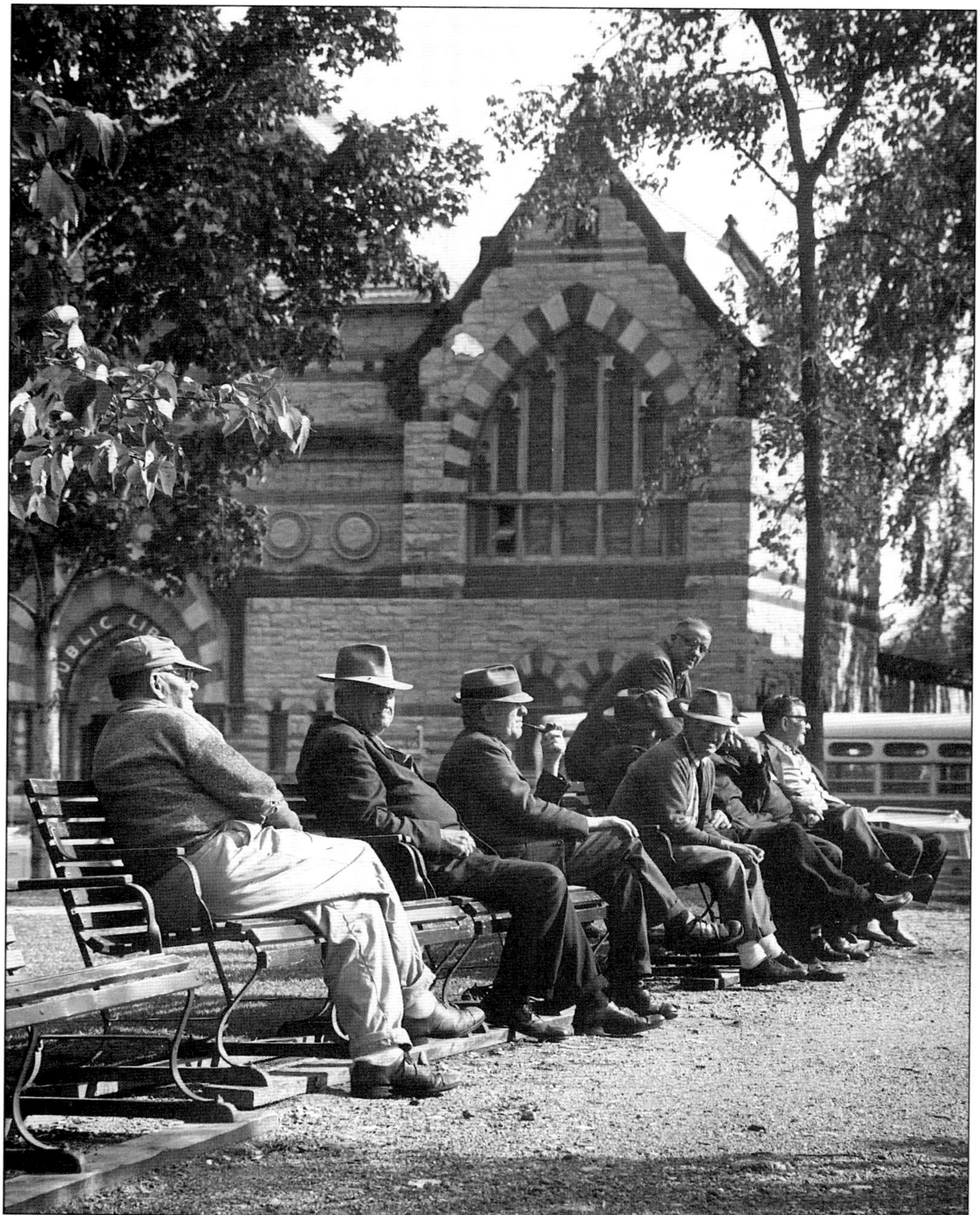

People don't seem to sit on park benches any more, as they did here in August 1956—most men wearing fedoras—soaking up sun outside the ornate Berkshire Athenaeum, the public library located at Pittsfield's Park Square.

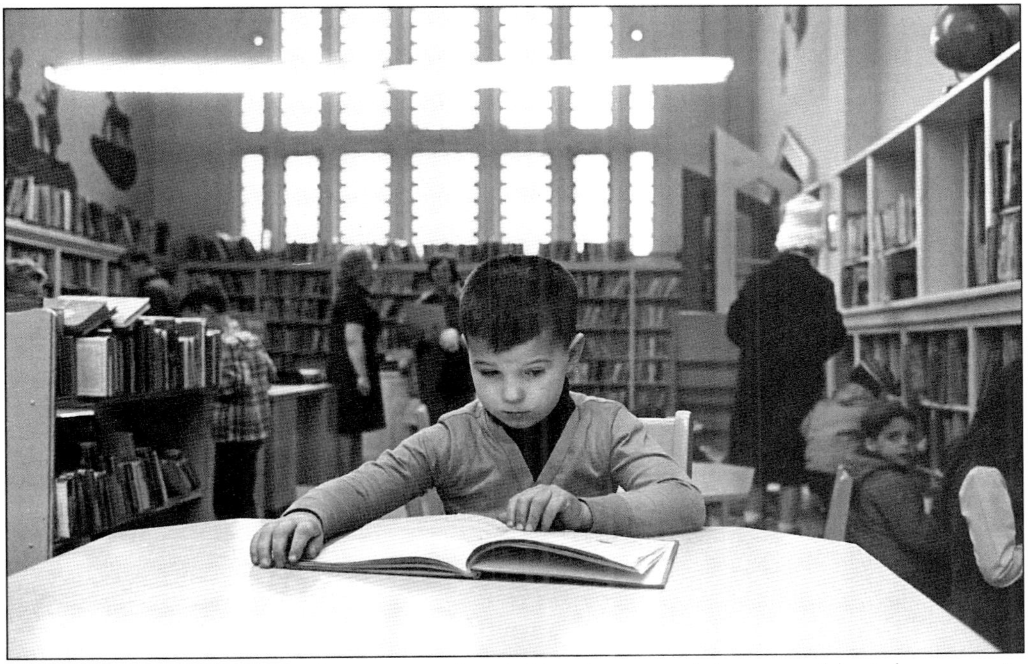

A small boy finds literary adventure in the children's room of the venerable Athenaeum in March 1967.

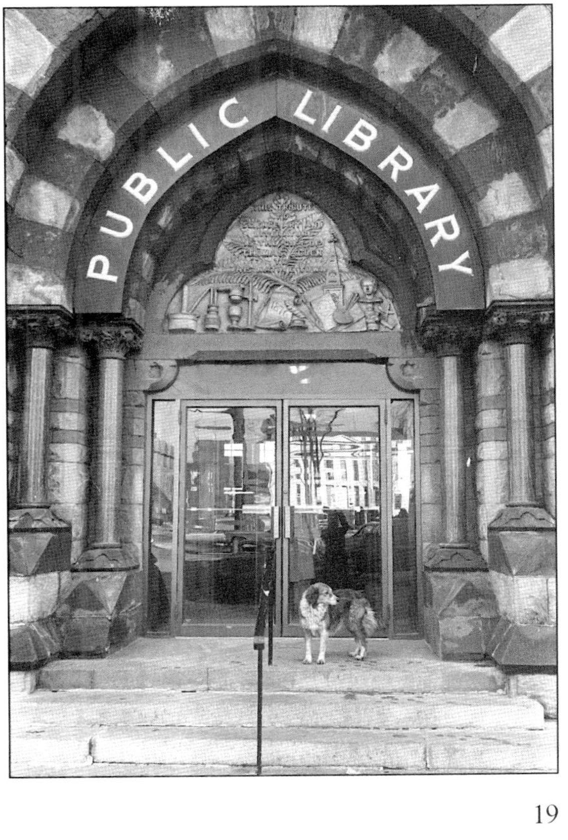

A dog awaits its more literate master outside the old library entrance. The Gothic building, fabricated of Great Barrington blue limestone and red Missouri granite, was taken over in 1980 by the Berkshire County Register of Deeds and Probate, while a new Berkshire Athenaeum was built in the next block as a far more adequate public library.

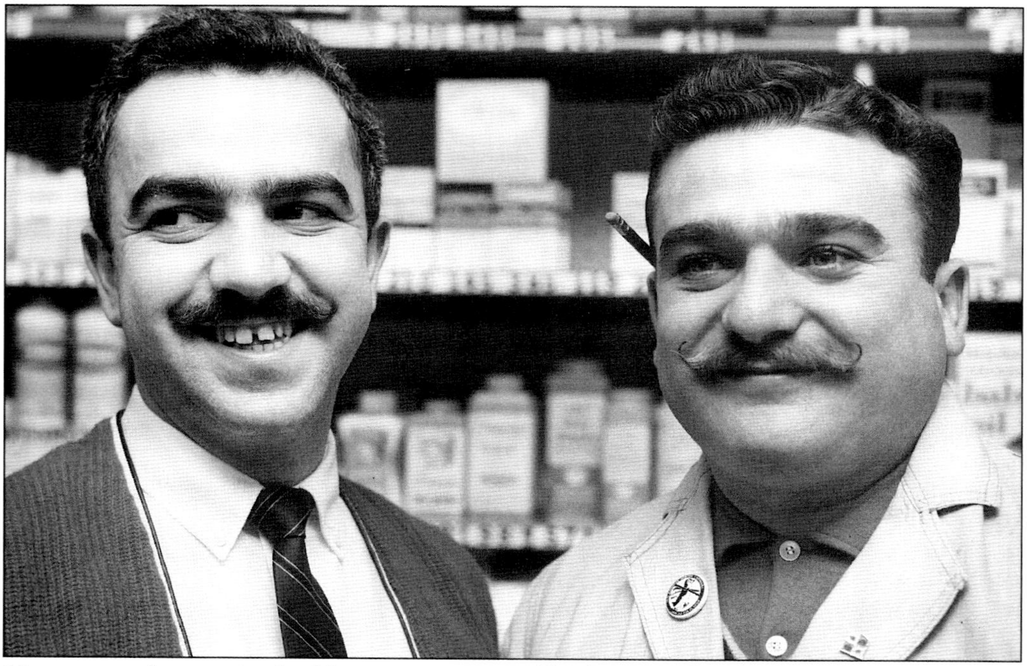

"Are moustaches coming back? is a question raised by these two fine-looking specimens. 'For no special reason,' they were grown by Nichols' Pharmacy proprietor Arthur J. Nichols, at left, who is the uncle of Nichols' Package Store clerk Francis G. (Nick) Nichols Jr., at right." —January 17, 1959.

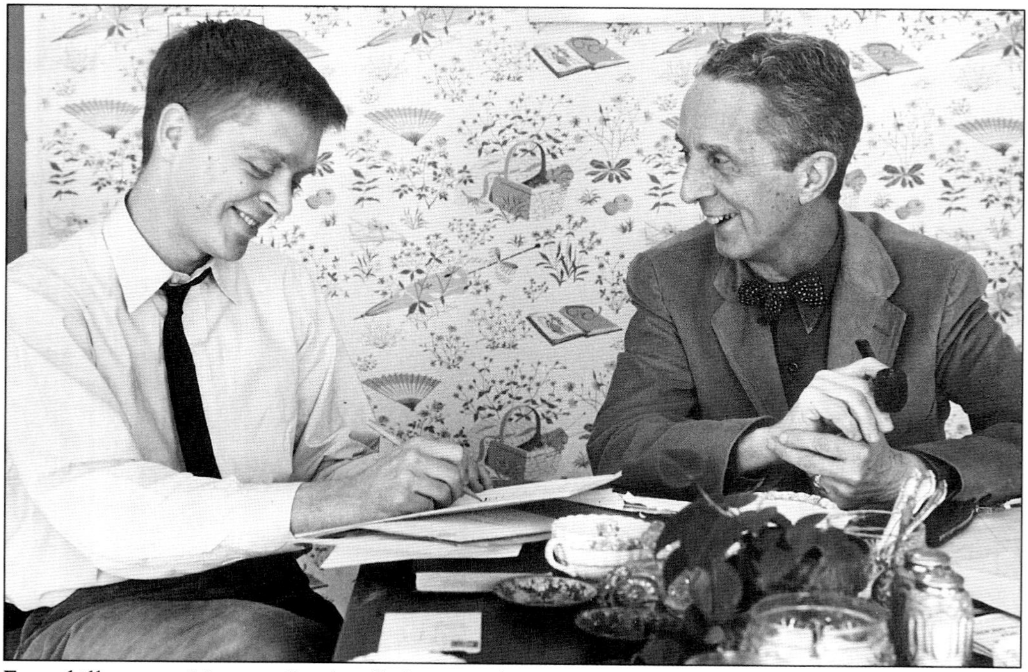

Famed illustrator Norman Rockwell shares a pleasant moment with his son Tom in the kitchen of their Stockbridge home in February 1960.

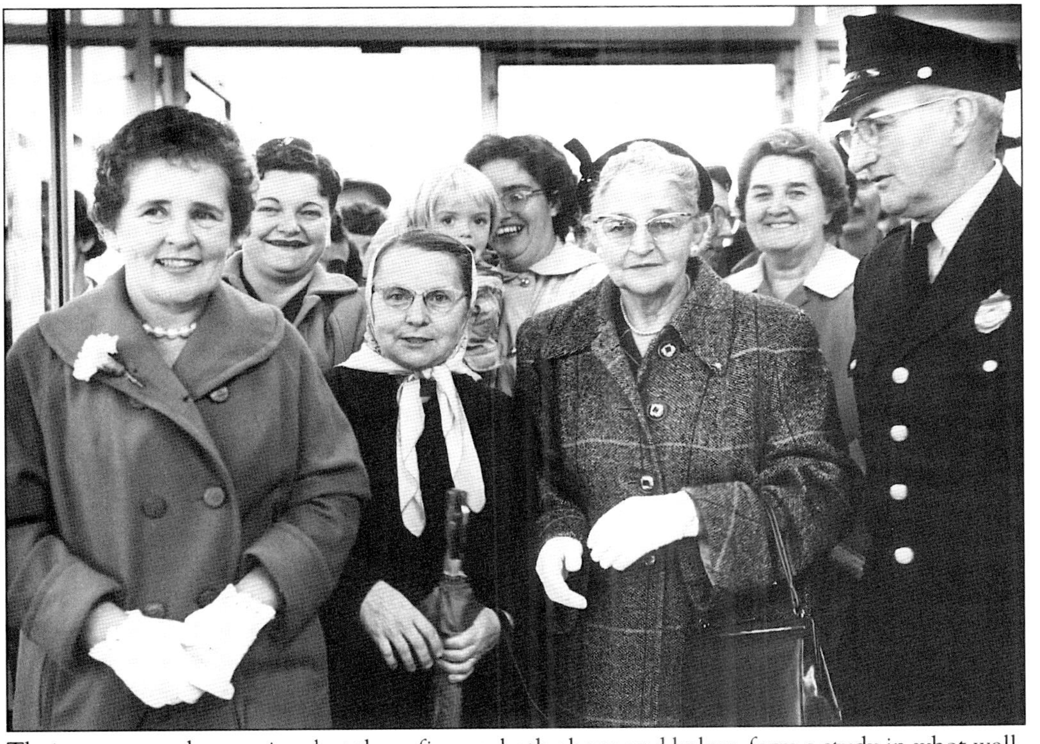

Their names are lost to time but these figures, both above and below, form a study in what well-dressed Berkshire ladies wore in the late 1950s. Remember when girls actually wore skirts?

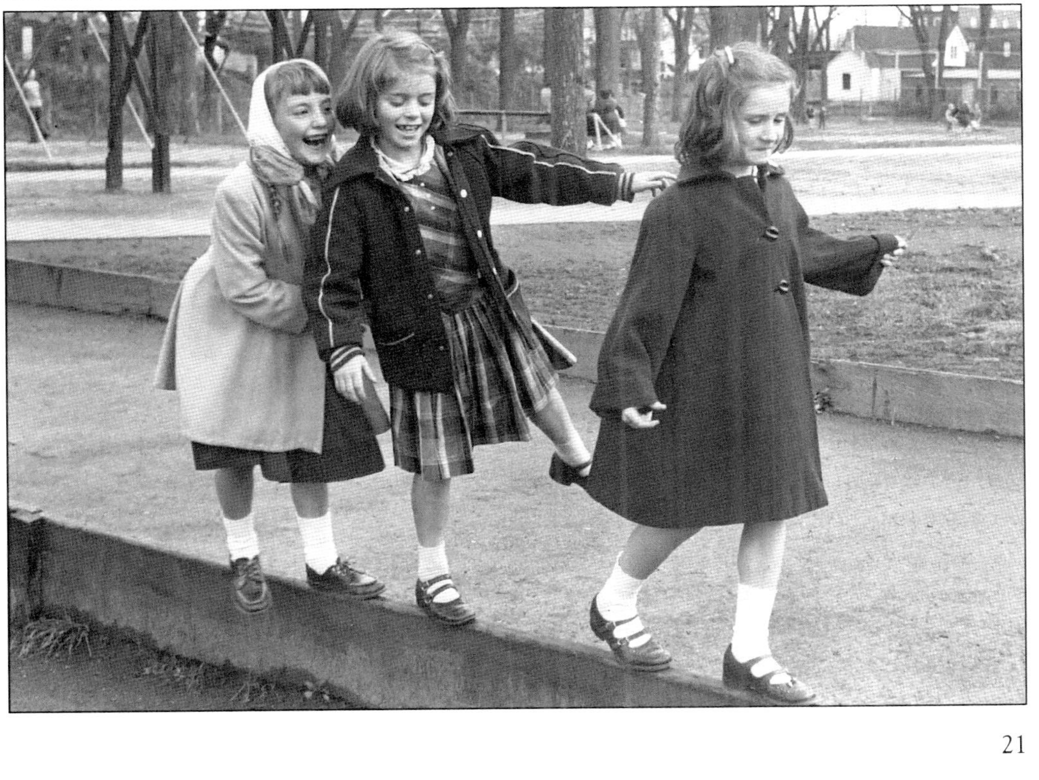

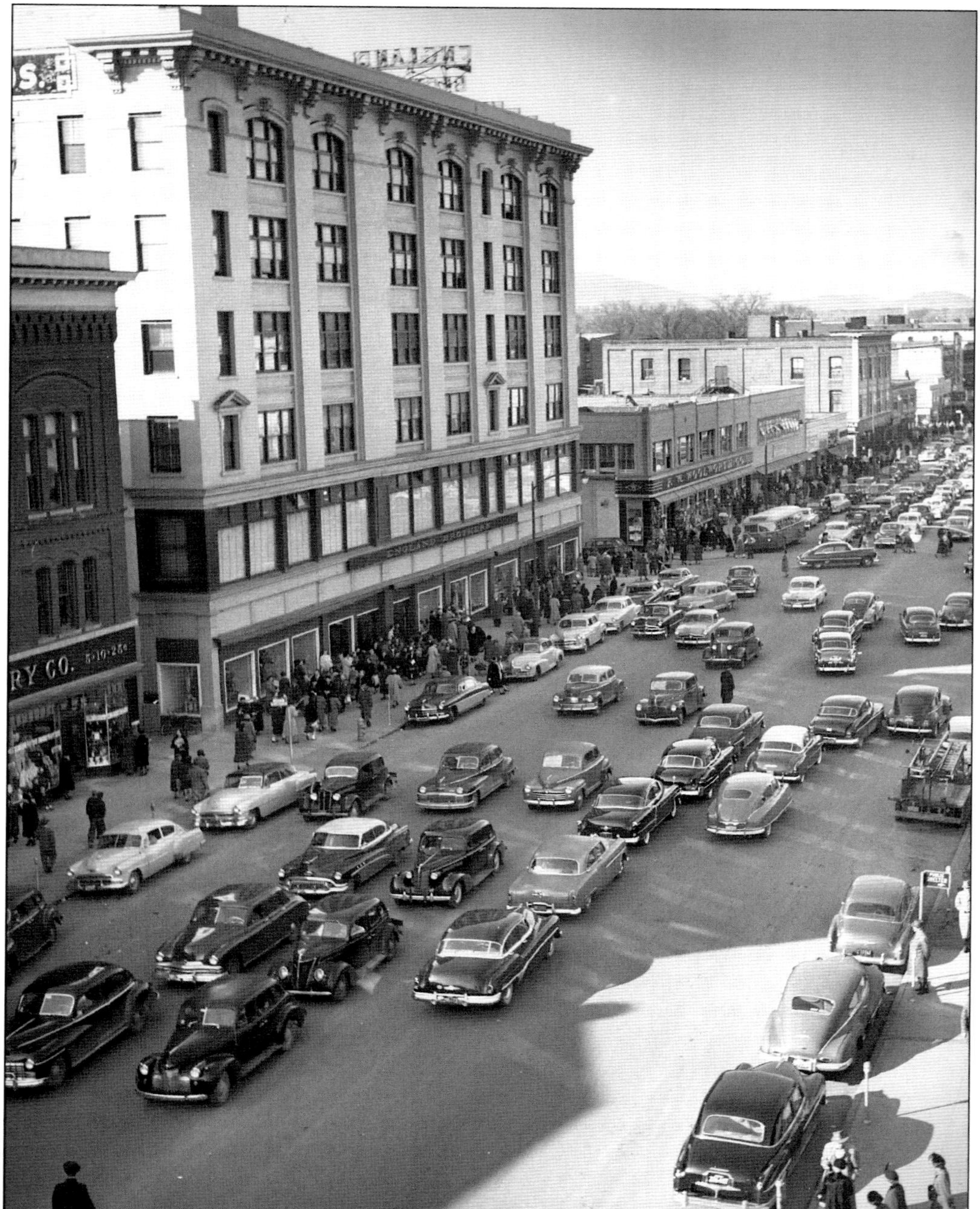
RY CO. 5-10-25¢

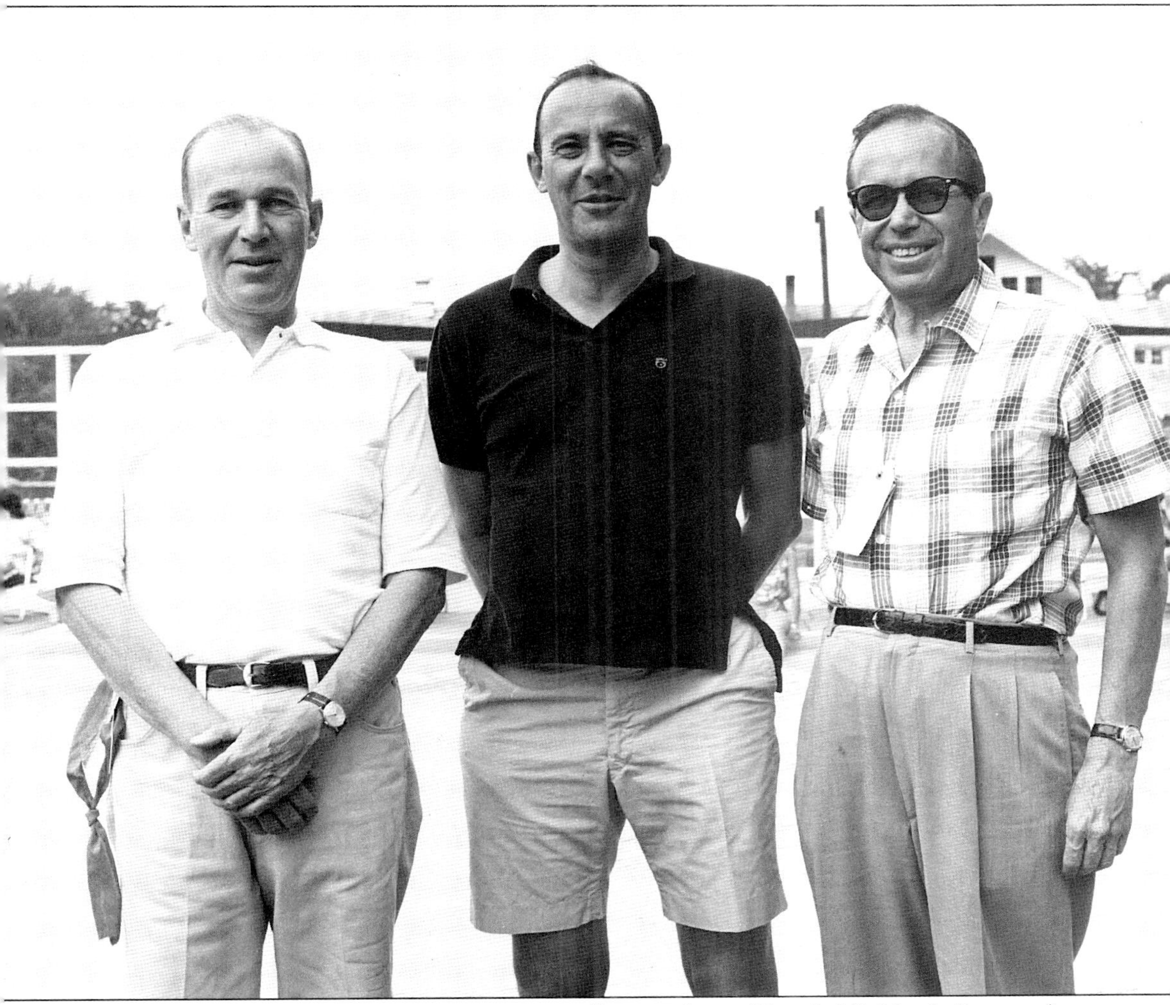

The England Brothers' department store was still an anchor of Pittsfield's North Street when the photo at left was taken in March 1953, surrounded by what now seems like a veritable parade of American automobiles from the late 1940s and early 1950s. Above, brothers Dan, Ben, and Simon England were photographed at a picnic for England Brothers' employees at Eastover in Lenox in July 1963. It was a major blow to the region's economy when the store closed its doors.

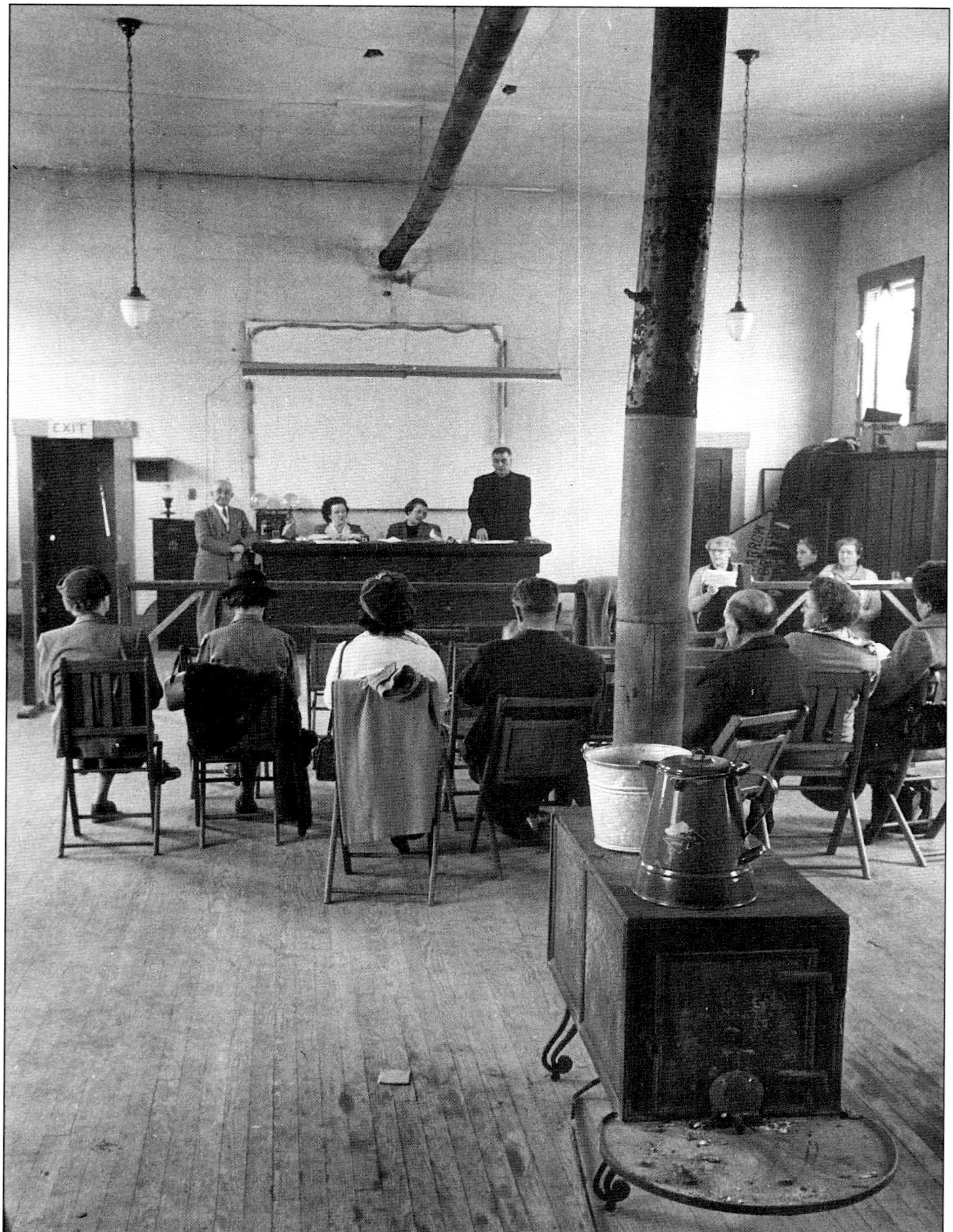

The scene seems more like something out of northern Vermont than southern Berkshire—it's a wood-heated town meeting in Sandisfield in the late 1950s.

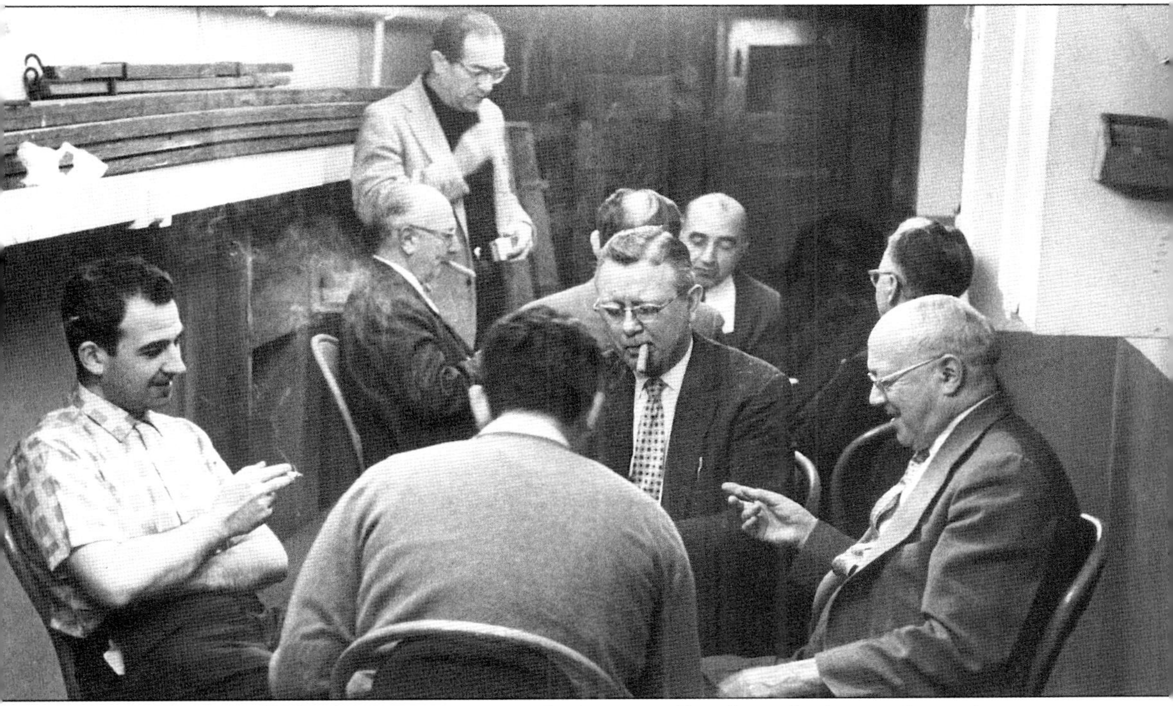

It was an era in which almost everyone smoked, especially when playing cards, as these gents are doing in a photo taken in May 1959.

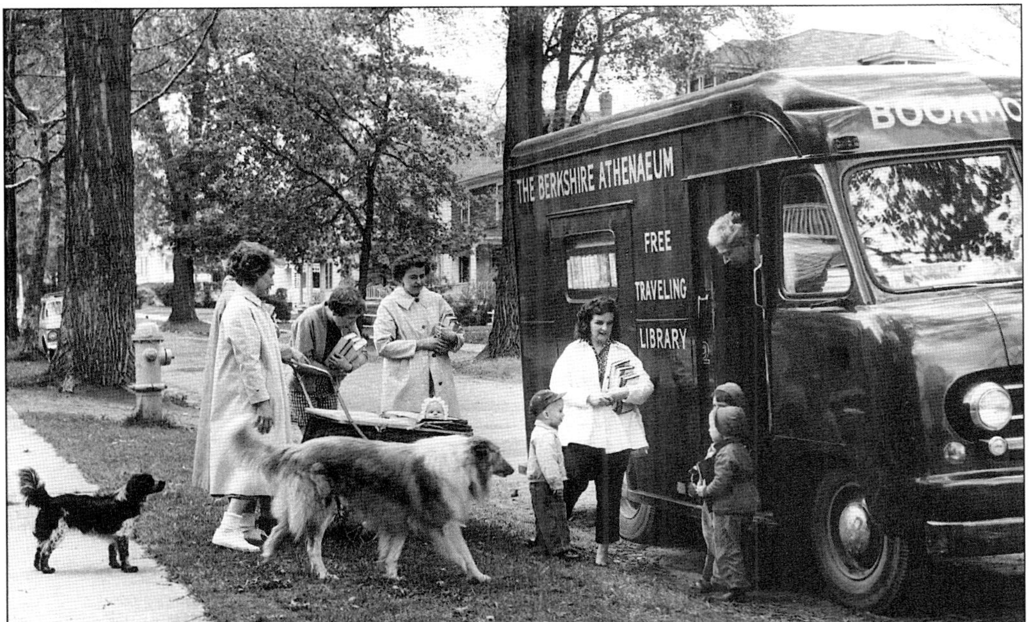

There was also a time when the library brought books directly to their readers. Greeted by dogs, a baby carriage, small children, and several young mothers, this visit of the Berkshire Athenaeum's "free traveling library" seems to define a more innocent era.

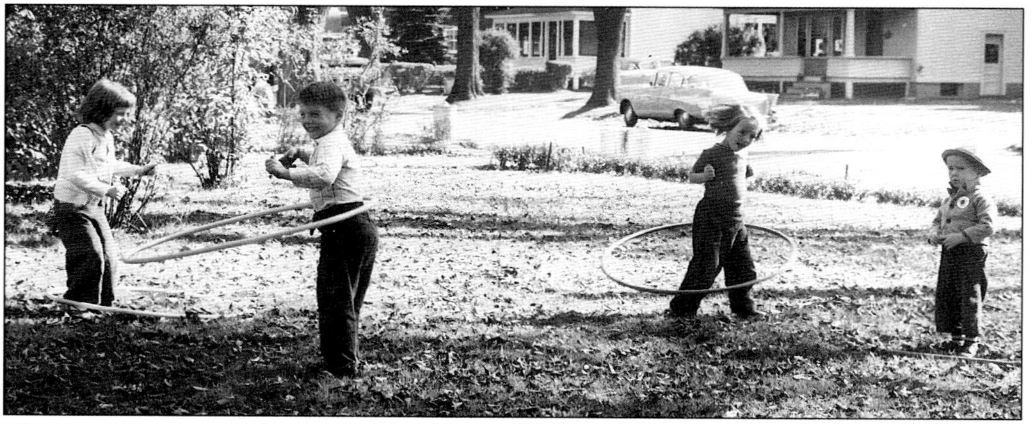

The hula hoop practically defines itself as the fad of the era 1957–58, and that is true in this photo taken in October 1958. The fins on the '56 Chevy parked in the background help authenticate the time frame.

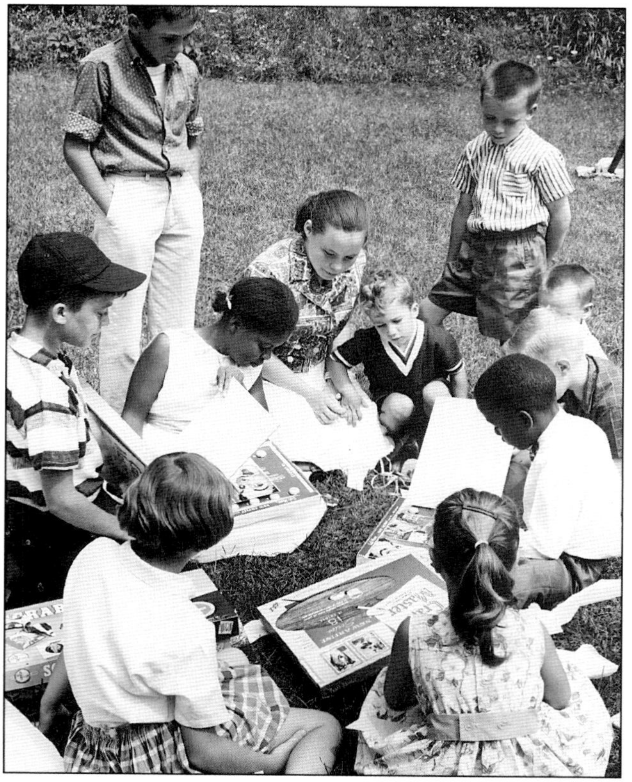

Fresh Air children are given a party in a Pittsfield neighborhood before they return to New York. The time is July 1960.

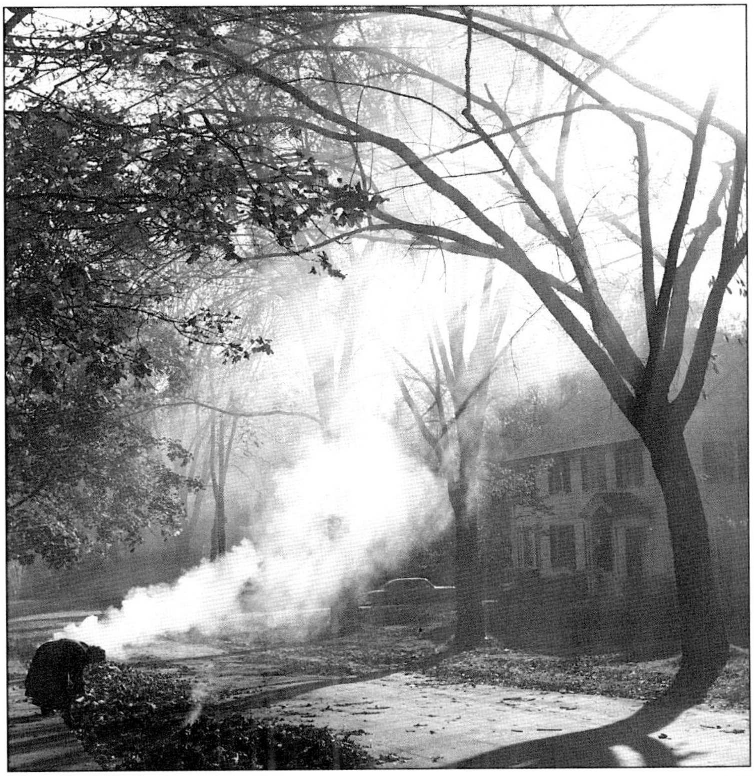

Burning leaves instead of composting them helps to date this neighborhood scene in Williamstown, taken in the late 1950s. Below, American Legion conventioneers prepare to enter Pittsfield's once-proud Wendell Hotel.

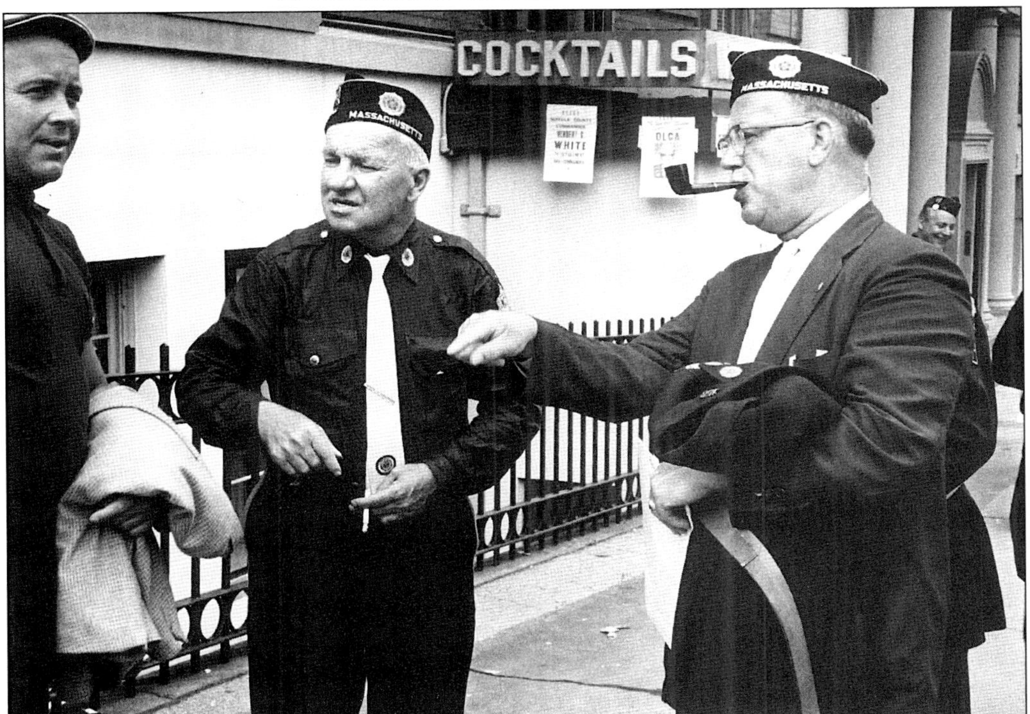

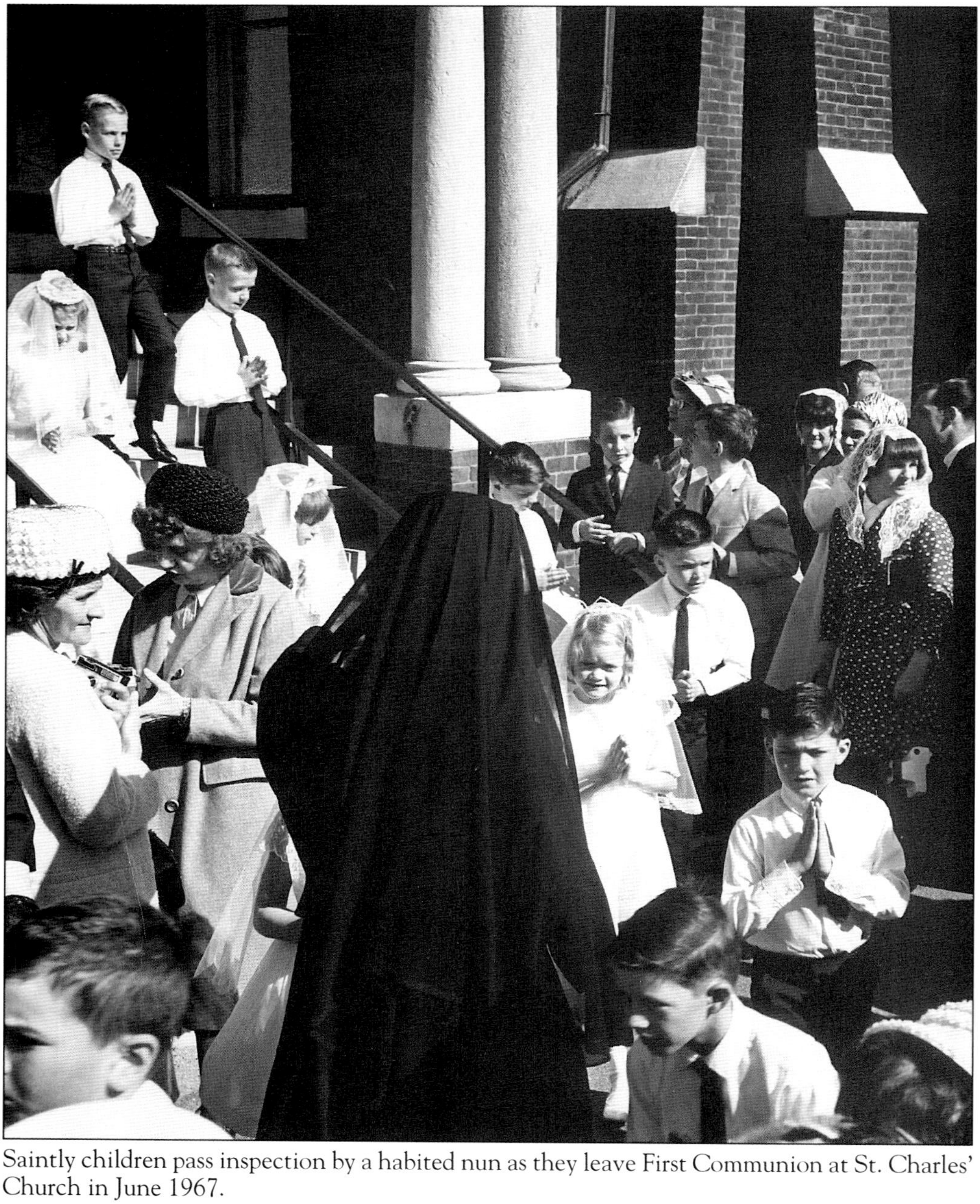

Saintly children pass inspection by a habited nun as they leave First Communion at St. Charles' Church in June 1967.

Berkshire Eagle colleagues of Bill Tague's were often the subject of his focus. At right, city editor Ted Giddings (who wrote the introduction to this book); at left below, political writer A.A. Michelson accompanying a group of children aboard the *Sheila* on Pontoosuc Lake; at right below, writer Ray Librizzi.

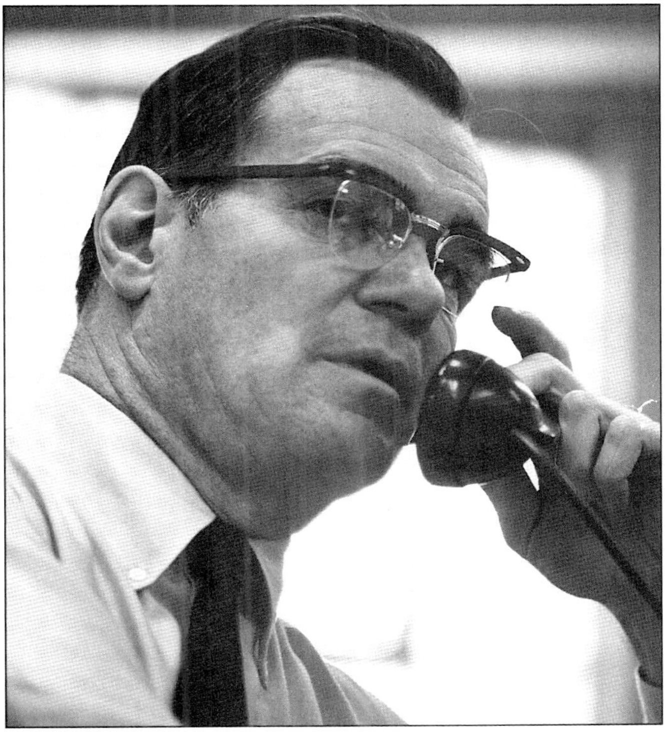

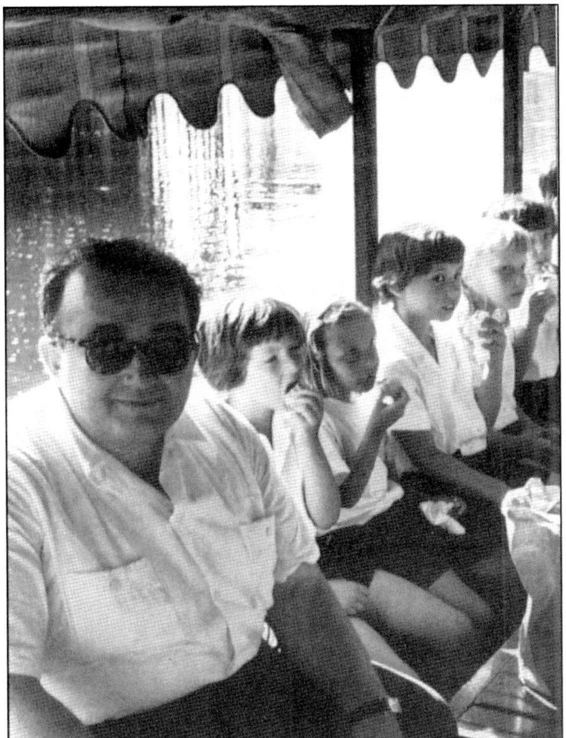

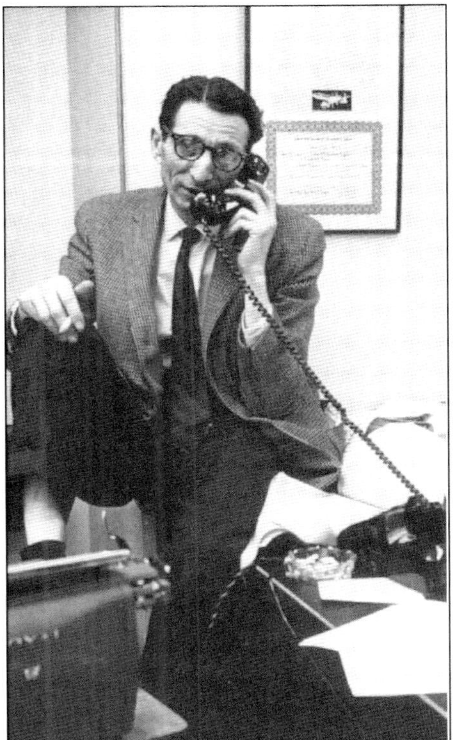

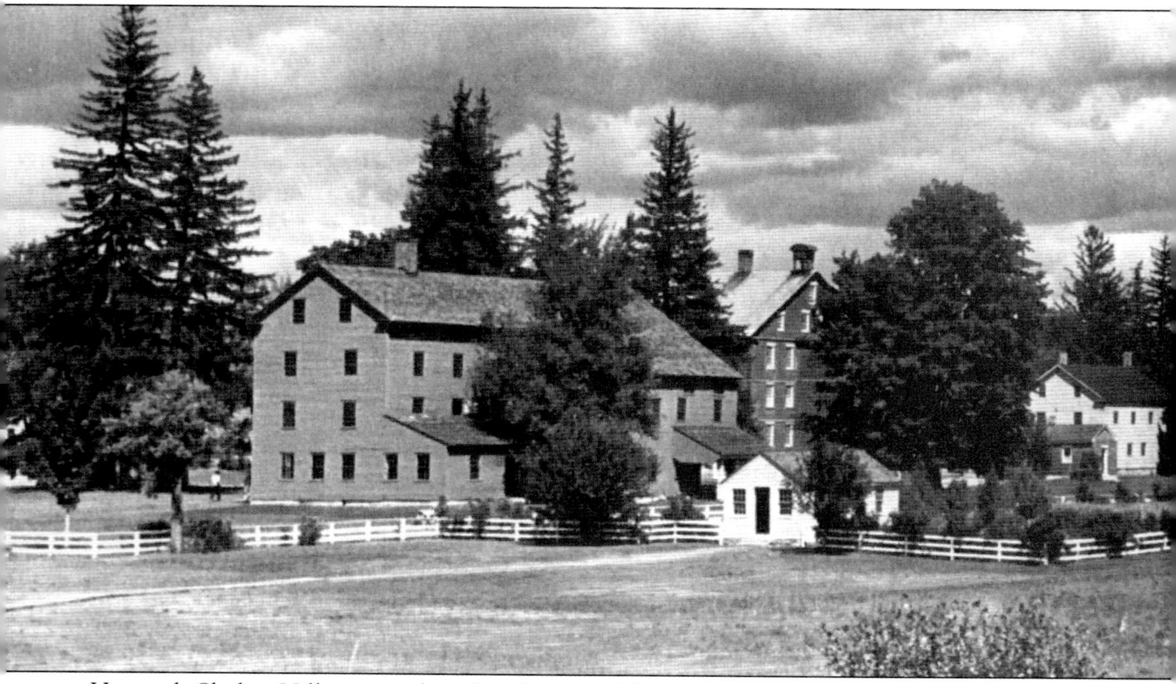

Hancock Shaker Village, purchased and restored by a private group in 1960, serves to evoke and interpret a simple, fascinating religious and agricultural community. A keystone to the

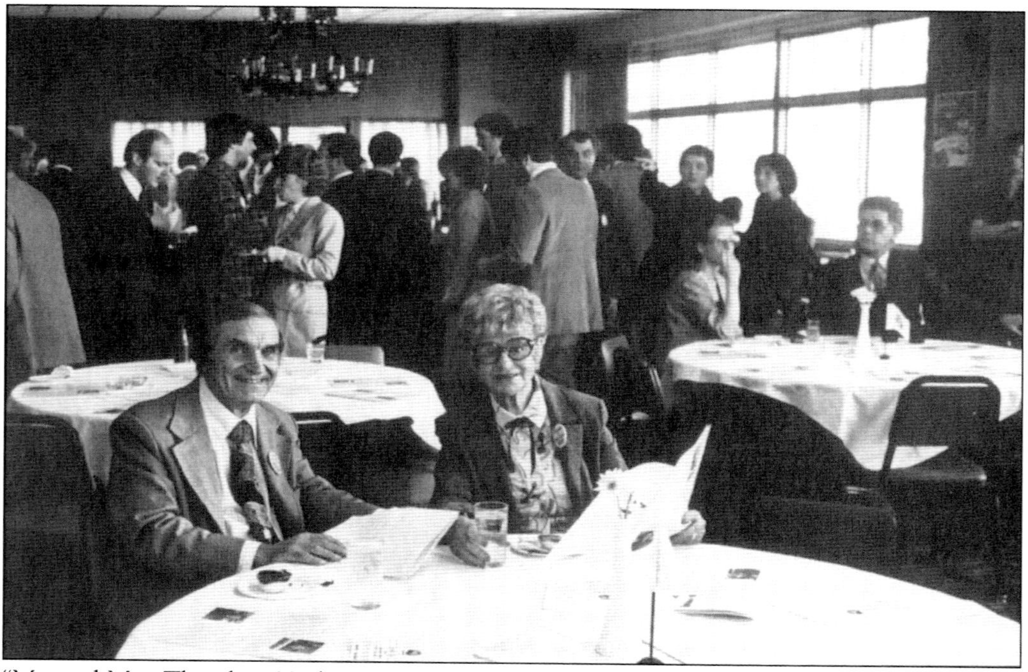

"Mr. and Mrs. Theodore Herberg, 78 Richard Drive, were among the many who attended the annual meeting of the United Way at Itam Lodge. United Way is gearing up for its biggest drive. The goal: $1 million" —April 12, 1980.

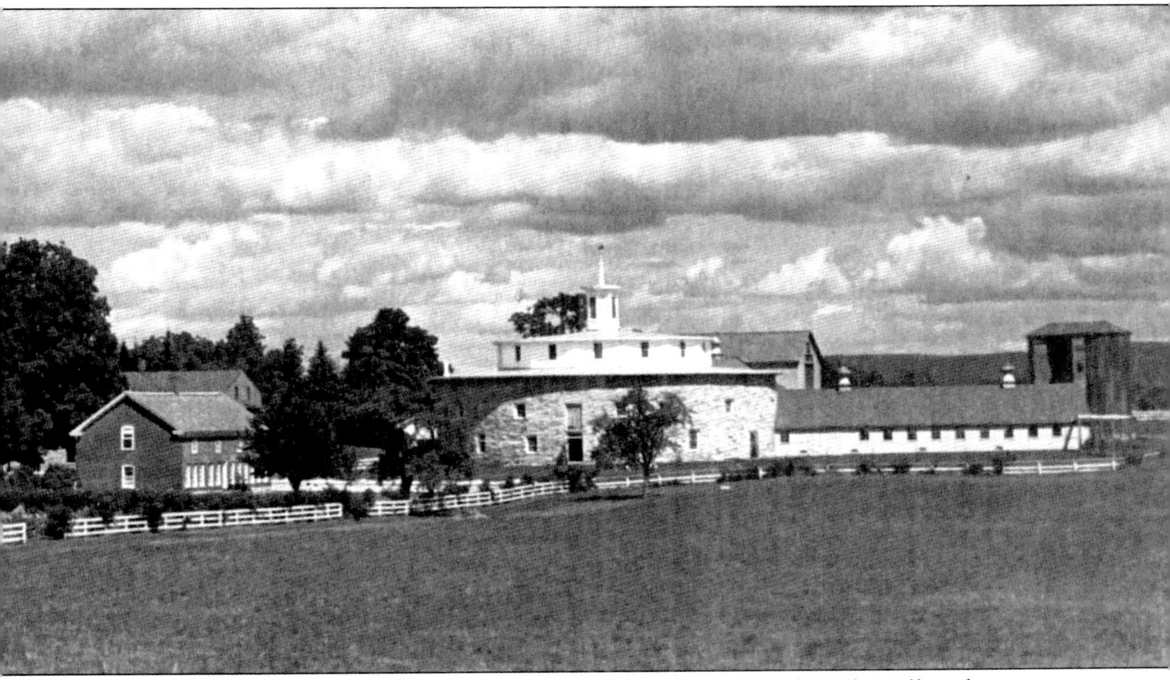

project was the restoration of the ingenious round stone barn at right. The village has proven itself as an educational and tourist attraction.

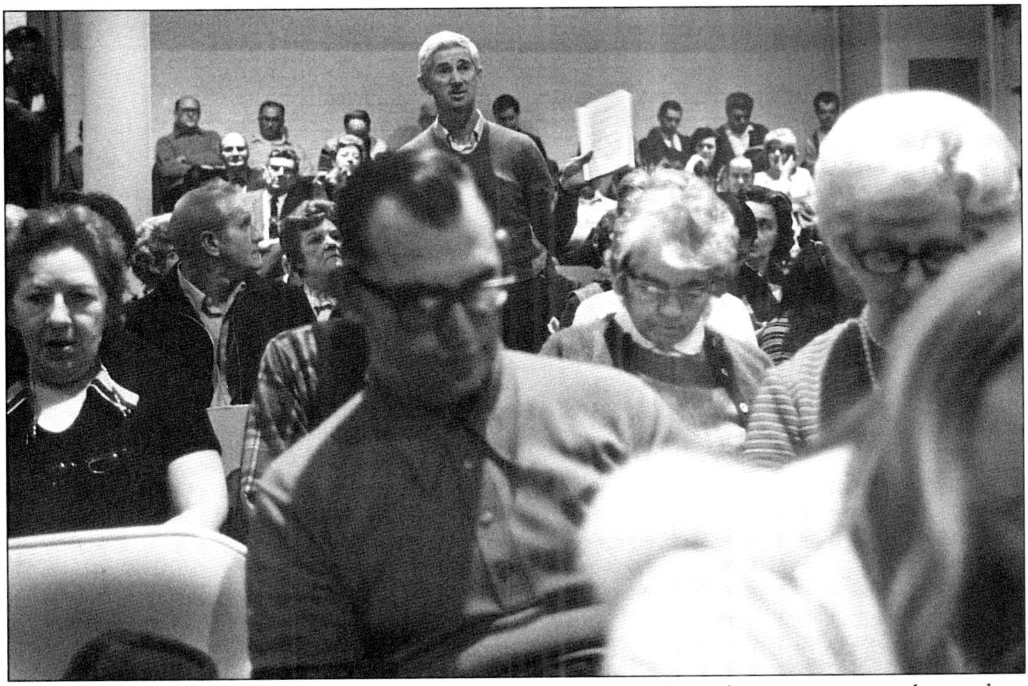

"Citizen Bertram J. Ramsay takes the floor at town meeting in Lanesboro to question the wisdom of adopting a town building code without first having it explained to the voters. A majority agreed and tabled the code" —February 20, 1971.

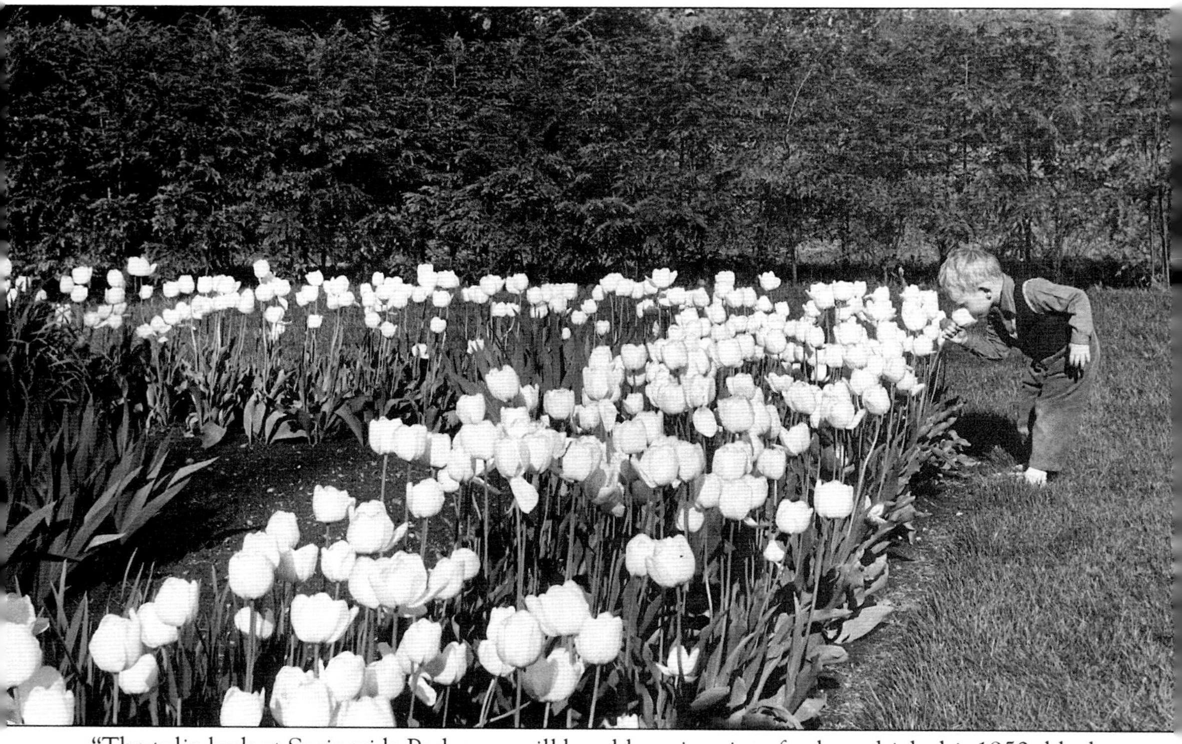

"The tulip beds at Springside Park soon will be a blooming riot of color, which this 1950s black-and-white version of the scene doesn't do justice to. You must see the display in person, and smell a blossom or two, as this tyke is doing, to fully appreciate it" —April 27, 1985.

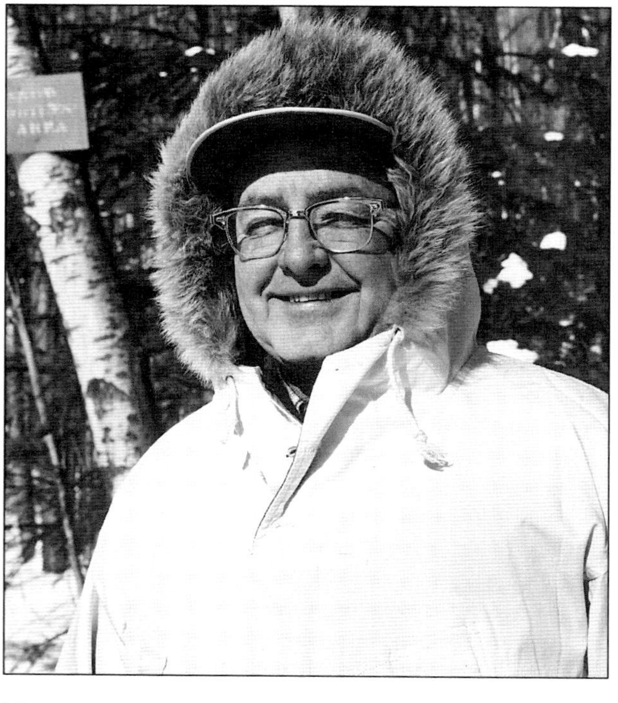

Vincent Hebert, superintendent of parks for Pittsfield, was responsible for the annual profusion of spring flowers. He was photographed here in January 1971.

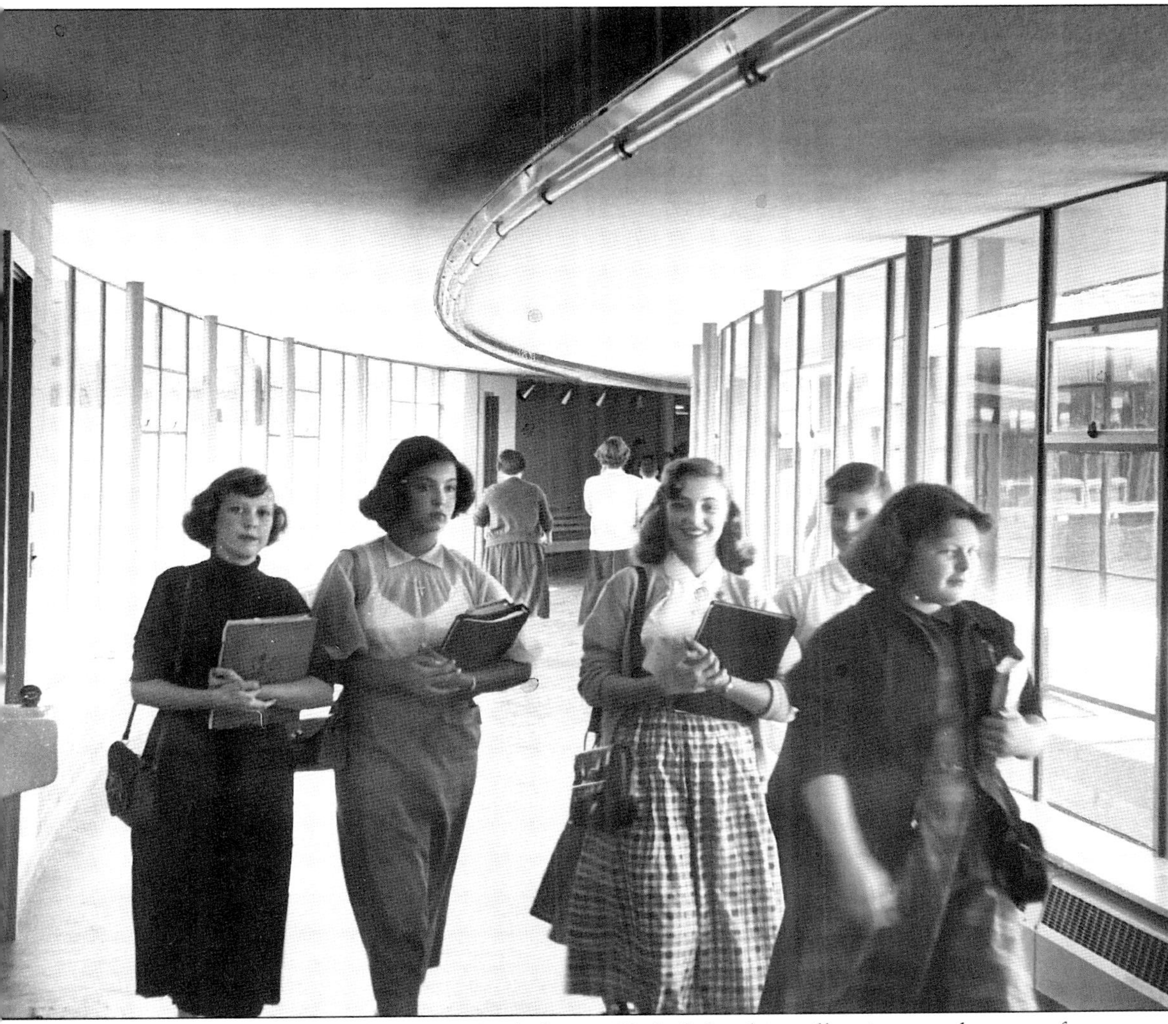

"Between bells: changing classes at North Junior High School is still quite an adventure for pupils finding their way around the new building. The girls are walking in glass corridor between the classroom and gym-cafeteria wings" —September 26, 1953.

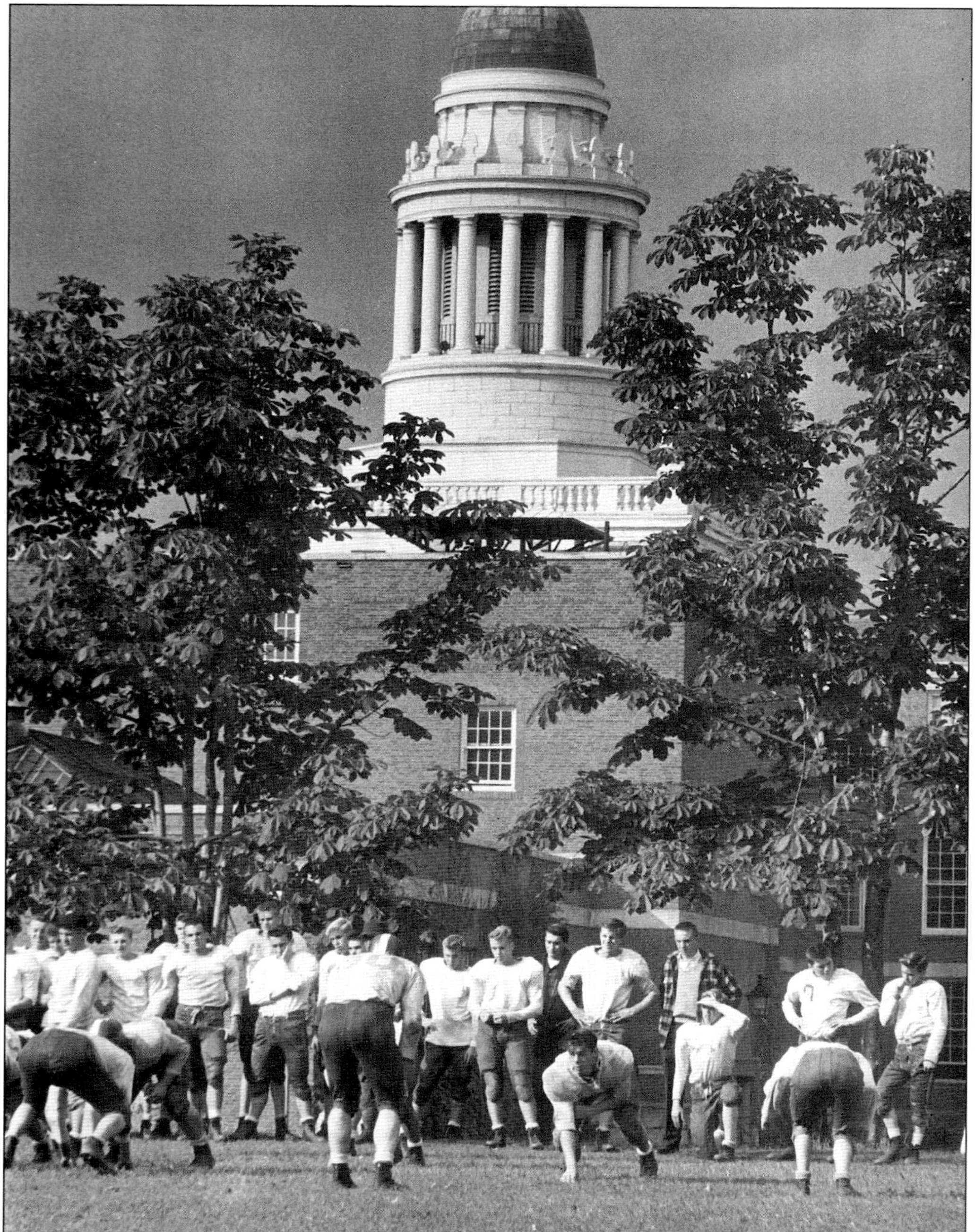

"Football practice, a sure sign of fall, is held at Pittsfield High behind the school building. Players are dwarfed by the great dome in this telephoto shot" —September 22, 1956.

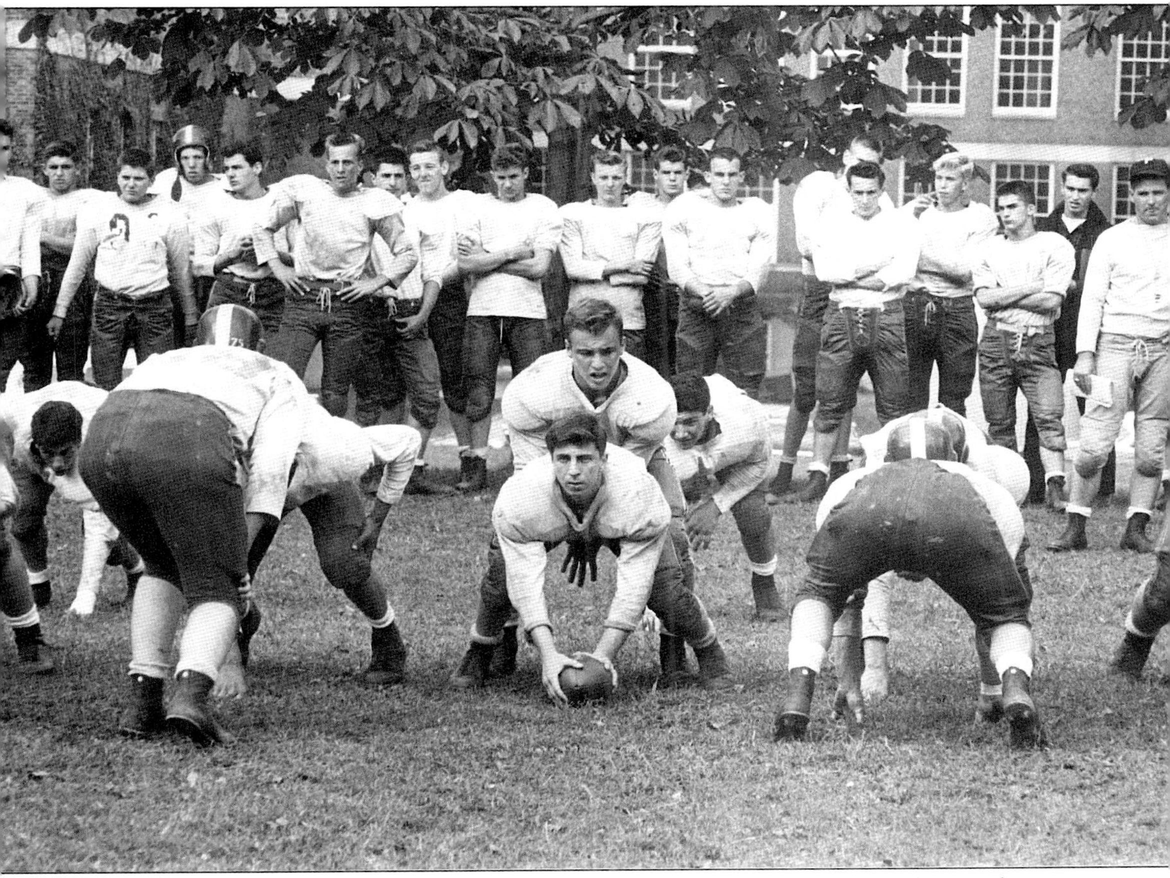

This closeup of football practice, revealing a wide array of serious faces, was taken at the same time as the one at left but not published for some reason.

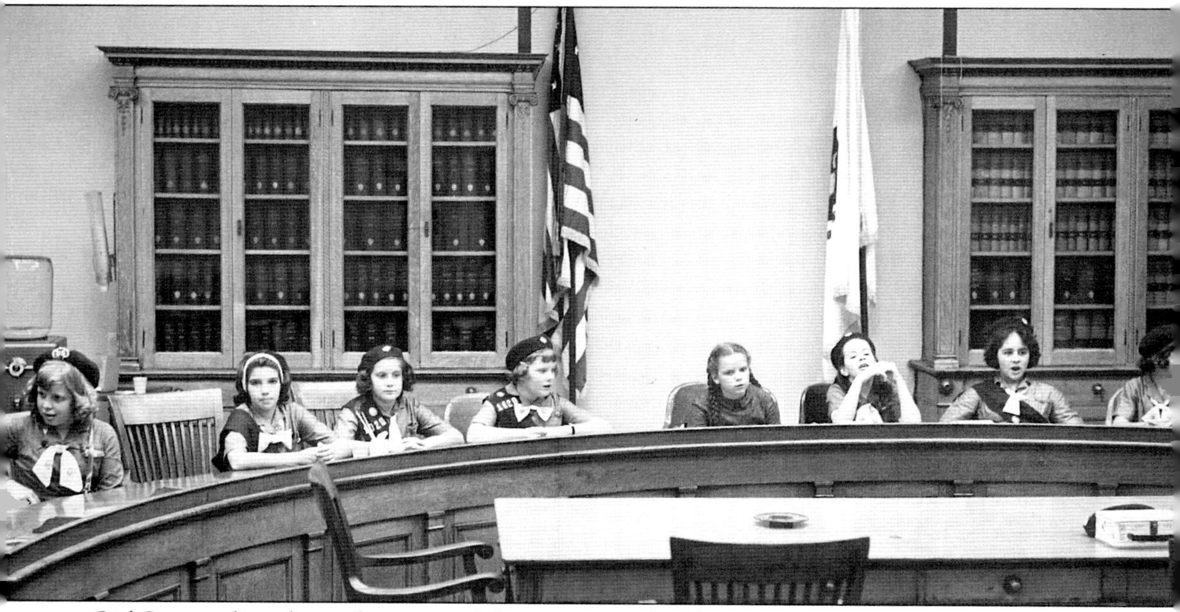

Girl Scouts align themselves around the city council table in October 1965.

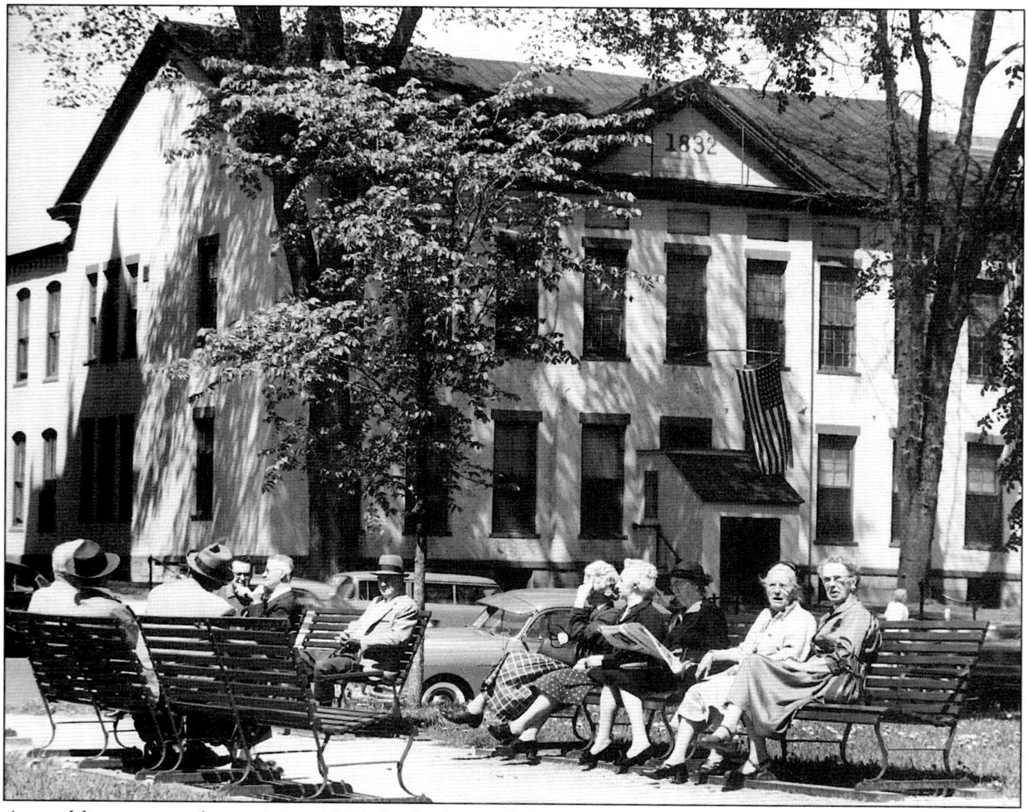

A cool but sunny day in May 1958 finds the park benches in heavy use outside the old Pittsfield City Hall on Park Square.

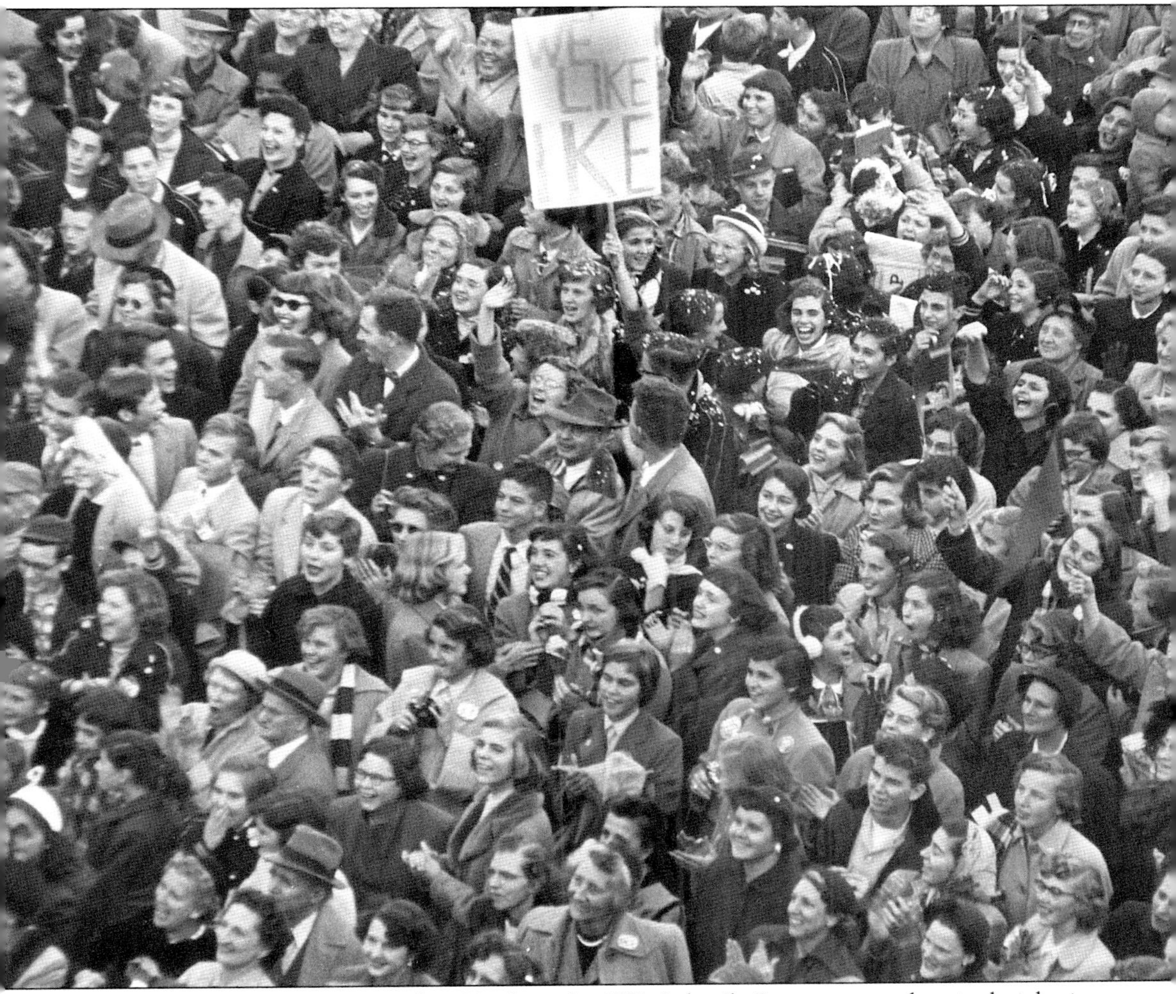

Who remembers the autumn of 1956 when the "We Like Ike" craze seemed at its height in the Berkshires? That year Gen. Dwight D. Eisenhower, the great World War II hero, defeated former Illinois Gov. Adlai E. Stevenson for the presidency for the second time.

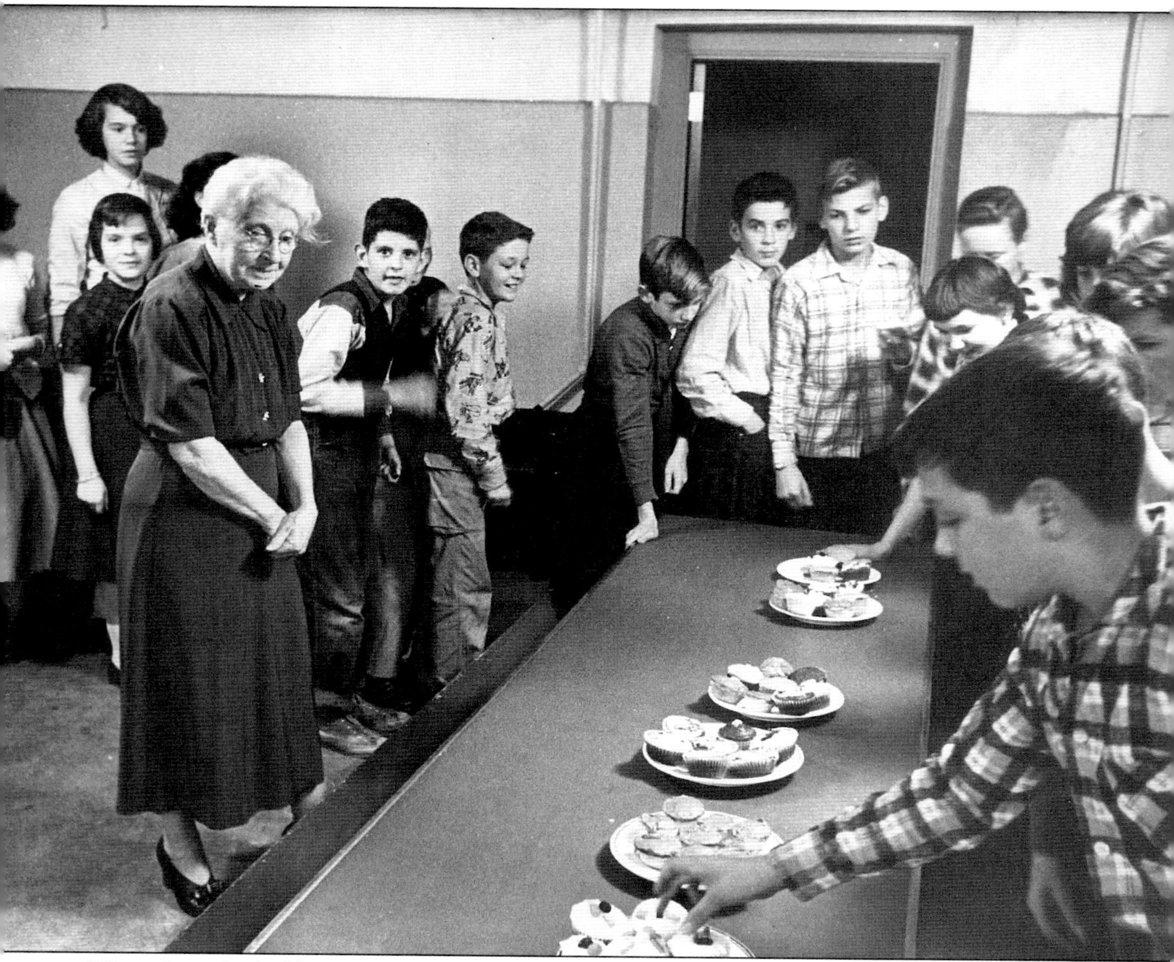

"Cupcake sale, held once a month at Kittredge School, Hinsdale, is a fund-raising project of the PTA. At left, Miss Rose Conley, retired school nurse, supervises pupils who may select one 5-cent cupcake each. PTA members make enough for all pupils in the school and invariably the sale is a success" —November 19, 1955.

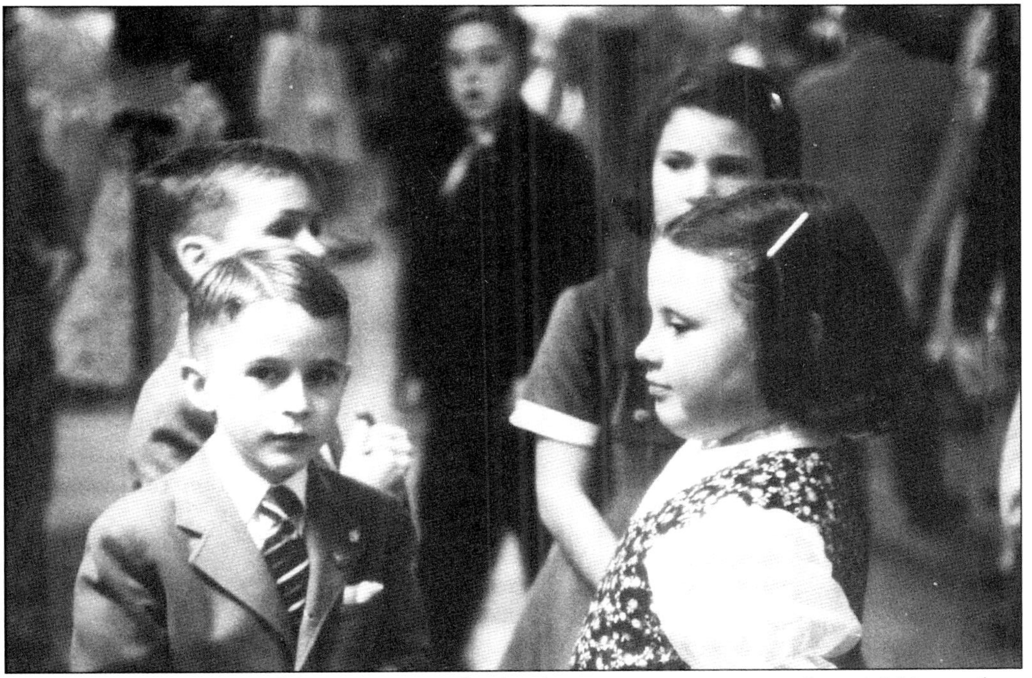

"Choosing partners, small boy pauses to think of correct way to approach a girl bigger than himself at dancing class cotillion. Boy at rear is also in doubt. Both are anxious to make a good impression and know a man has to be careful in addressing a woman" —December 11, 1954. The event took place at the Hotel Wendell-Sherwood ballroom for pupils of the Richardson dance classes. The photo below was taken at the same event.

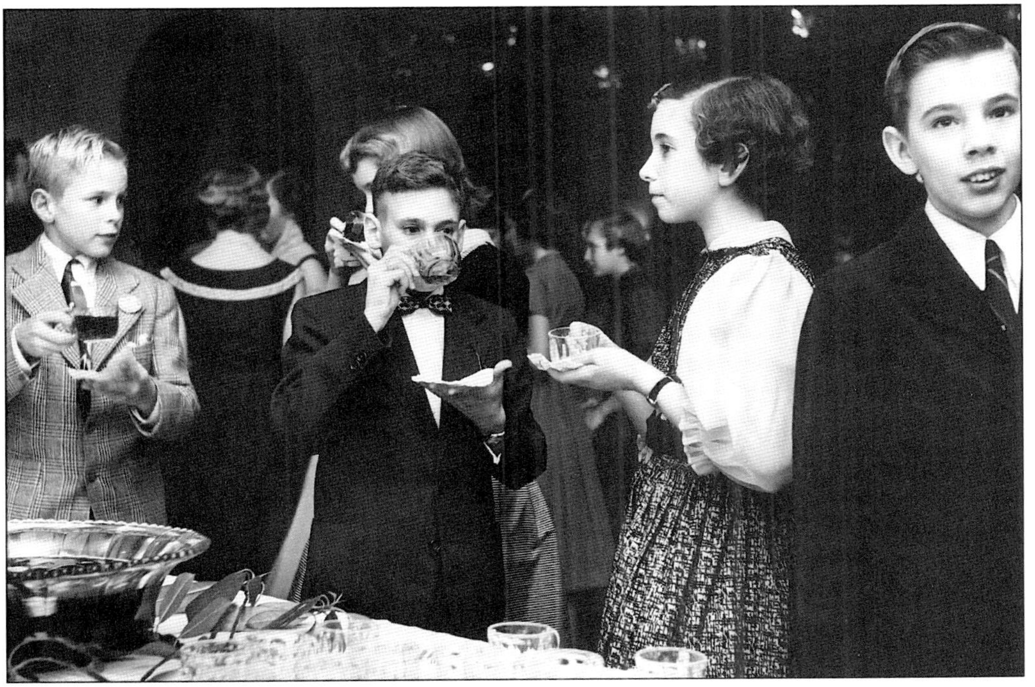

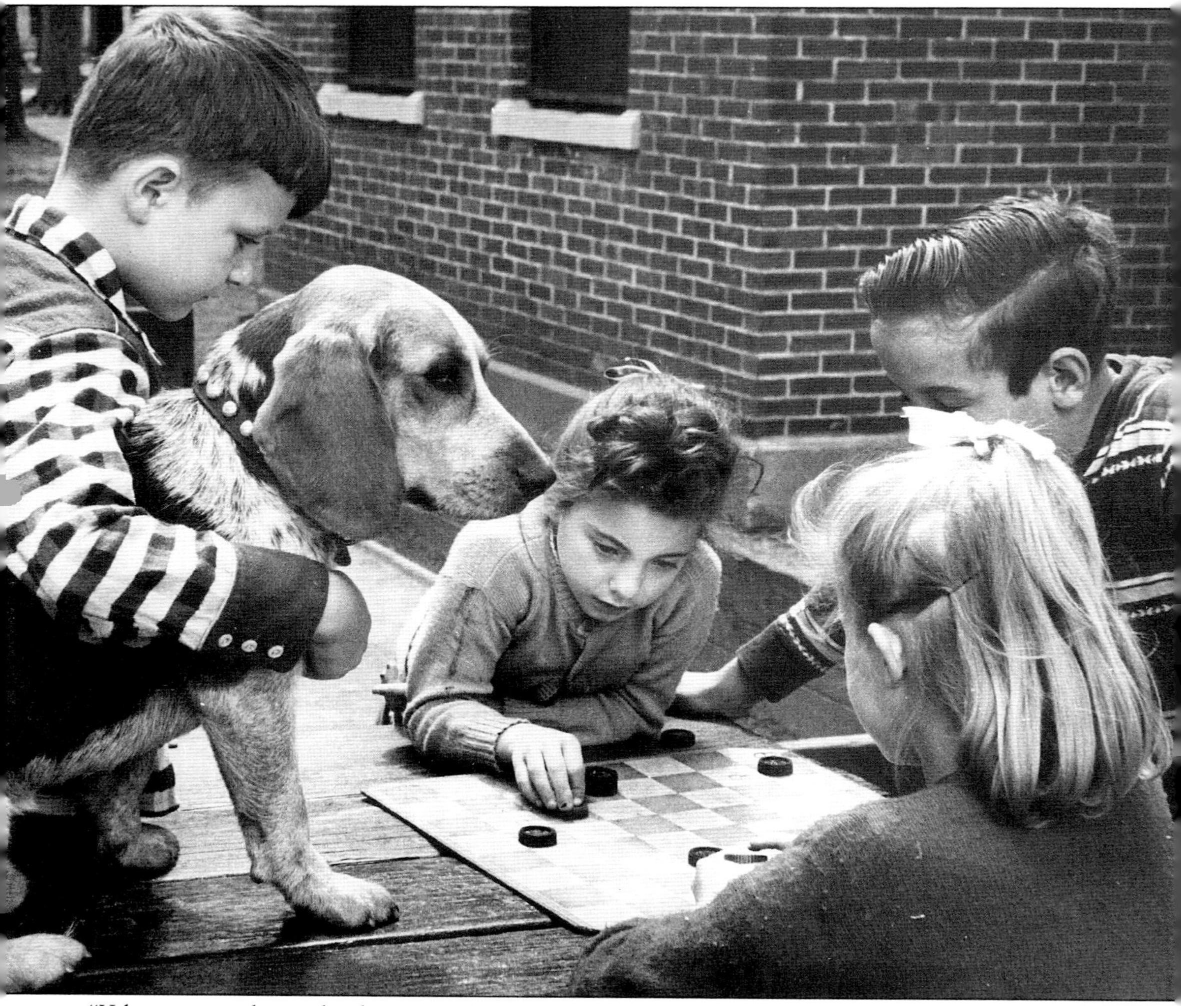

"Kibitzers watching checker game between Jean Sobato and Nancy Wyman at the Common playground include two boys, Tommy Fleming, Robert Mayo and friendly dog 'Nifty.' Game went on in serious fashion until broken up by argument over rules" —July 3, 1954.

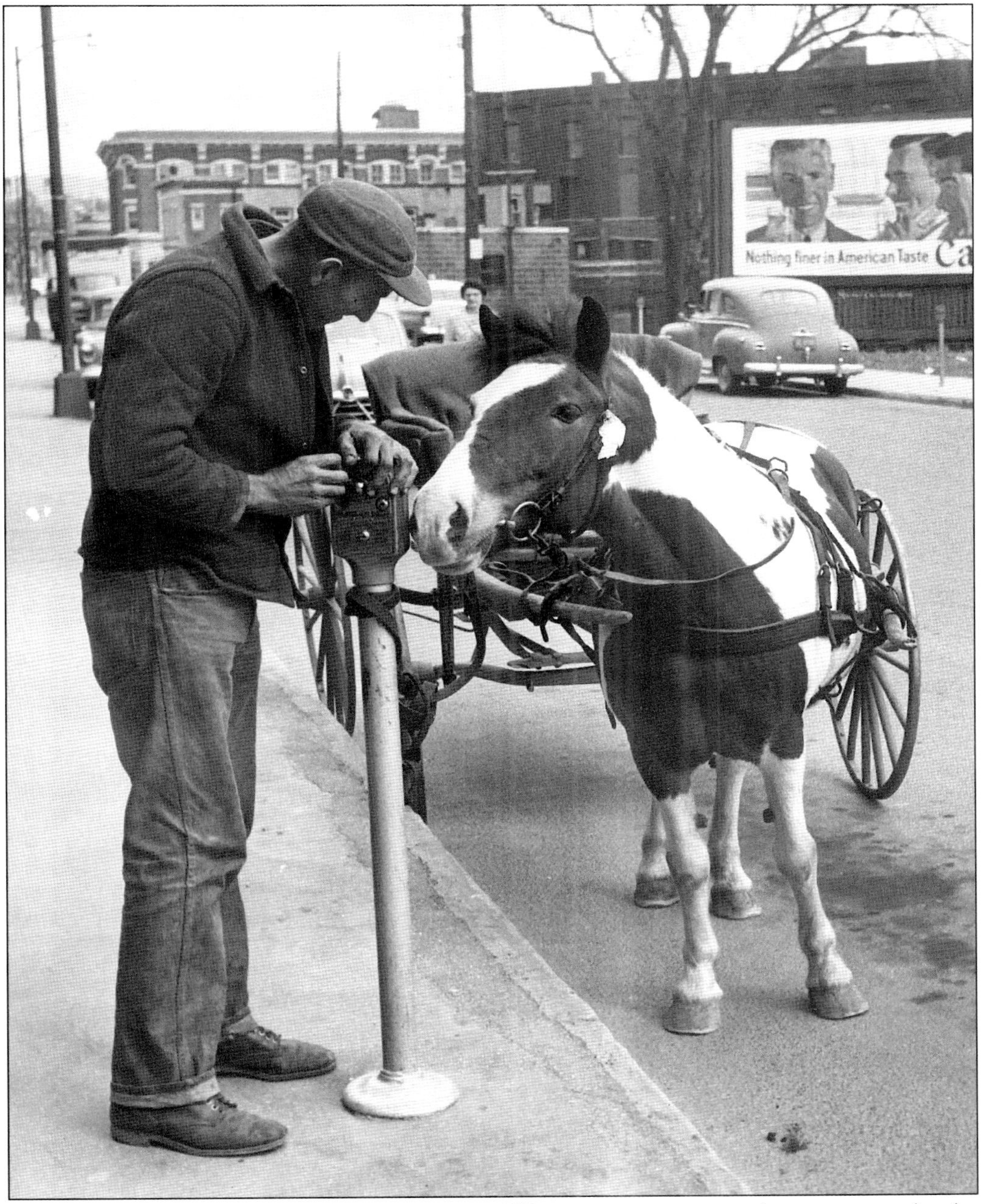

"A driver on Pittsfield's Columbus Avenue in 1957 puts a coin into a parking meter under the approving gaze of his power plant. Horse and buggy transportation would seem to be insurance against parking tickets. How would an enforcer go about ticketing a horse?" —October 7, 1989.

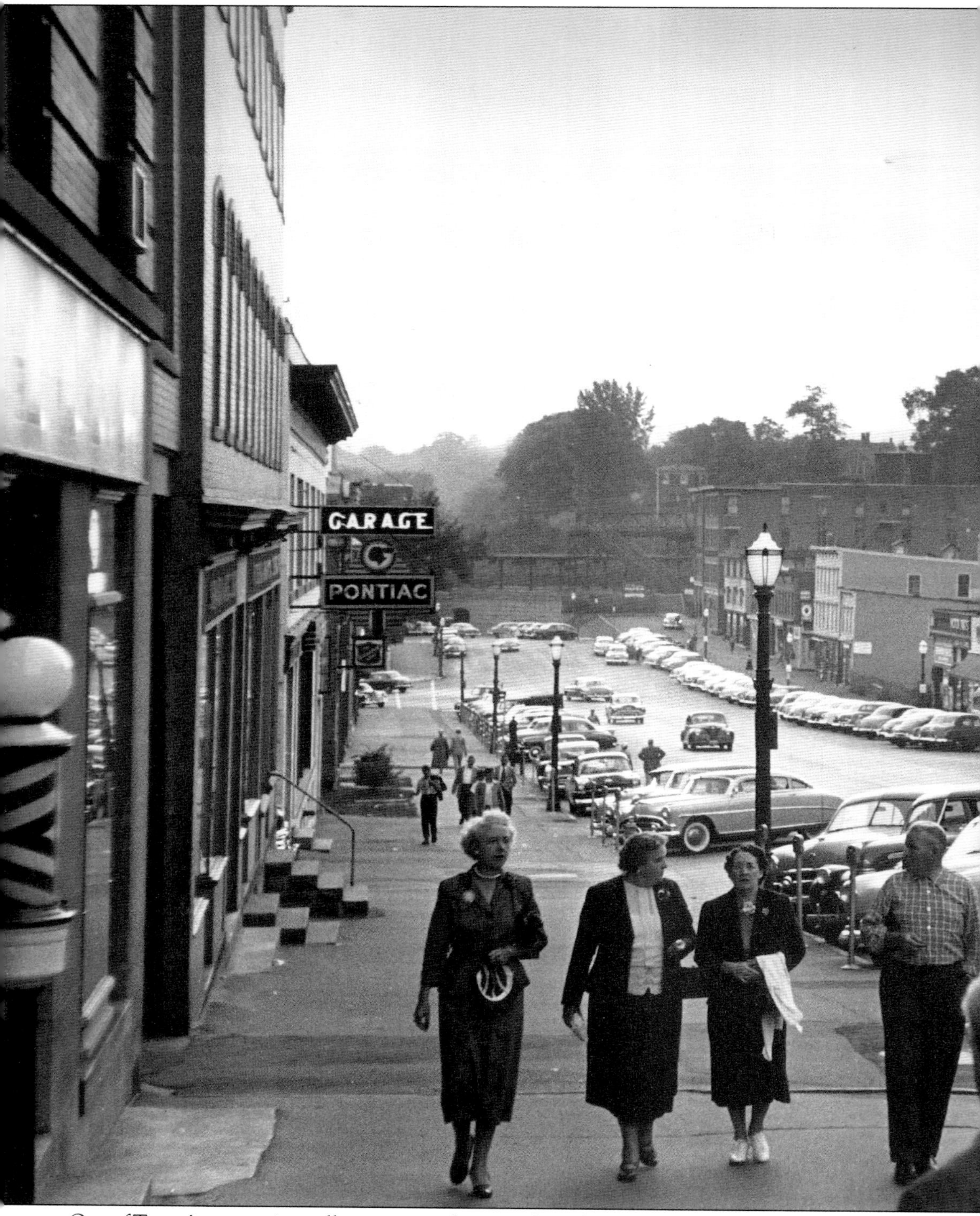

One of Tague's most universally evocative photographs is this scene looking west along Pittsfield's West Street in 1953. The reason is that all these buildings have been demolished and if one

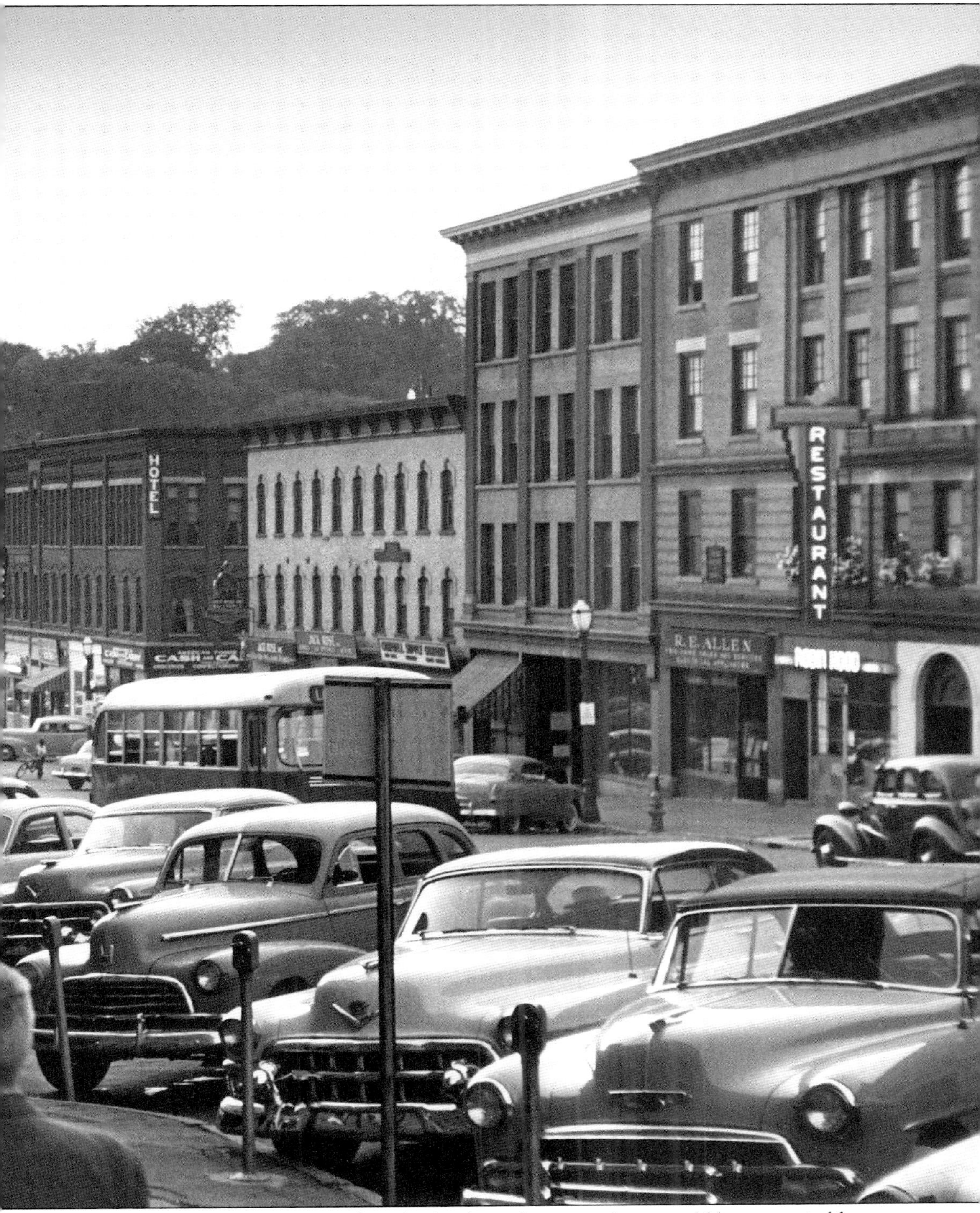

took a photo at the same spot today, absolutely nothing seen here would be recognizable.

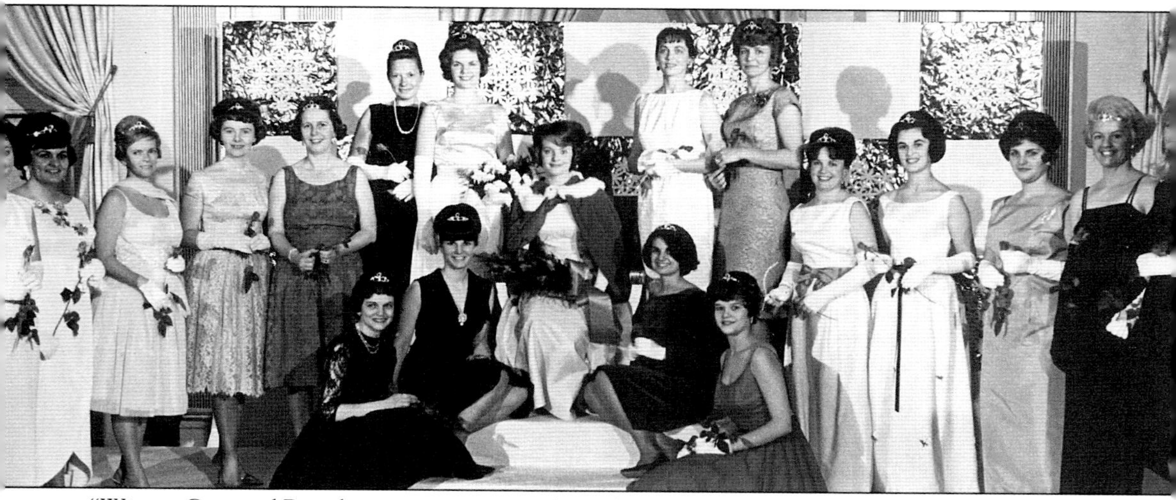

"Winter Carnival Royalty poses in unprecedented numbers at the 20th Anniversary Coronation ball last Saturday night. The group includes 14 queens. From left, standing: Mrs. William Tague (Irene Lanthier), 1951 queen; Mrs. Francis Sanginetti (Patricia Taglieri), 1957 queen; Mrs. Richard Maxon (Barbara Weston), 1955 member of court; Mrs. Walter Duda (Connie Bierdrzcki), 1949 lady in waiting; Mrs. Fred Love (Judy Ziemba), 1947 lady in waiting; Mrs. Edward Reynolds (Mary Voci), 1948 lady in waiting; Mrs. Wayne Galletly (Jerri Dietrich), 1946 queen; Mrs. Winthrop Piper (Emilou Starke), 1946 queen; Mrs. Paul Burke (Theresa Tsyziewski), 1946 queen; Mrs. George Yannone (Connie Dillon), 1953 queen; Mrs. Albert Coury (Barbara Todt), 1956 queen; and Miss Maaja Sildoja, 1963 queen. Seated, from left: Mrs. Edward Ziemba (Rose Marie Iorio), 1952 member of court; Mrs. Alexander McGovern (Carol-Sue Marby), 1962 queen; Miss Maureen Lowry, 1965 queen; Miss Kathleen Marby, 1960 queen; and Mrs. Peter May (Kathleen Nichols), 1961 queen. Dancing followed and a delightful time was had by all" —February 13, 1965.

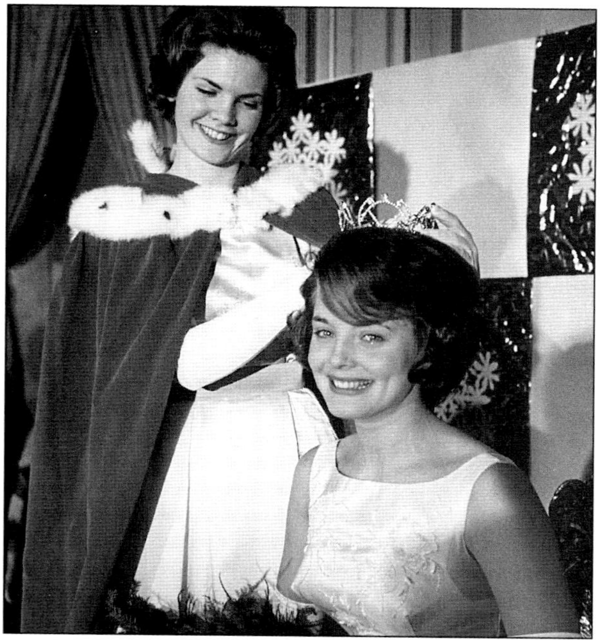

"Coronation of 1965 Winter Carnival queen Maureen Lowry is performed by Mrs. Wayne Galletly (Jerri Dietrich), the 1964 queen."

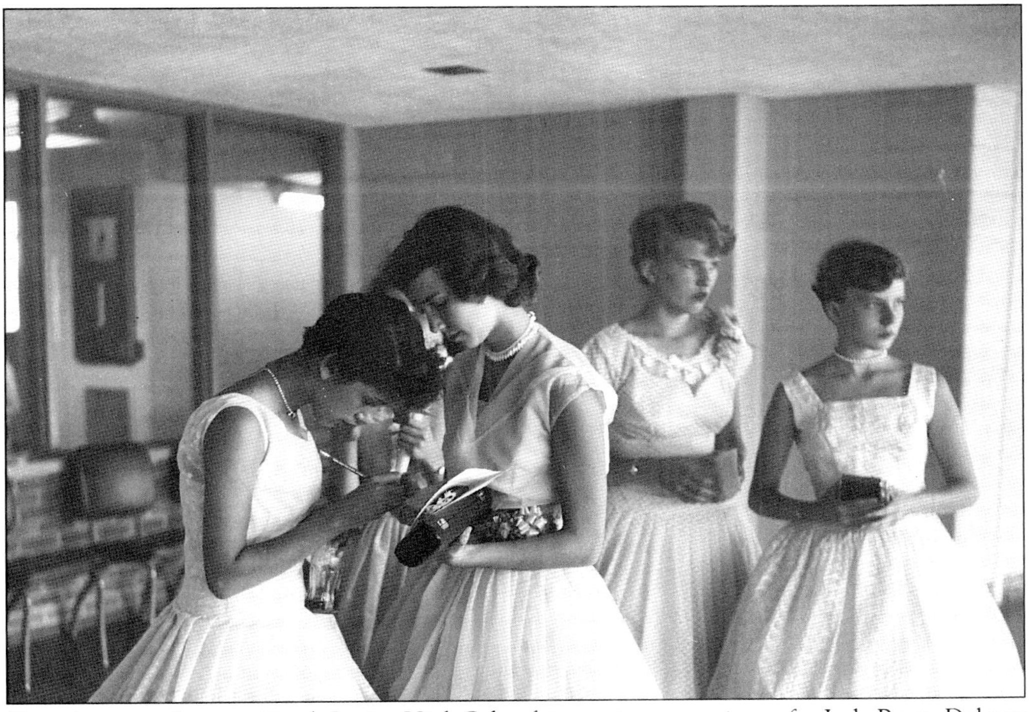

"Last day as students at North Junior High School is a serious experience for Judy Bove, Delores Watt, Barbara Milensky and Lynne Ochieano. Wearing their best frocks, they're just graduated and will be leaving shortly. Judy is giving Delores her autograph" —June 25, 1955.

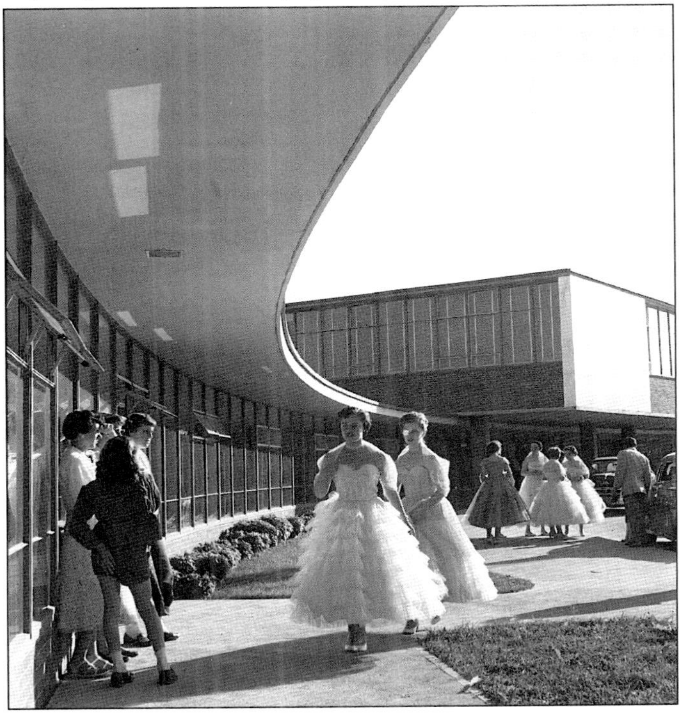

"Ninth grade prom at North Junior High School was a brilliant affair as girls in their formal gowns paraded back and forth outside the entrance, looking at each other before the dance began" —June 23, 1956.

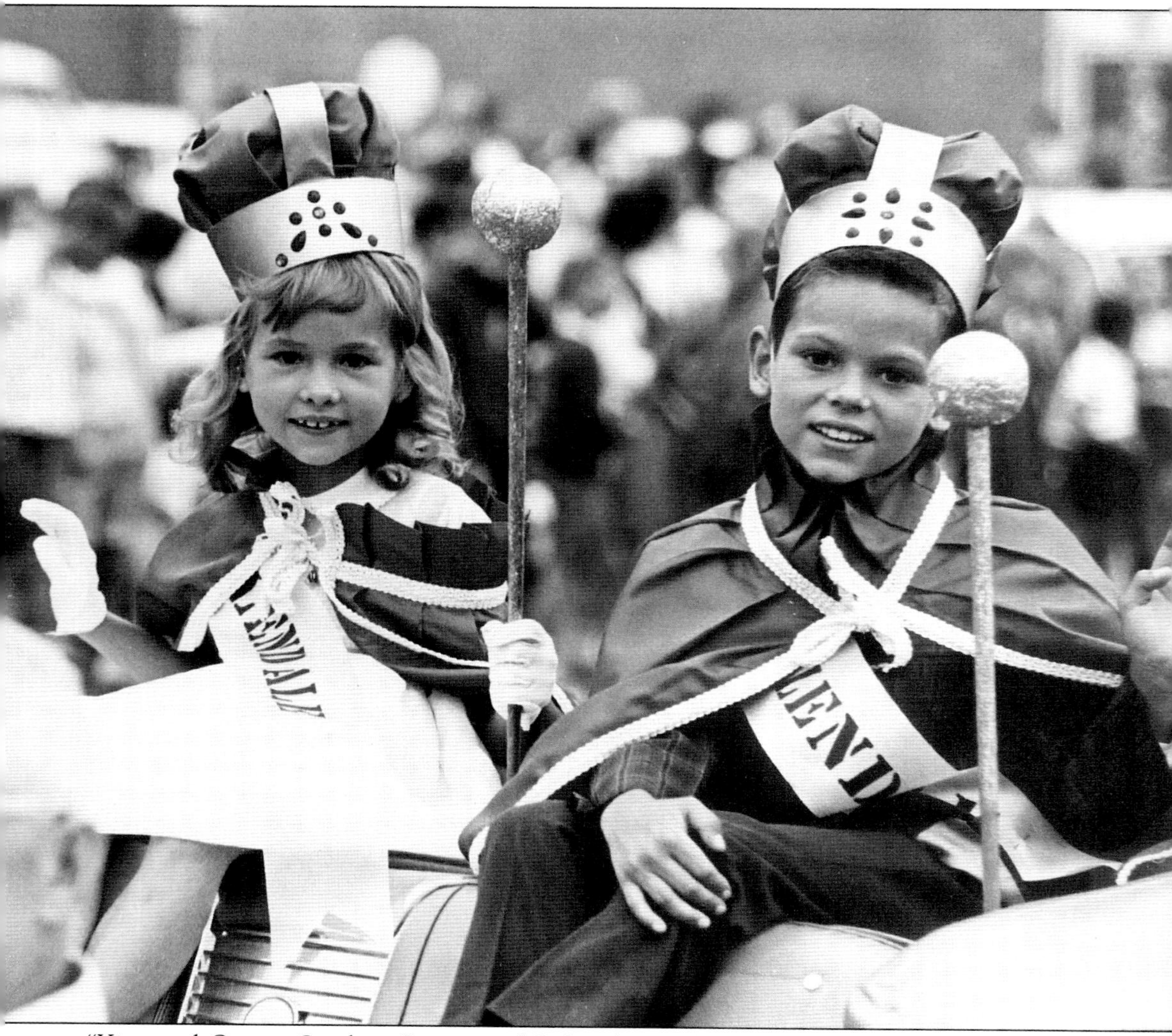

"King and Queen, Stephen Strauss and Deborah Winslow, ride in a convertible during the annual Mardi Gras Parade of the Pittsfield Parks Department." —August 13, 1966.

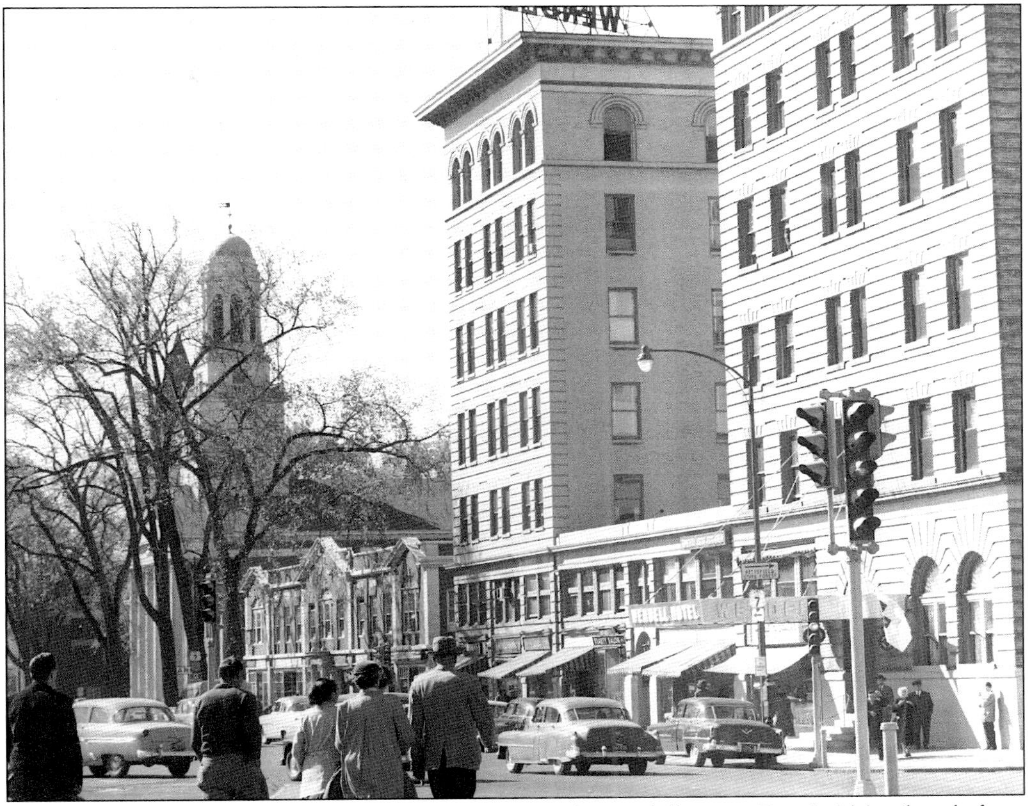

At the corner of North and West Streets, the Hotel Wendell was a Pittsfield landmark from its opening on September 30, 1898, to its demolition in 1965. It was replaced by the Berkshire Common and Hilton Inn.

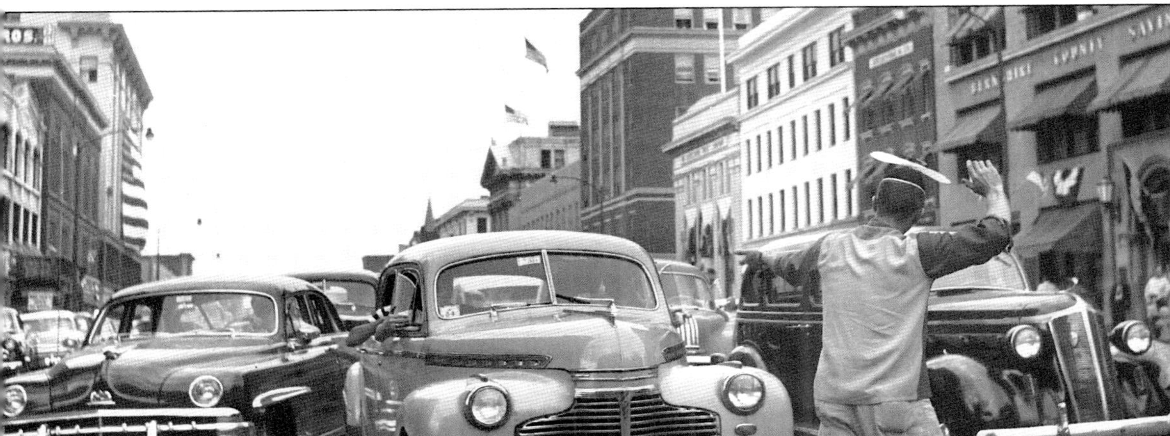

A brief fad during the 1950s was the beanie with the propeller on top. Thus clad, this fellow stops traffic along North Street in June 1954. The cars in foreground are a '49 Lincoln, a '41 Chevy, and a Studebaker of the late '30s.

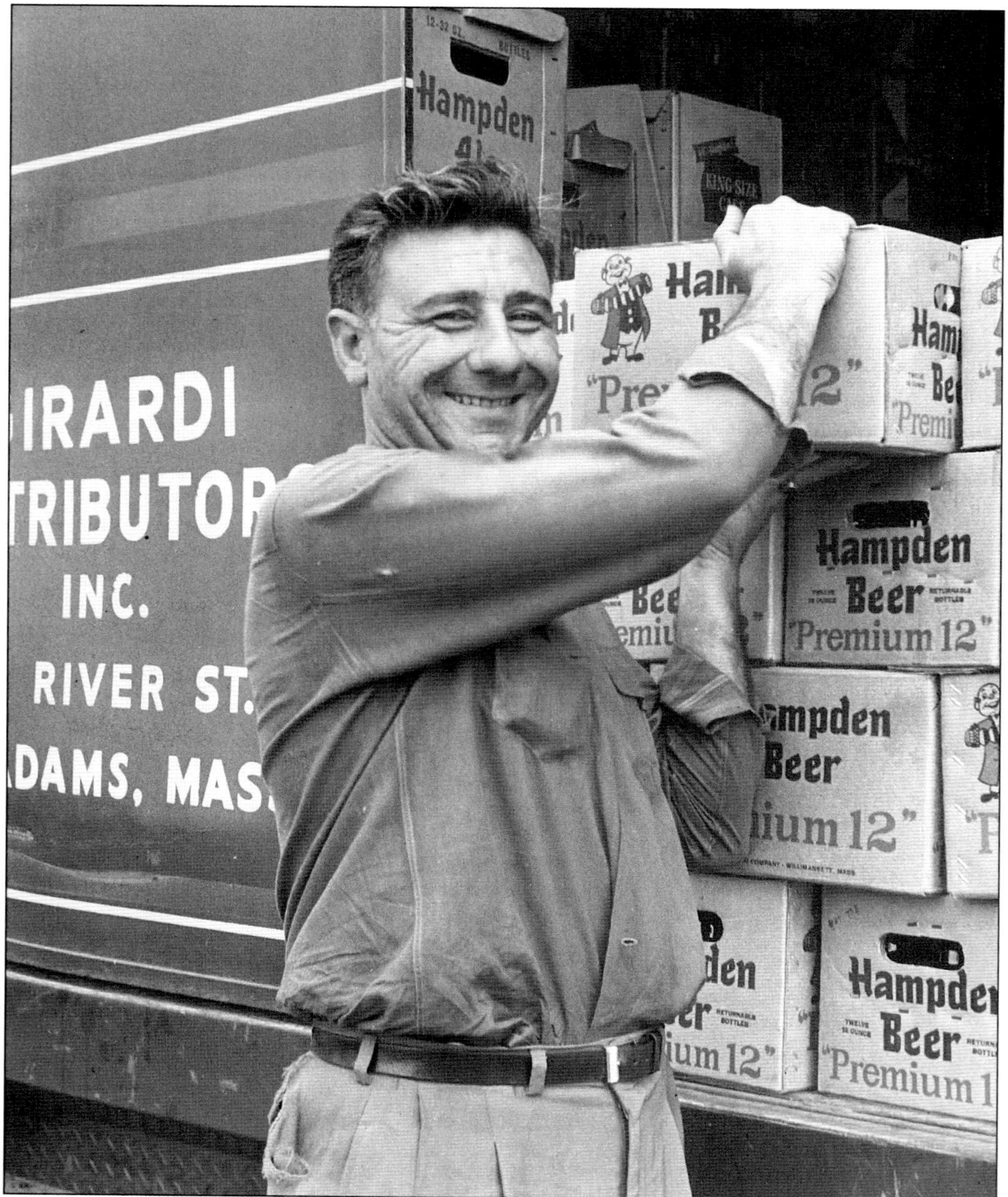

"Unloading bottled goods is Pasquale A. Bruni, sixth grade teacher at Hibbard School. He's a truck driver for the Girardi Brothers Distributors" —July 27, 1957. This was part of a series Tague did after discovering that 90 percent of the region's public school teachers got extra jobs during the summer vacation.

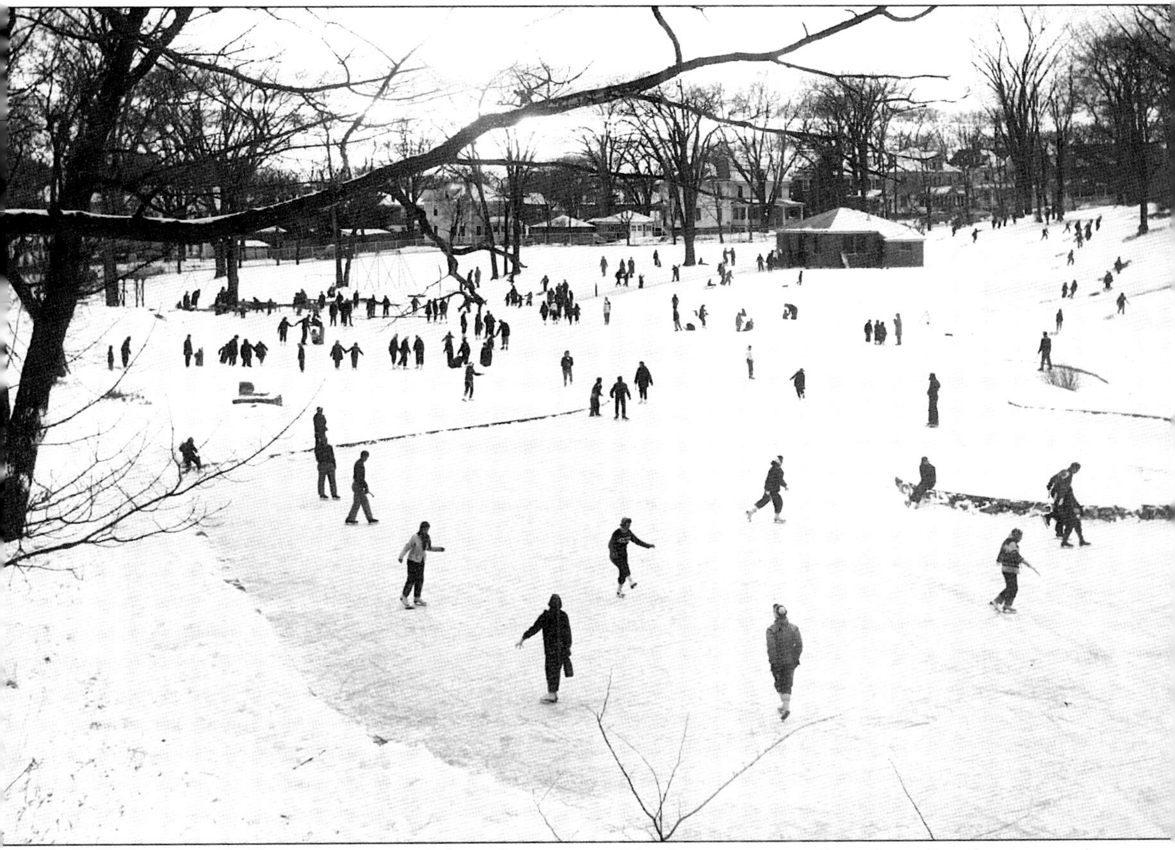

"Springside Park in winter is a definitely unspringlike but very popular place for skating and sliding, both of which have been good lately. The biggest crowds appear near the end of the afternoon when the children are out of school and ready for recreation" —January 7, 1957. Can anyone refrain from commenting on the Brueghel-like nature of this scene?

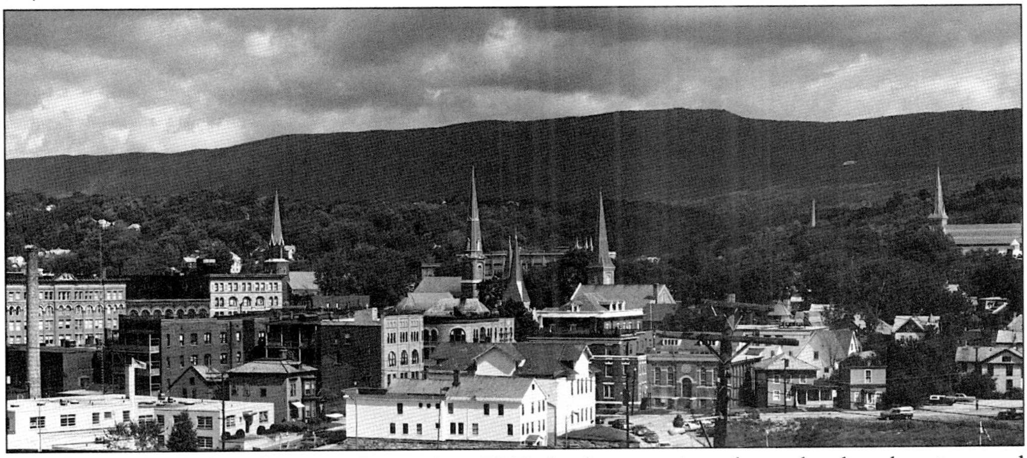

This view of North Adams in September 1969 discloses a city of mostly church spires and chimney stacks. A large swath of its built environment had been wiped out earlier in the decade by urban renewal.

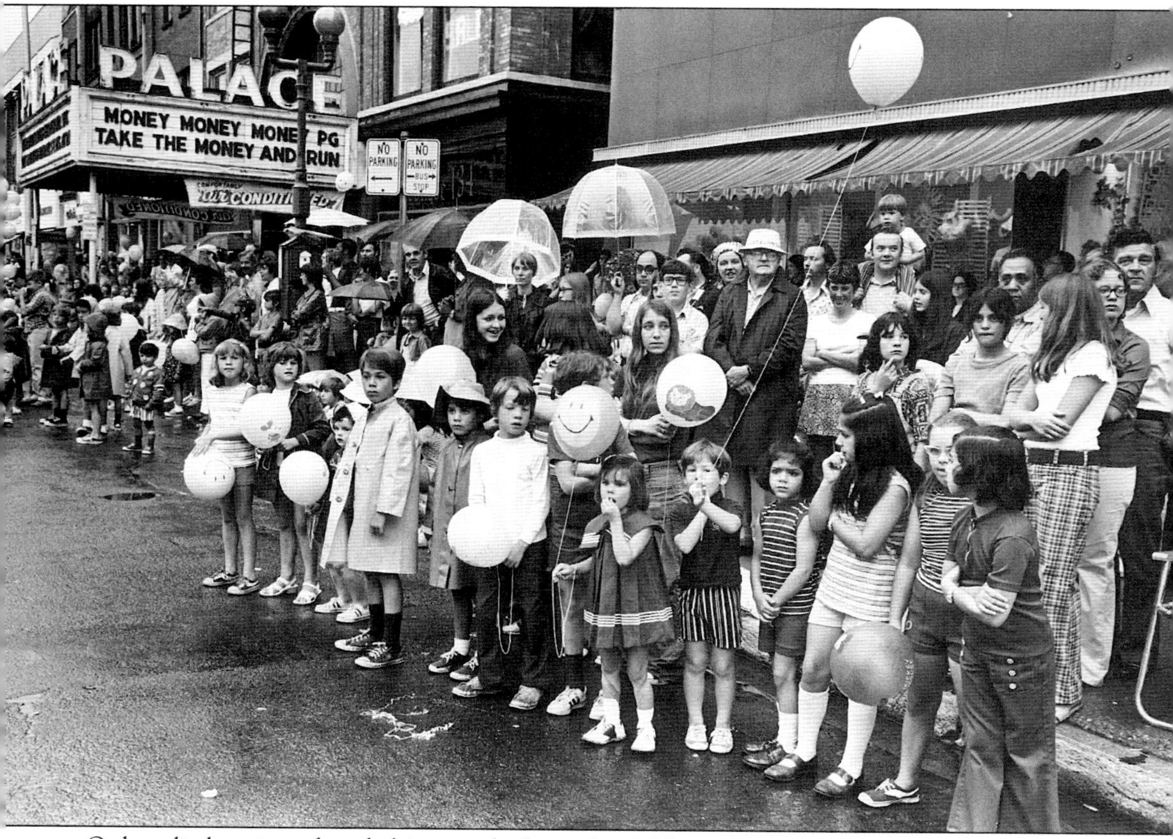

Only a little rain reduced this crowd of mostly children along North Street waiting for the Fourth of July parade to come along in 1973.

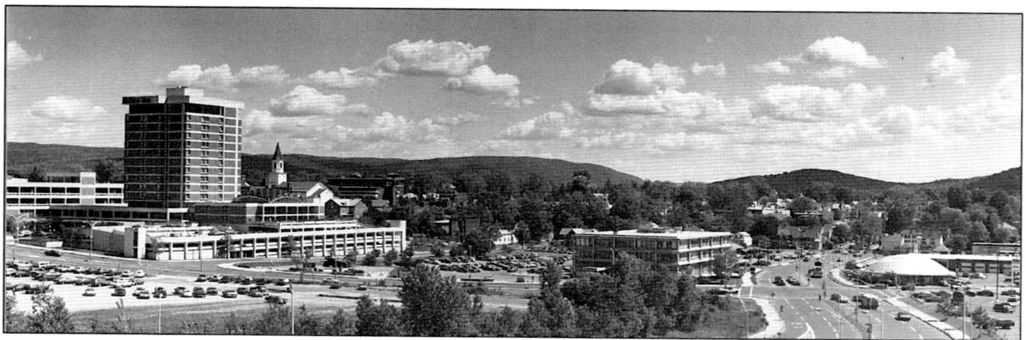

The Berkshire Common, at left, a complex that included the 14-story Hilton as well as a three-story office building and shopping arcade, was what replaced the buildings and scene of the old West Street shown on pp. 42–43.

Three

Recreational Pursuits

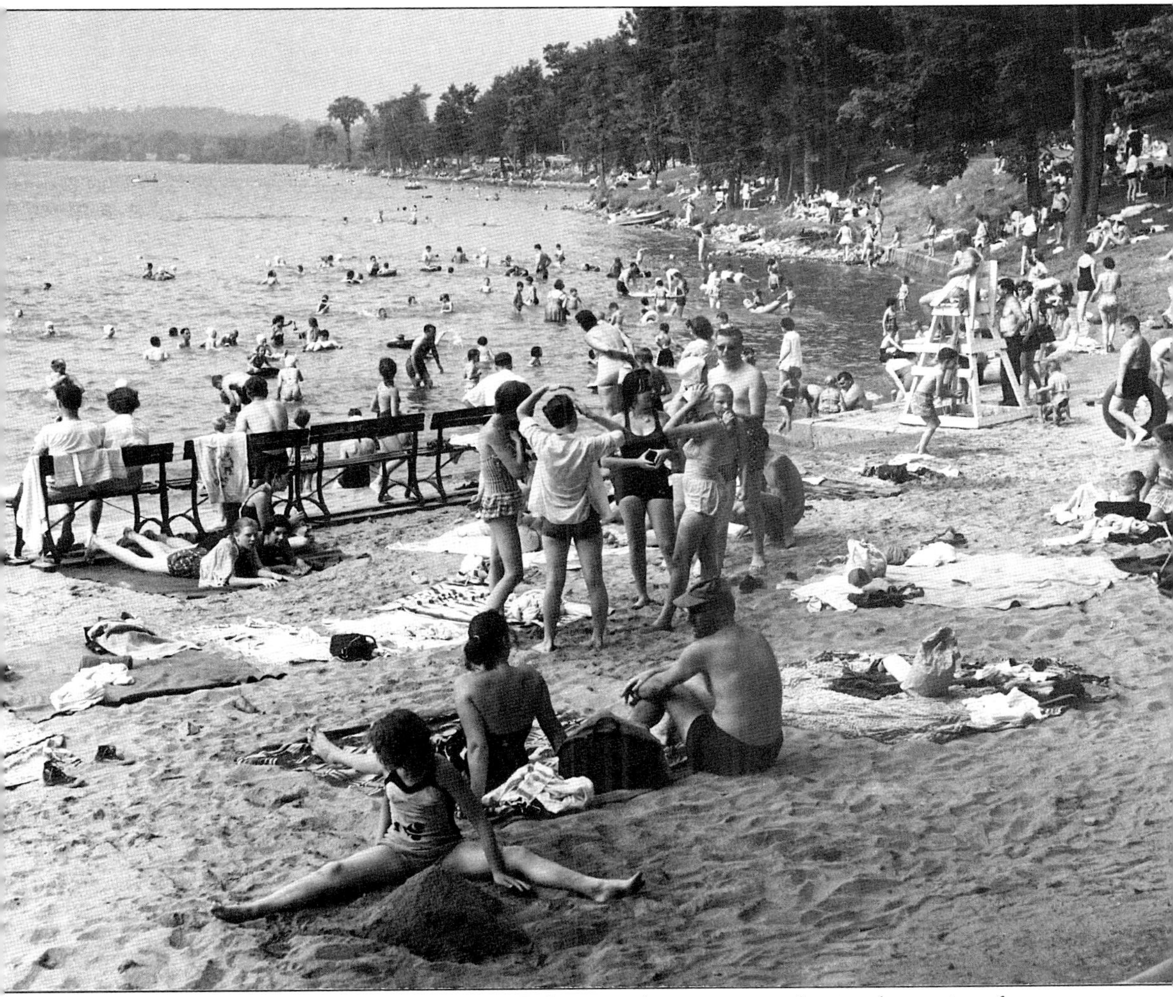

The beach at Burbank Park on Onota Lake was the most popular in the region for many summers. This photo was taken in July 1957.

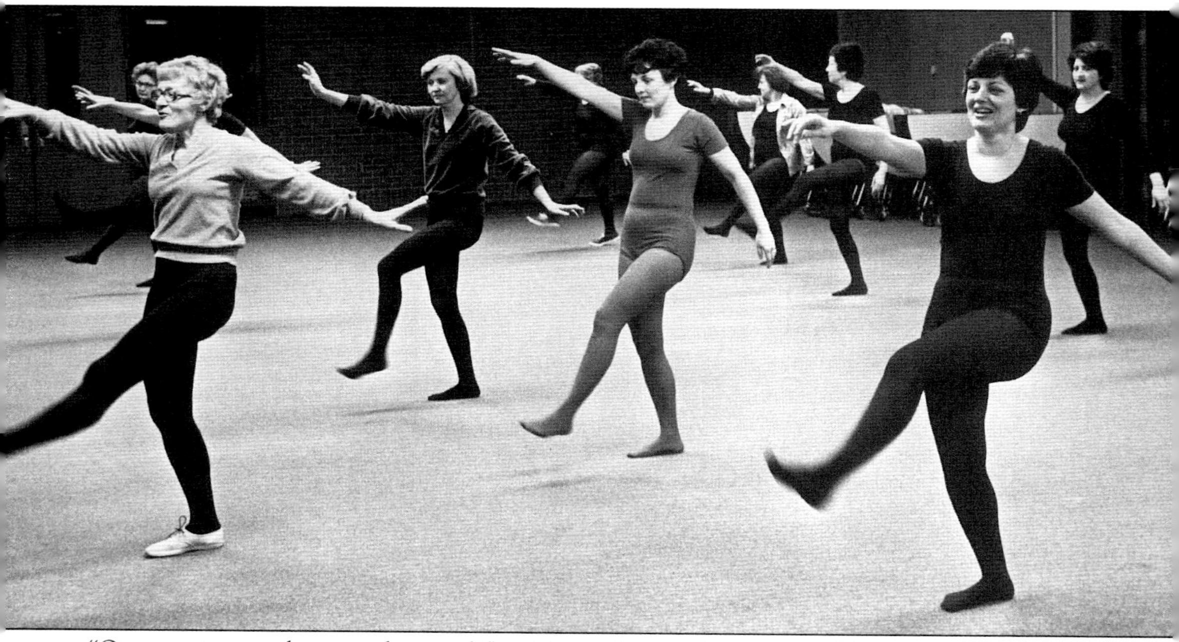

"Overcoming surplus poundage and flaccid muscles can be an enjoyable experience when one does it to music in a congenial group, as here at the West Side Community School. The women are students of Celia Conuel in a 'jazz exercise' course given by the adult continuing education program. It runs 20 weeks, which ought to be enough for a significant shrinkage" —January 12, 1980. The photographer also focused on the difficulties of exercise without a congenial group, as below.

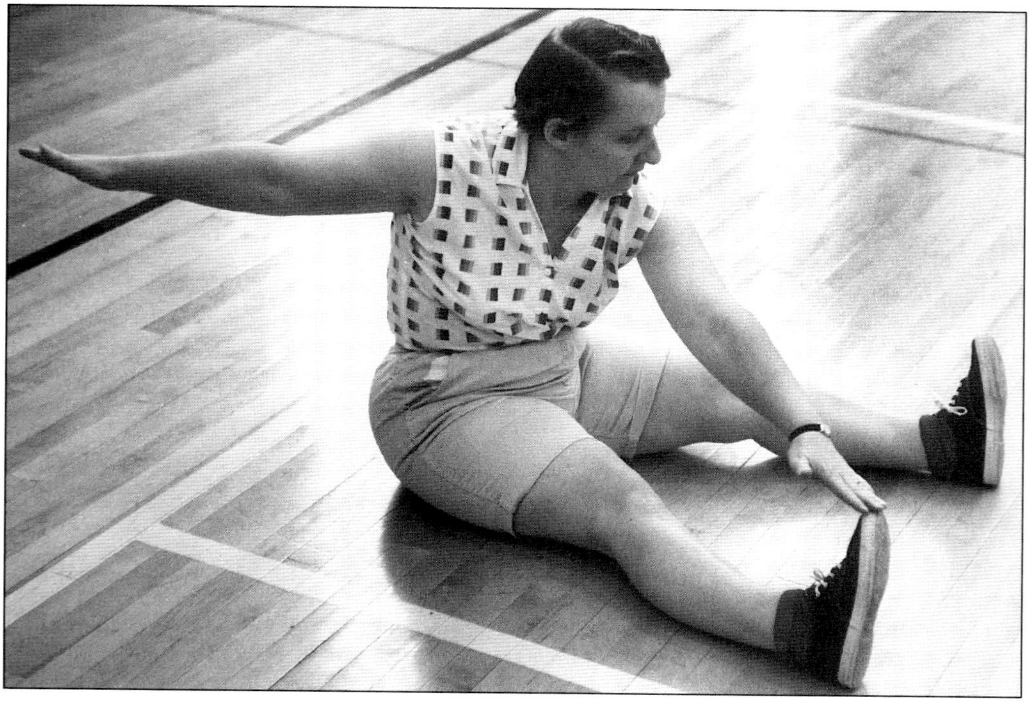

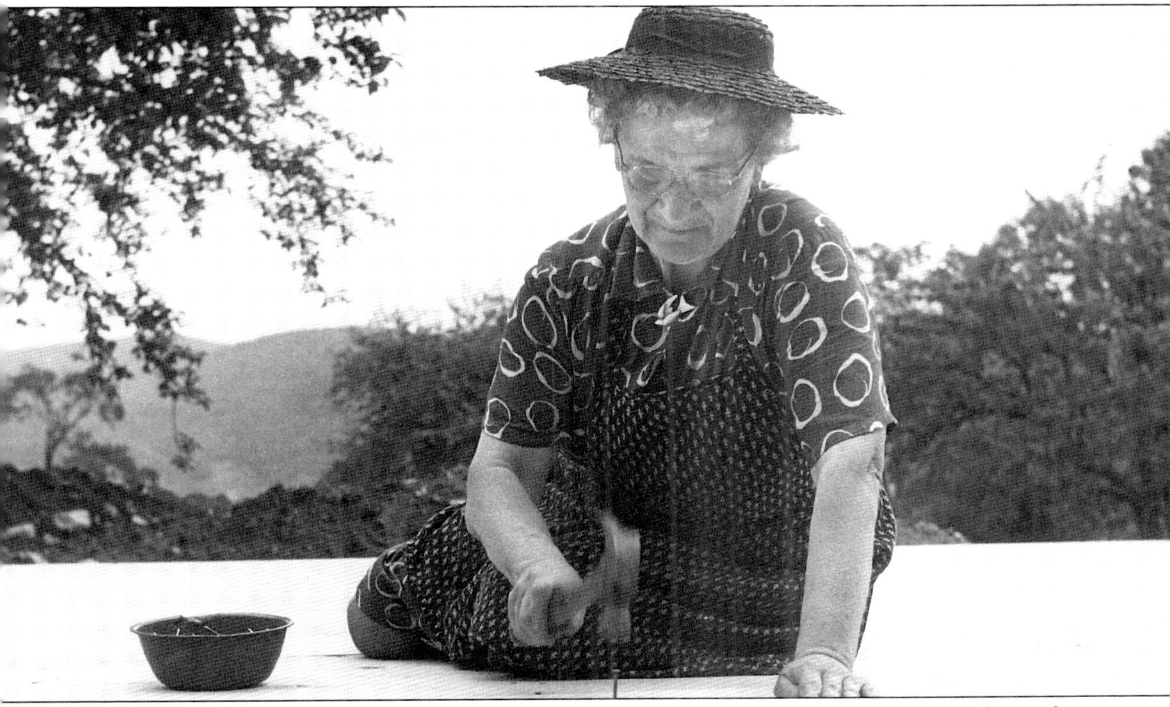

"Never too old to tackle a new project, Mrs. Margaret M. Taylor, 63, pounds nails on first floor of a new four-room house she and her husband Eli are building by themselves next to their present home on East Street in Lenox. Mrs. Taylor has seven children, 23 grandchildren, and 2 great grandchildren and has never done any carpentry before. Mr. Taylor, a farmer, has had some house-building experience, but doesn't claim to be an expert. Nevertheless, they're making progress and expect to move in by spring" —June 4, 1955.

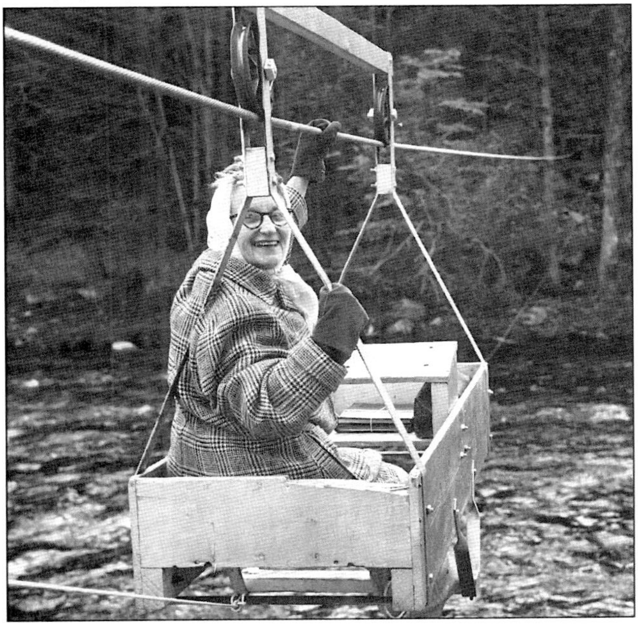

Neither this woman happily sailing across a stream on homemade tramway nor the site is identified, but the date is October 1955.

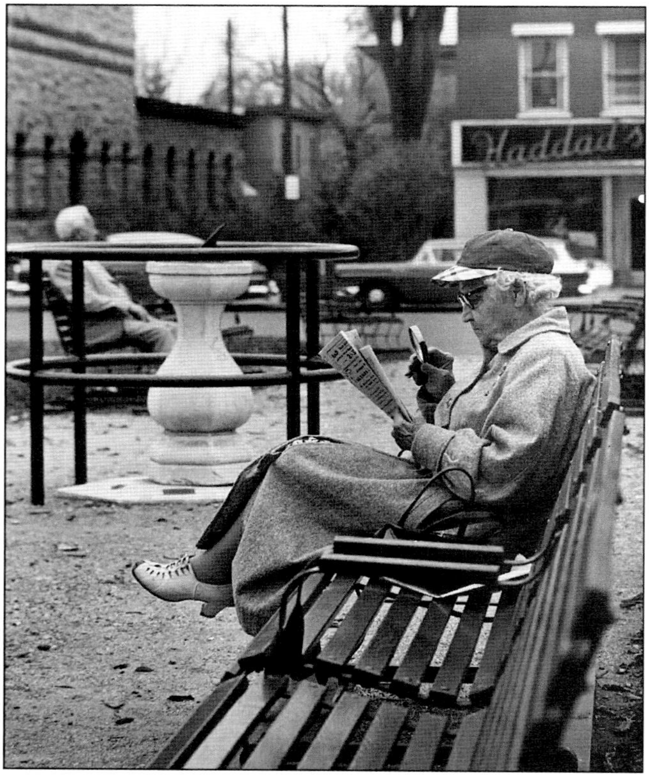

Park benches provided captive audiences for Tague, especially when the subjects were dozing or deeply engaged. Such was the case with this woman at Park Square, and the photographer's colleague, Jay C. Rosenfeld, who was the *Eagle*'s music critic, napping with his Boston Symphony Orchestra program.

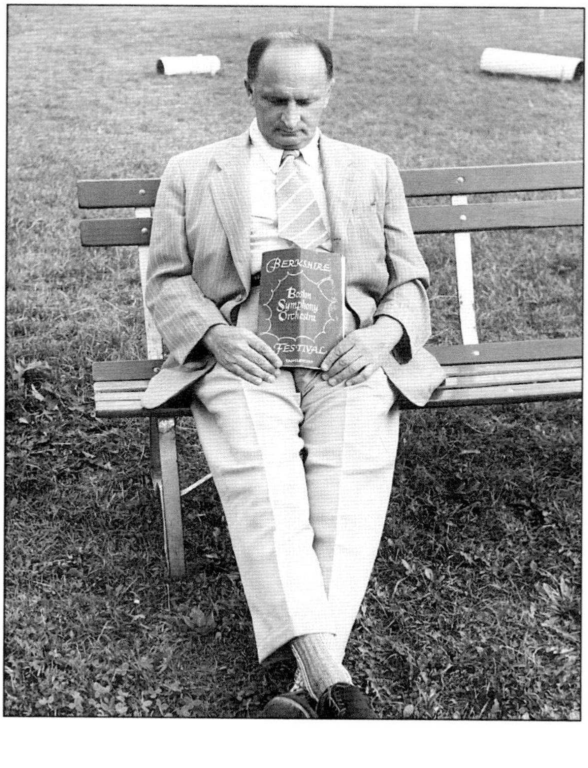

The men absorbed by the *Morning Telegraph* probably never realized they were being photographed. They didn't seem too happy, anyway. The photo is dated September 1958.

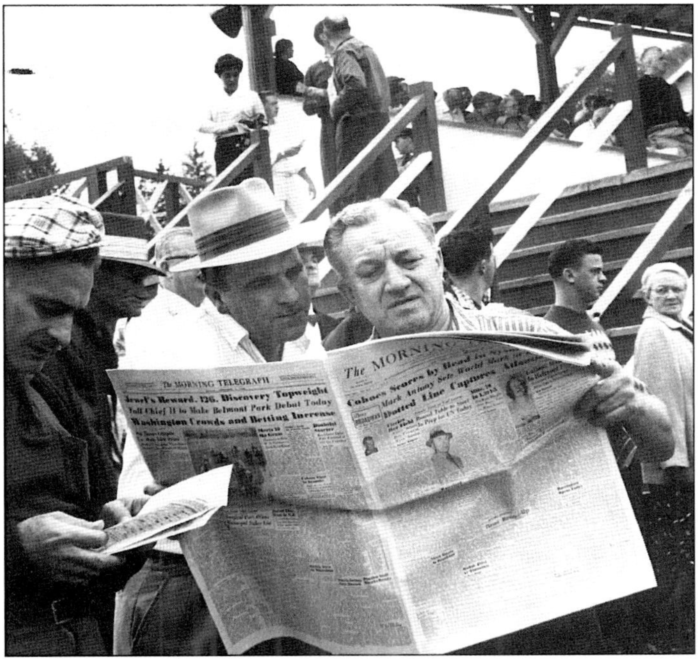

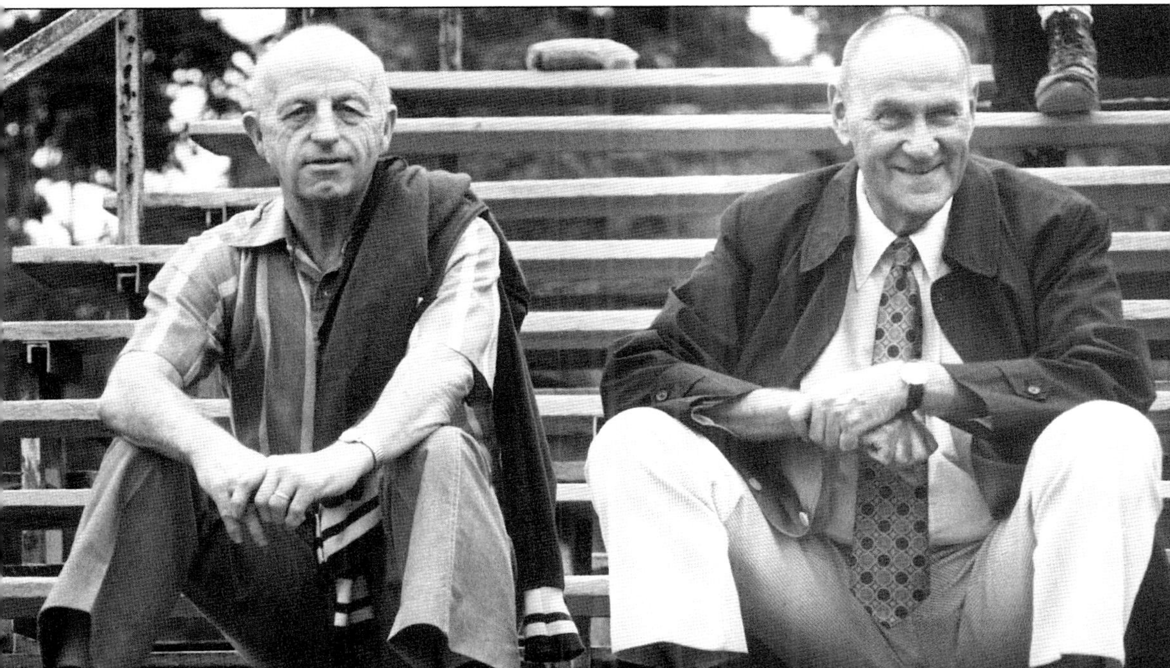

"This is the last picture I took of Randy Trabold, the man on the right, as almost everyone in North Berkshire knows. He's watching a Williams College football game with Ray Merrigan, a former colleague on the North Adams Transcript, which Randy served for 44 years as a photographer. He died last week, much too soon, but his pictures will long survive" —March 1, 1980.

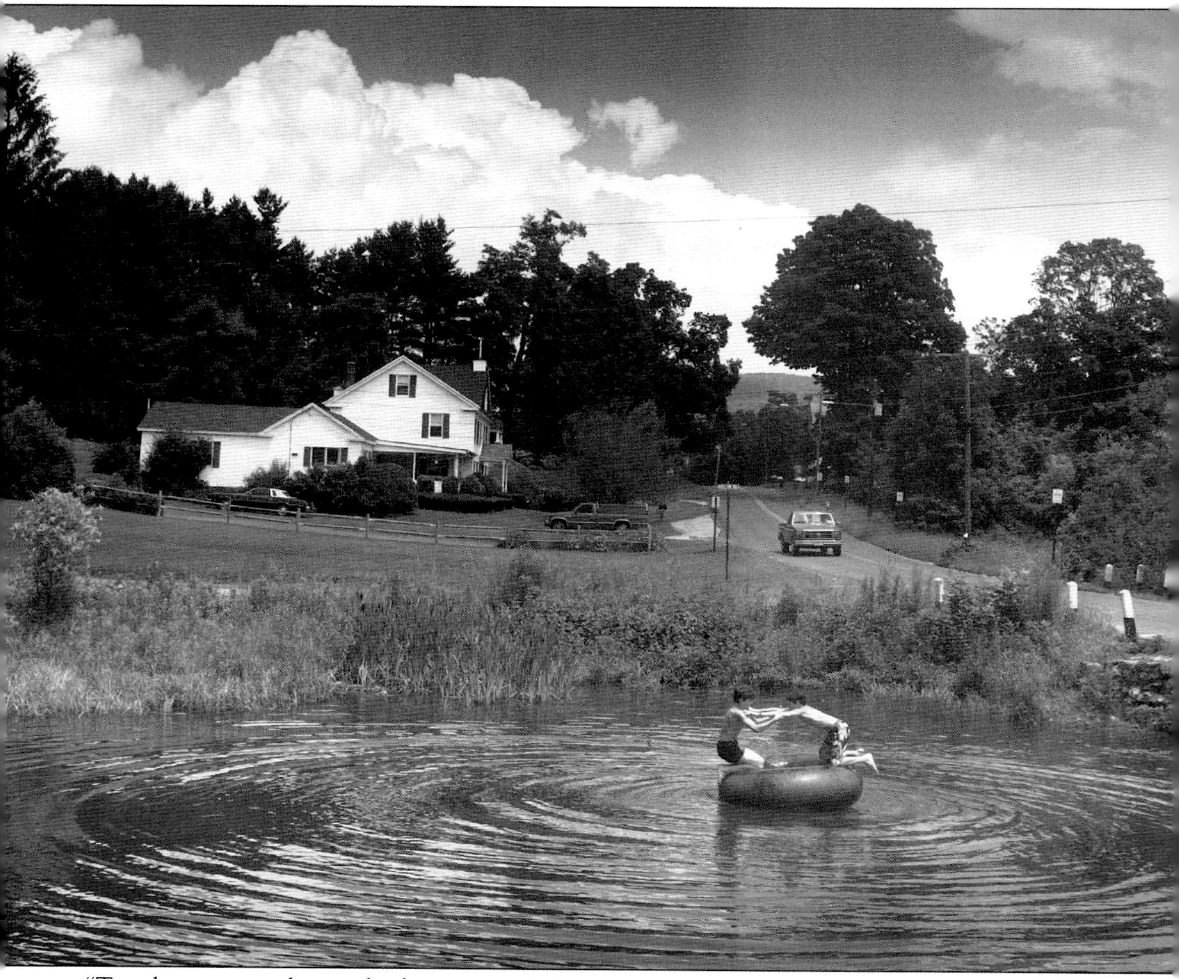

"Two boys on a tube ripple the waters of the old swimming hold in Berkshire Village, which probably has been a source of childhood fun for a century or so" —July 15, 1989.

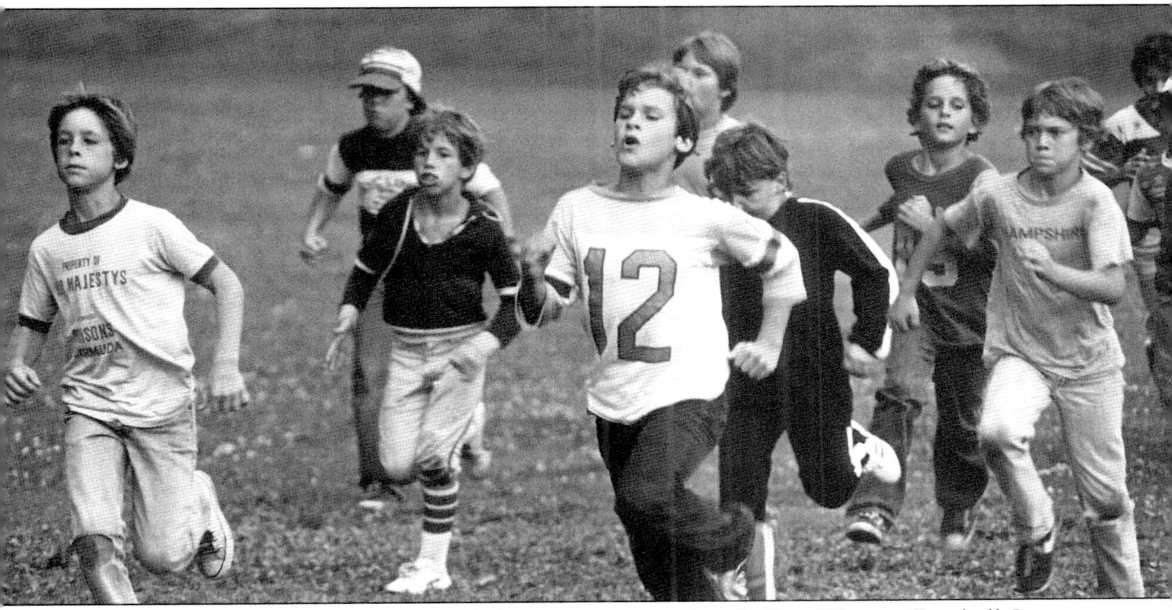

"Young fellows going out for one of the teams in Pittsfield's Pop Warner Football League are determined to impress the coach during practice . . . Some of these lads sprinting on the Common will be picked for the backfield and some for the line. And who knows? One day one of those here might even become a professional" —August 25, 1979.

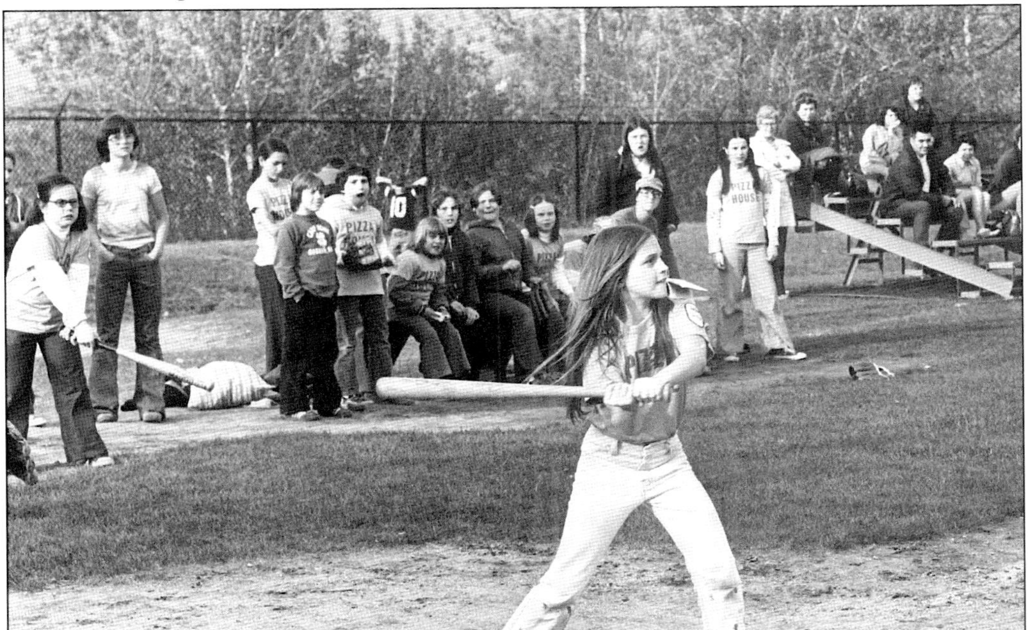

Wearing decorative bell-bottoms, this strong-hitting girl is the focus of everyone's attention in a photo dated May 1976.

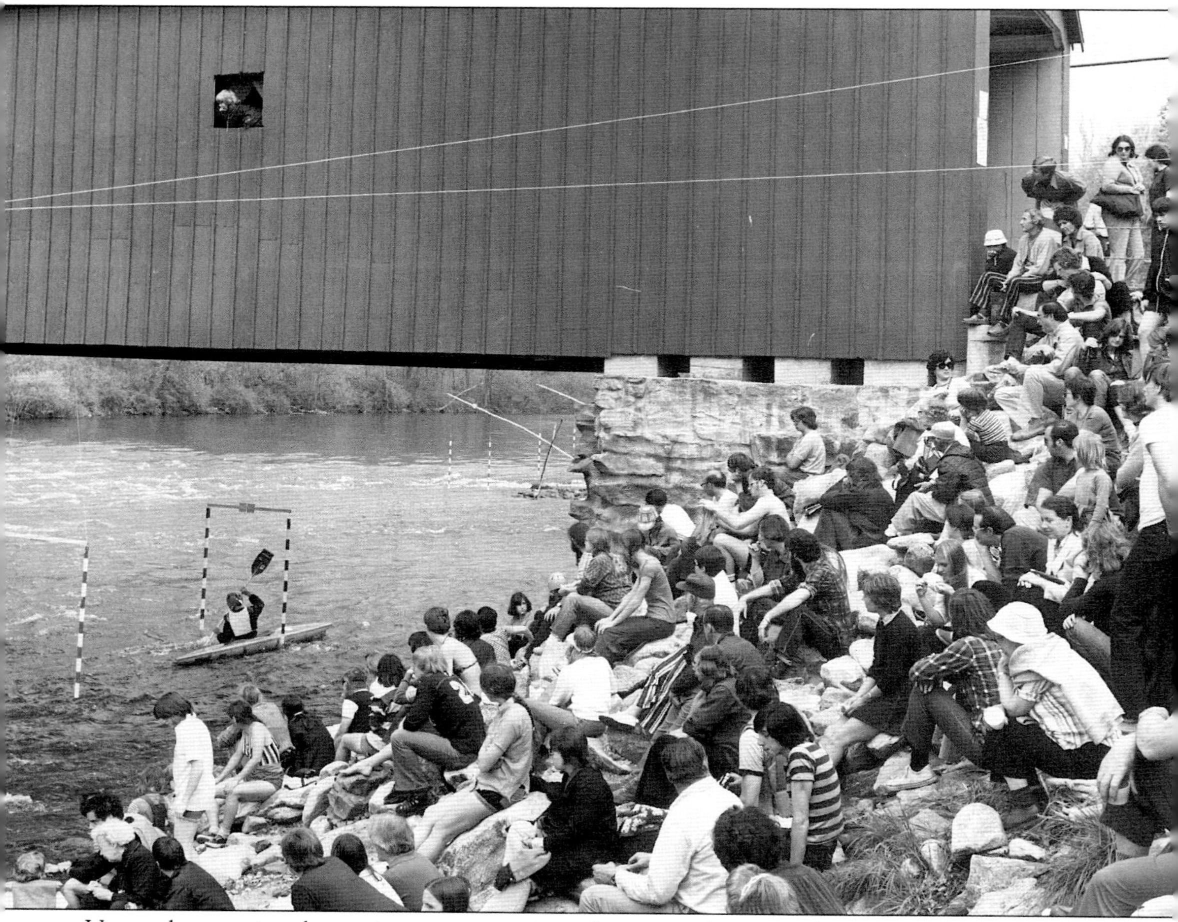

Unusual recreational pursuits were attractive subjects, as photos on these pages suggest: above is a whitewater kayak race at the famous covered bridge in West Cornwall, Connecticut, in May 1975; below, the new Alpine slide is inaugurated at the Jiminy Peak ski area in May 1977.

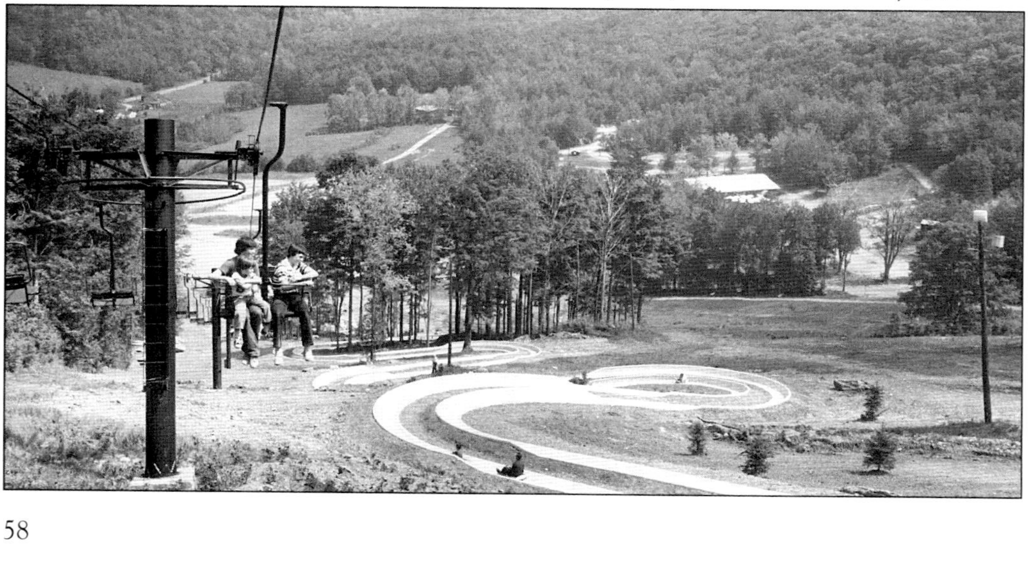

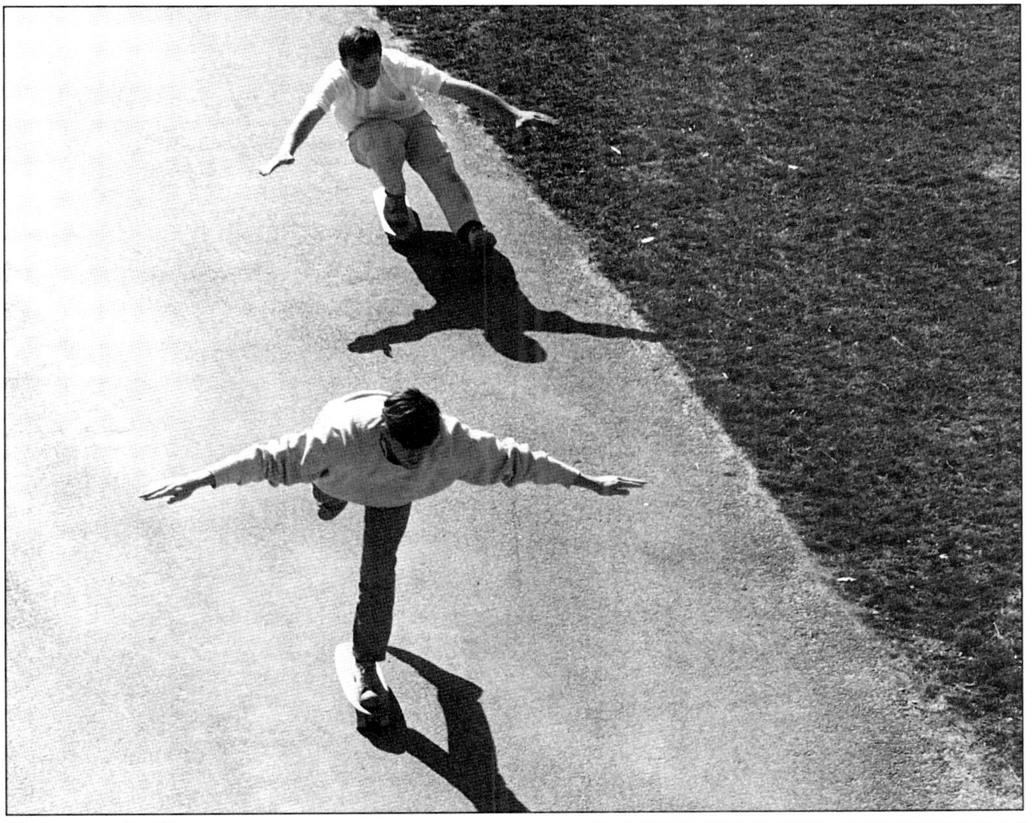

Two eras of rolling fun are conveyed in these photos: at top, Williams College students try out the then-new sport of skateboarding in April 1965; right, boys along a suburban street in an earlier time enjoy old-fashioned roller skates.

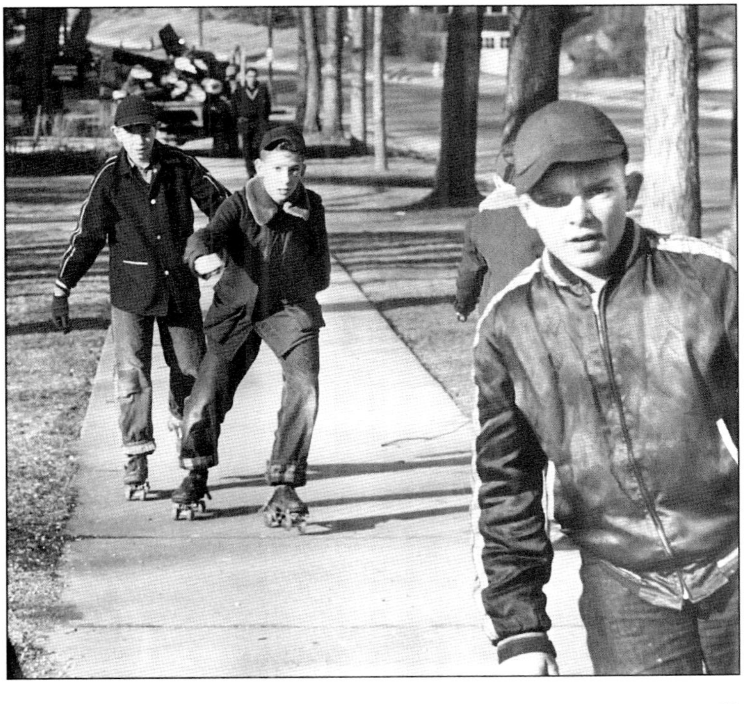

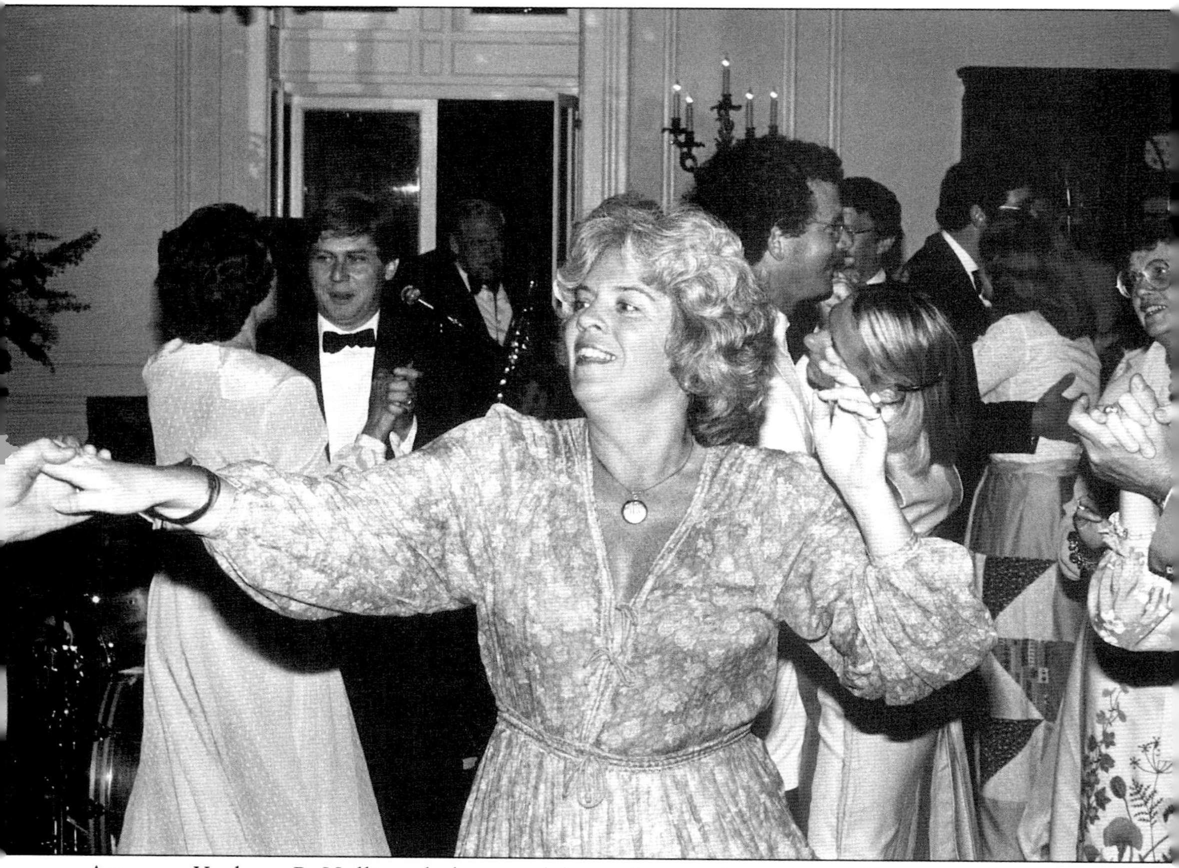

Attorney Keyburn P. Hollister helps to celebrate the grand opening of Blantyre in Lenox as a full-service hotel in May 1981.

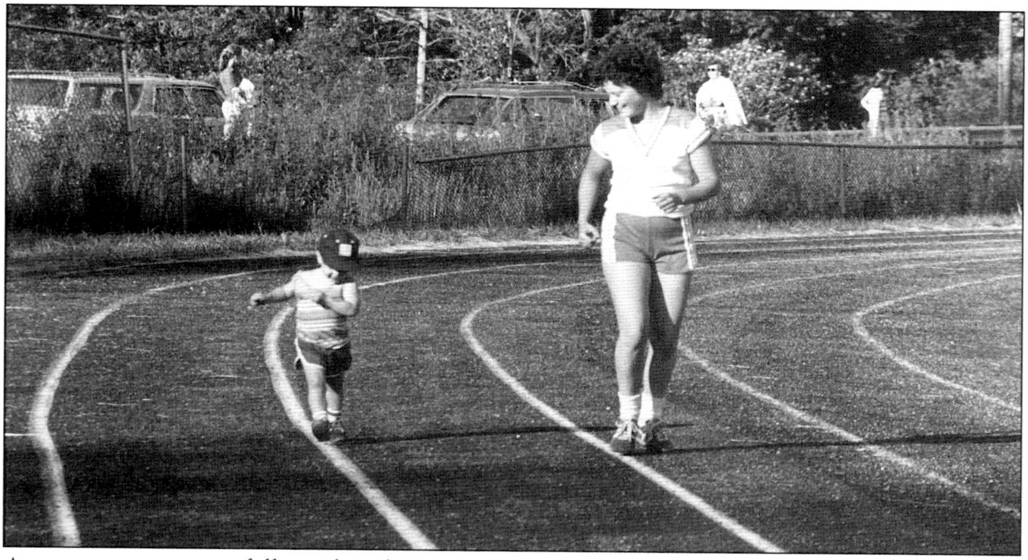

A young recreationist follows the white line on a track with his mother in June 1979.

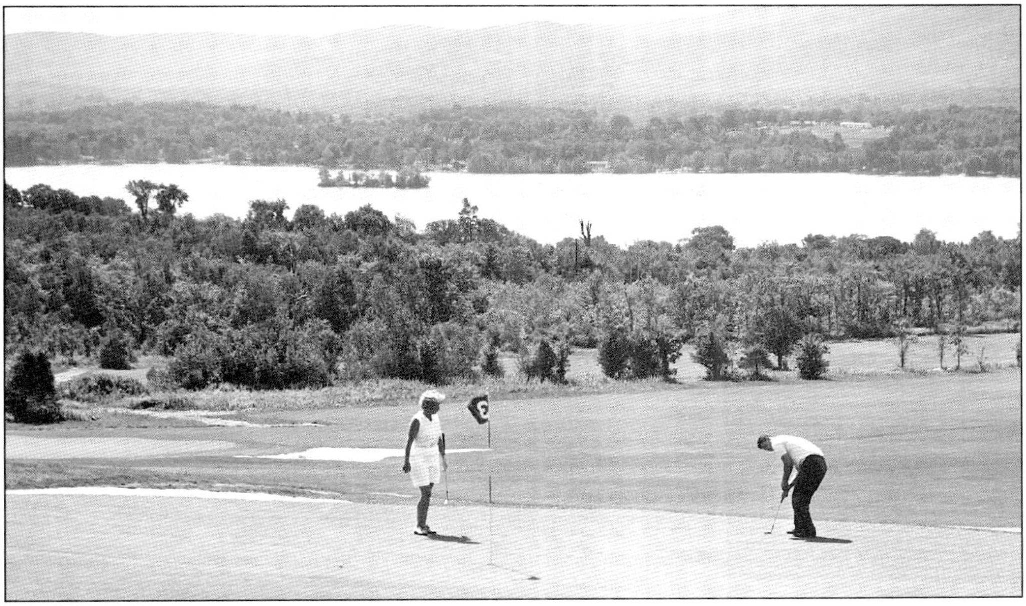

Golfers take in a great view of Pontoosuc Lake and the Taconic mountain range as they putt at the Skyline Country Club in Lanesboro in August 1962.

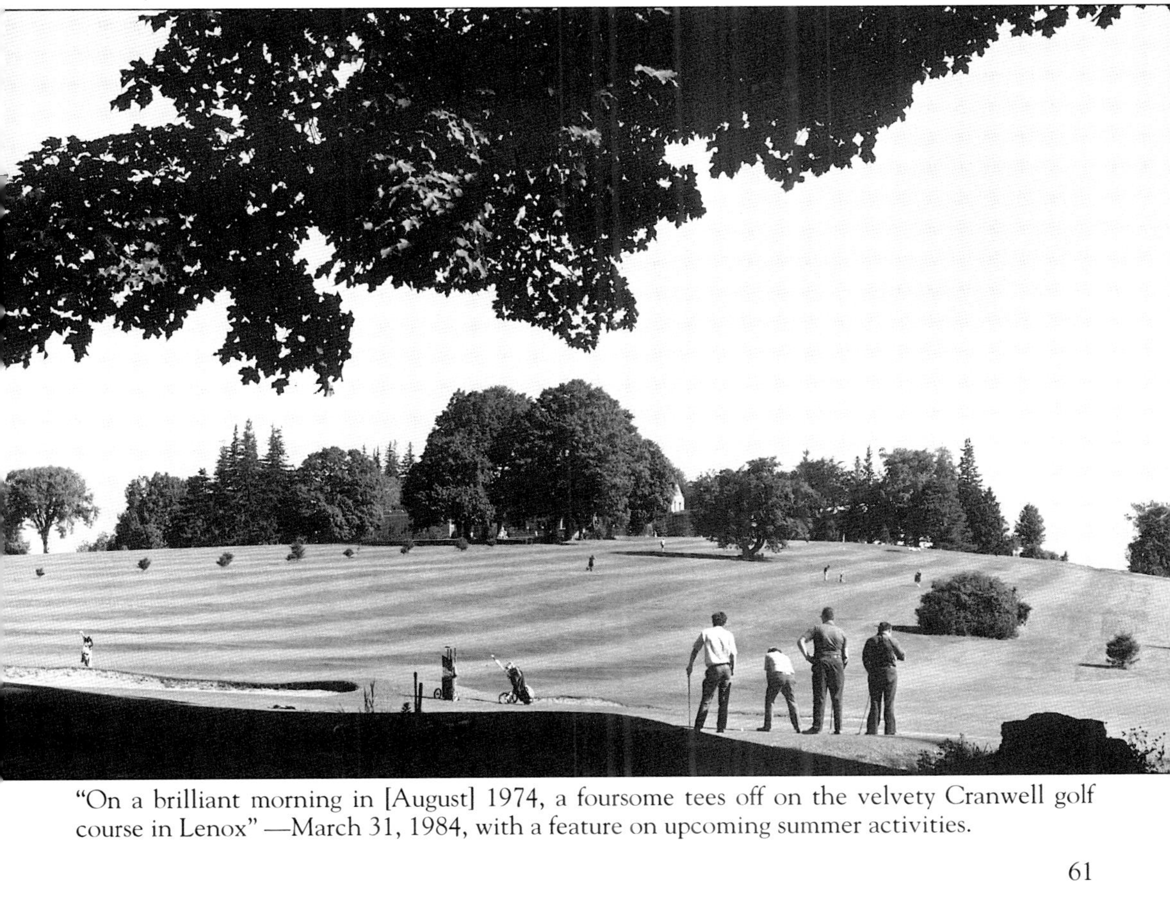

"On a brilliant morning in [August] 1974, a foursome tees off on the velvety Cranwell golf course in Lenox" —March 31, 1984, with a feature on upcoming summer activities.

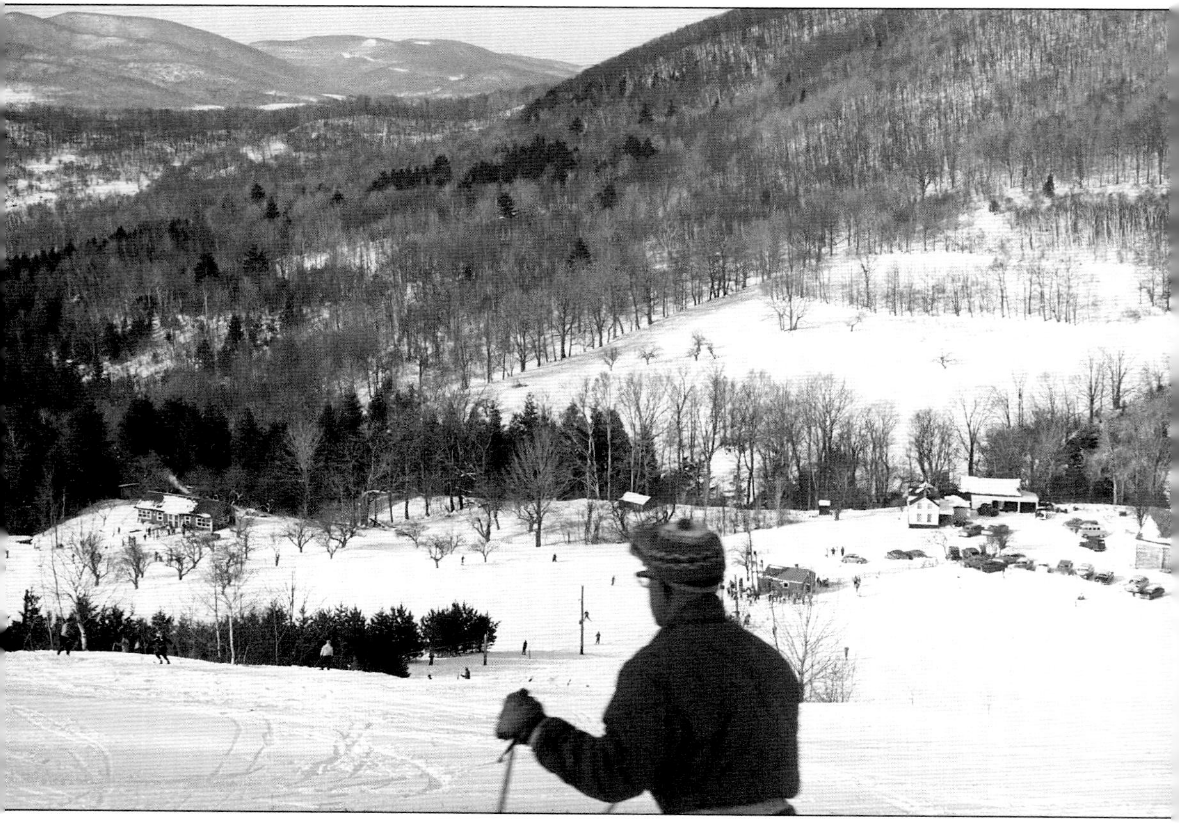

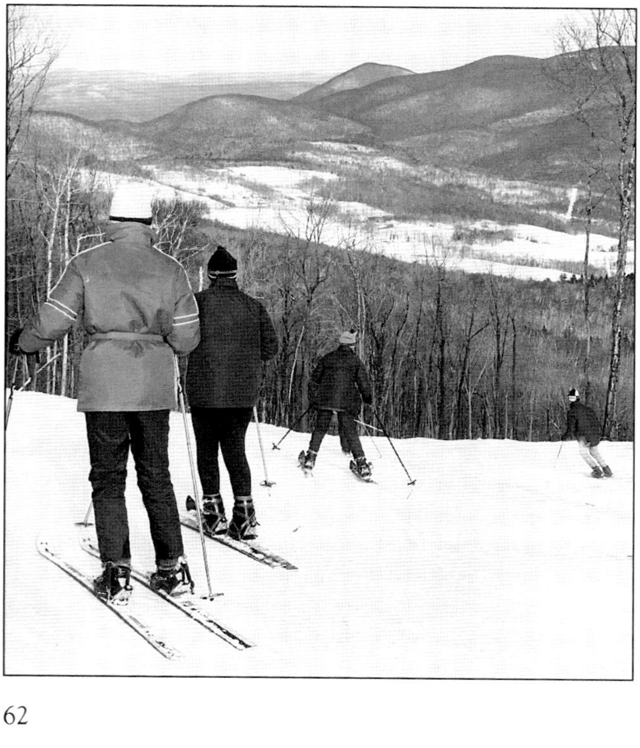

The qualities of perspective in this photo of Goodell Hollow—distant mountains, the size of trees, diminutive cars and buildings, ski tracks, and the figure in the foreground—are enough to induce in the viewer a sense of special reality. Goodell Hollow in South Williamstown is the home of the Greylock Ski Club. The photo was taken in February 1962.

A view from the top of the mountain at the Brodie ski area in New Ashford, January 1970.

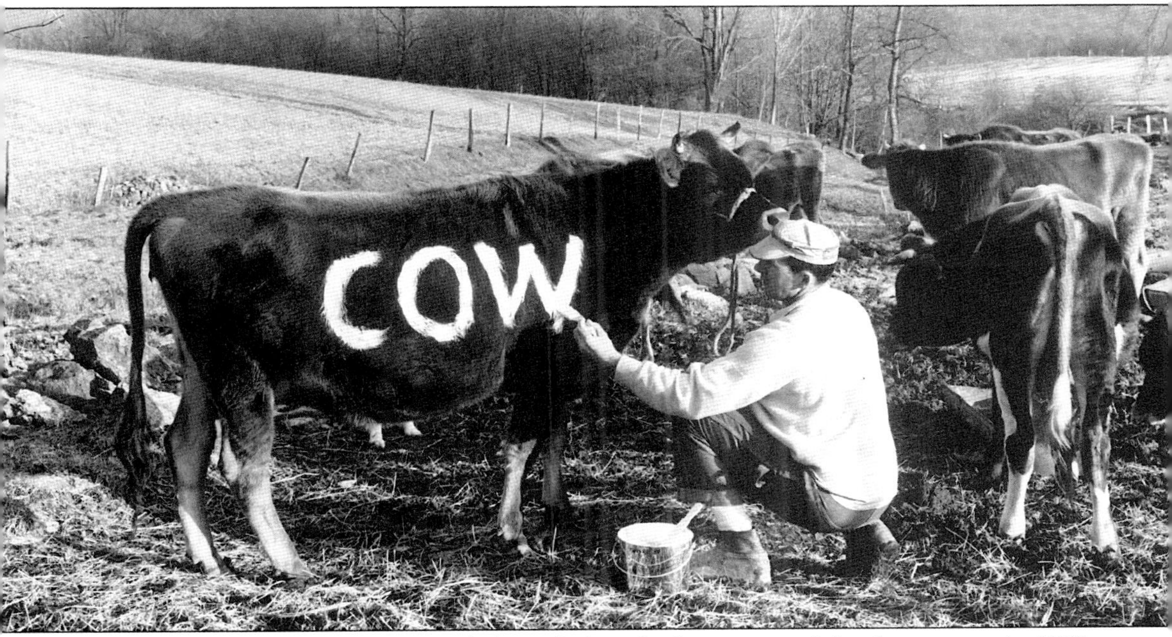

"Helpful hint for hunters was provided just before the beginning of the deer season in 1959 by Lanesboro farmer Earl D. Fletcher. The picture was carried on the AP network, and Earl received clippings from all over the nation" —September 20, 1969.

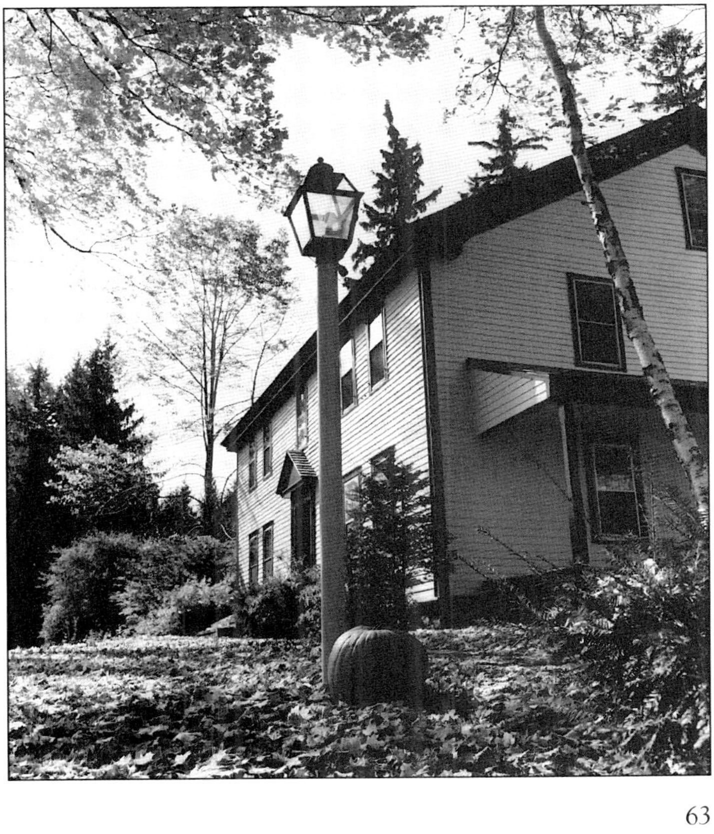

"Autumn at Arrowhead: bright leaves and a pumpkin are trappings of fall at Arrowhead on Holmes Road in Pittsfield, former home of Herman Melville and now headquarters of the Berkshire County Historical Society" —October 19, 1985.

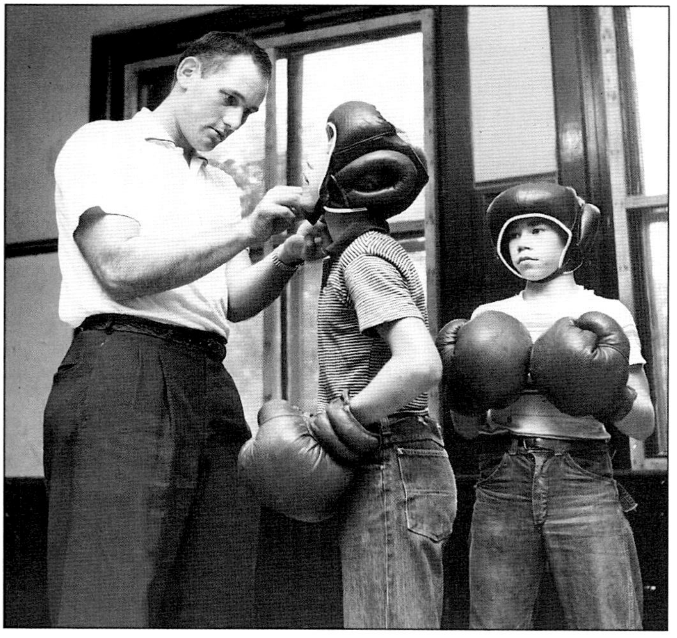

The Boys Clubs in Pittsfield and Williamstown always provided good material for Tague's cameras: at left, young boxers are outfitted for combat at Williamstown in September 1956; below, wrestlers' gyrations appear to make things a real challenge to the ref's decision-making powers during this match, which took place in Pittsfield in January 1974.

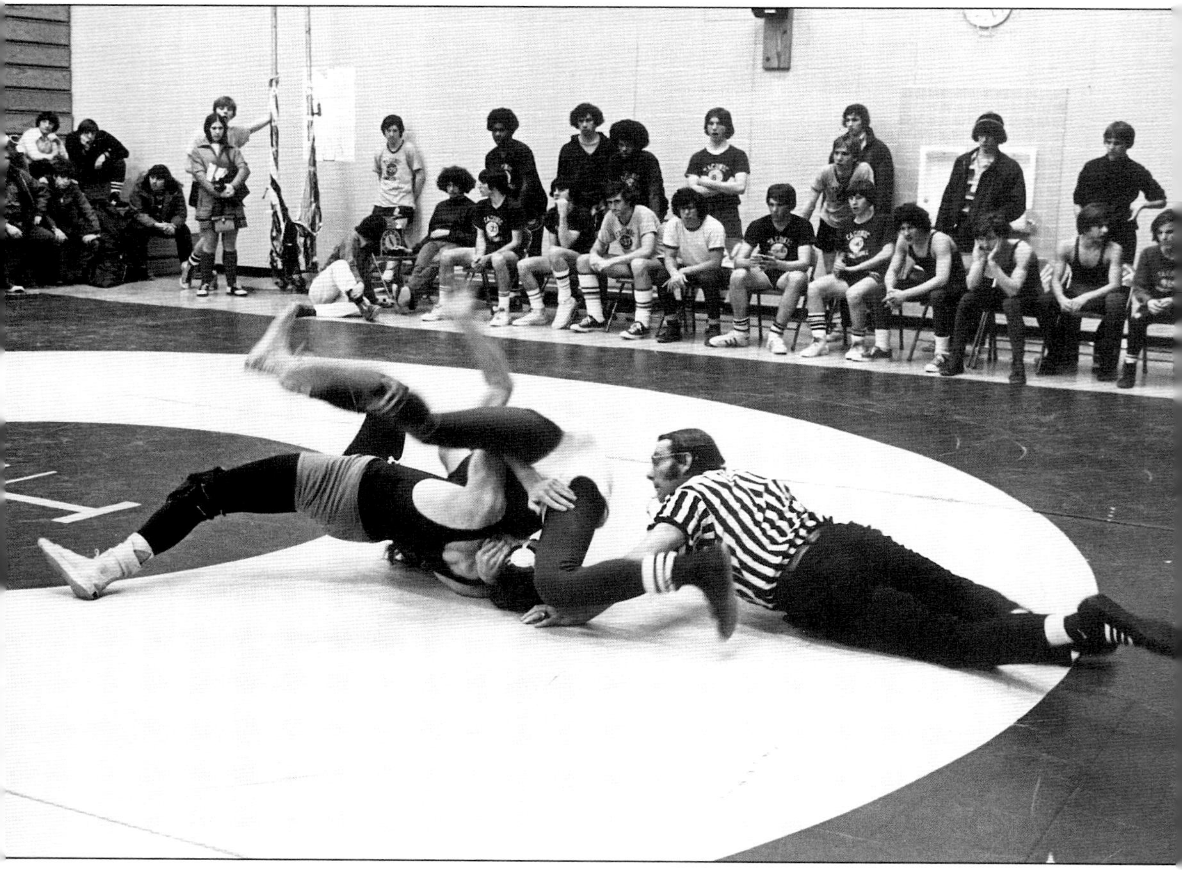

Four

Canny and Crafty Cats

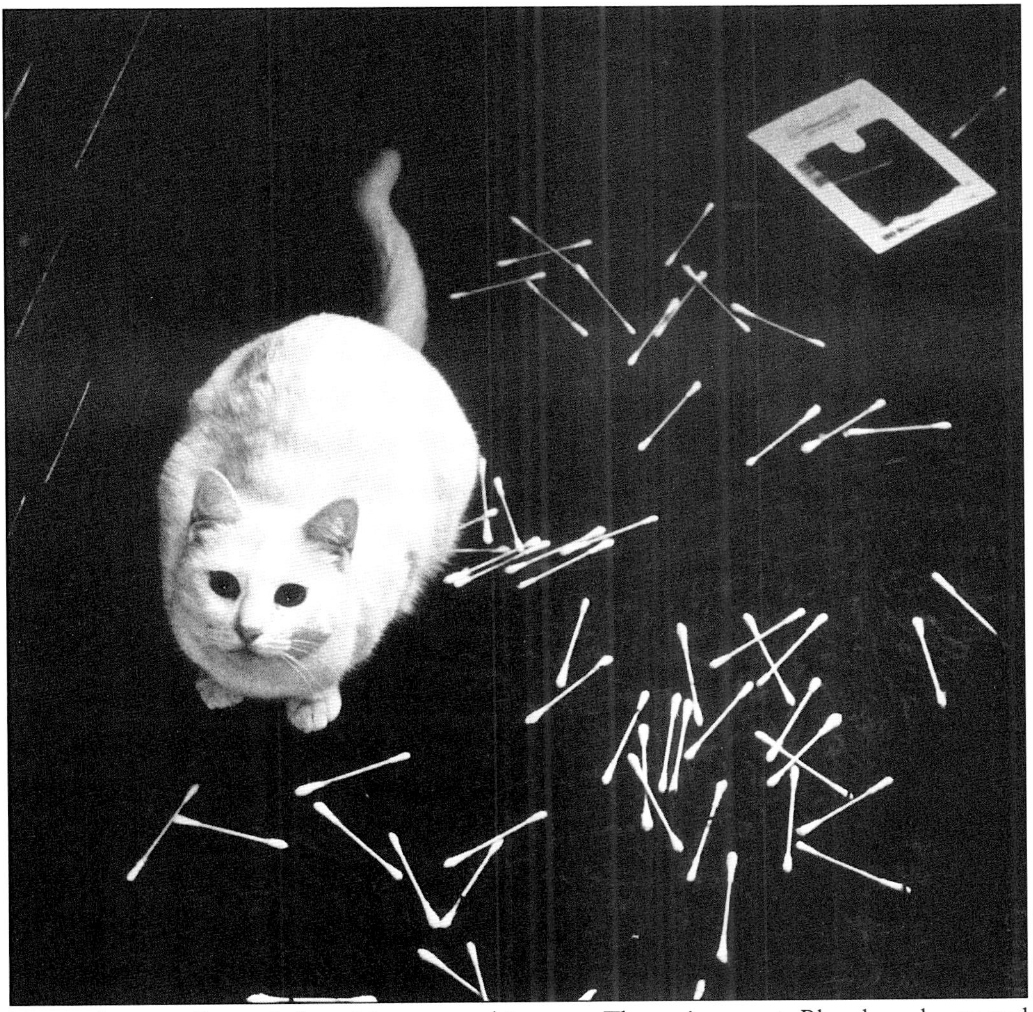

No words are really needed to elaborate on this scene. The cat's name is Blanche, who starred in many Tague photos.

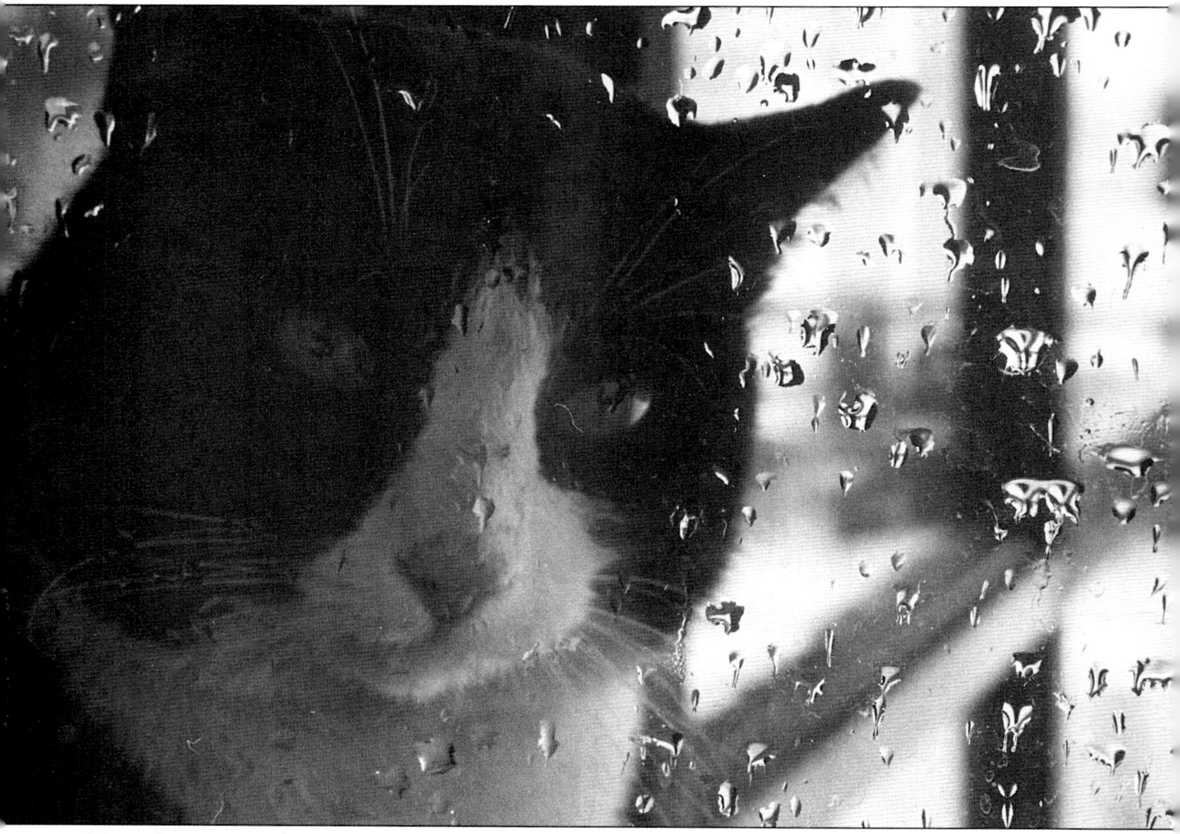

"Raindrops: Weatherwise, March has been behaving like the traditional lion this week, or at least like a fairly large cat such as our George. He's lurking outside the kitchen window whose glass is spattered with rain" —March 23, 1974.

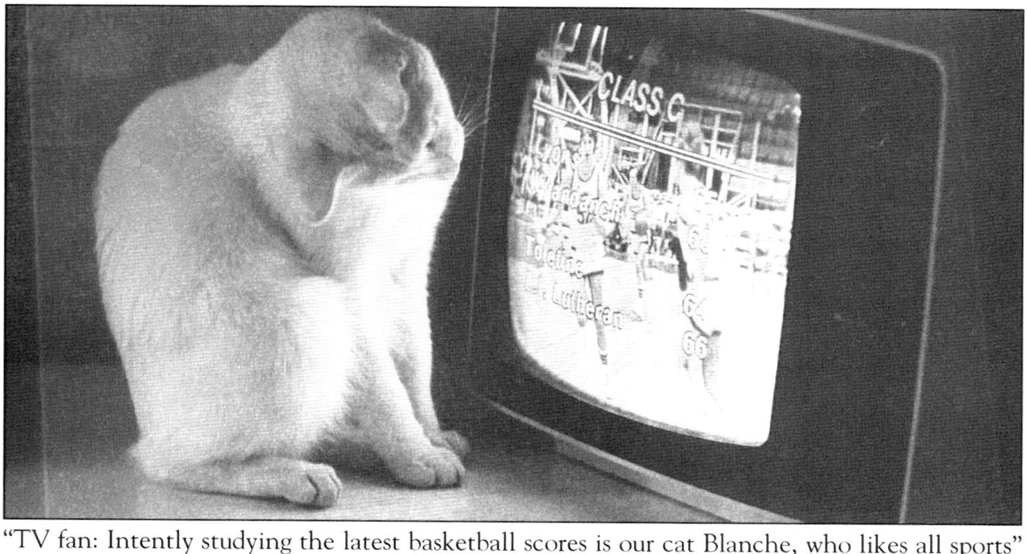

"TV fan: Intently studying the latest basketball scores is our cat Blanche, who likes all sports" —April 10, 1982.

"Easter Bonnet: For the big parade tomorrow, Mary Lloyd Gross, 10, of 105 Bartlett Avenue, picked out a tiny bonnet for her extremely tolerant cat, Abigale, who had nothing to say. Incidentally, we're always on the lookout for funny or unusual pets, so let us know if you have one" —April 4, 1953.

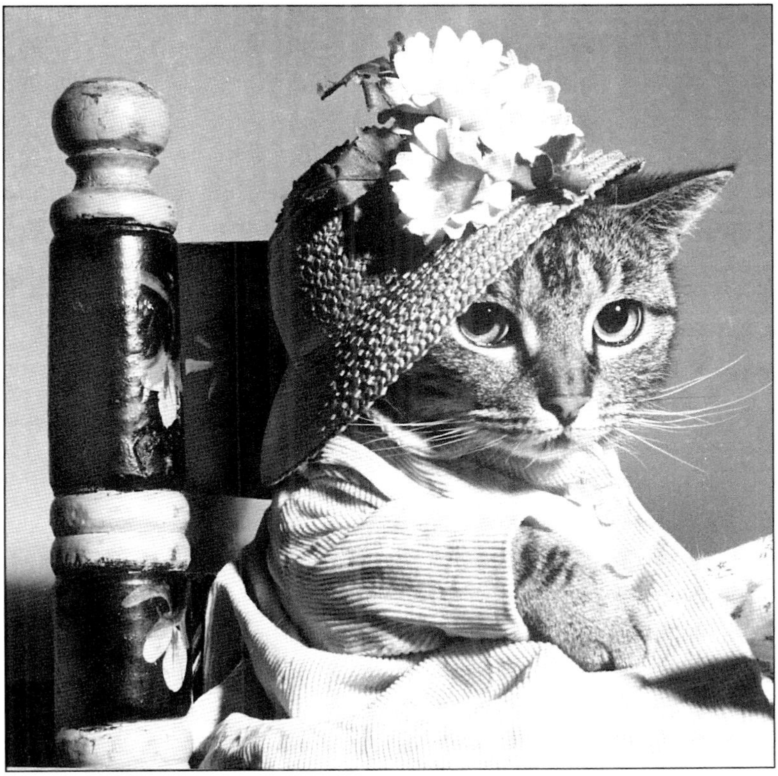

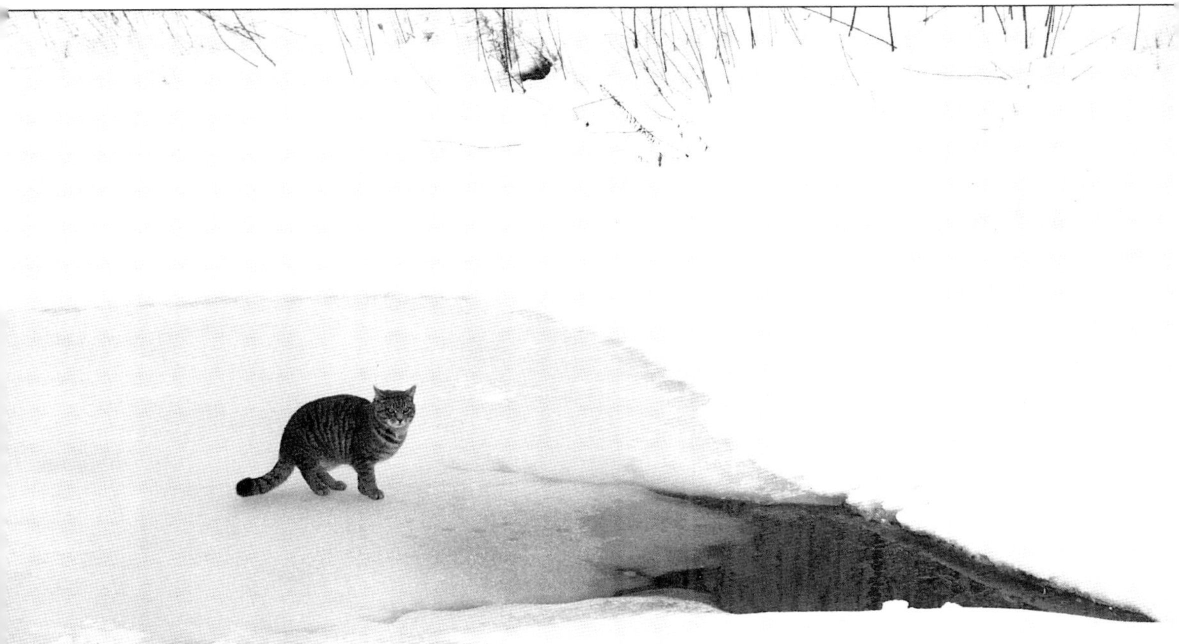

This cat's name was "Streaker," and it does not appear to be enjoying its thin-iced predicament. The date was January 1975.

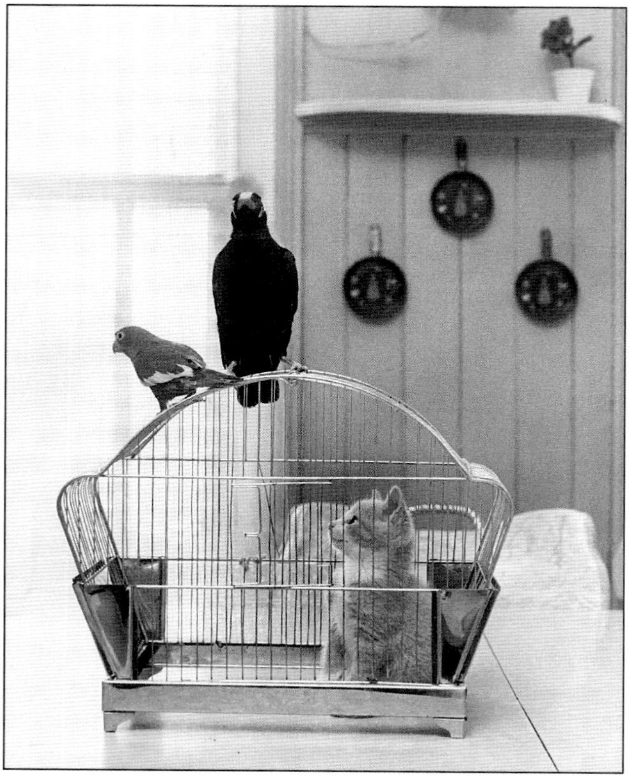

"Something went wrong: Kitty has achieved an awkward role reversal by going hunting in a bird cage. The birds have returned, looking aggressive, and kitty feels trapped. This took place back in 1959. Kitty eventually escaped with only a scolding" —May 1, 1982.

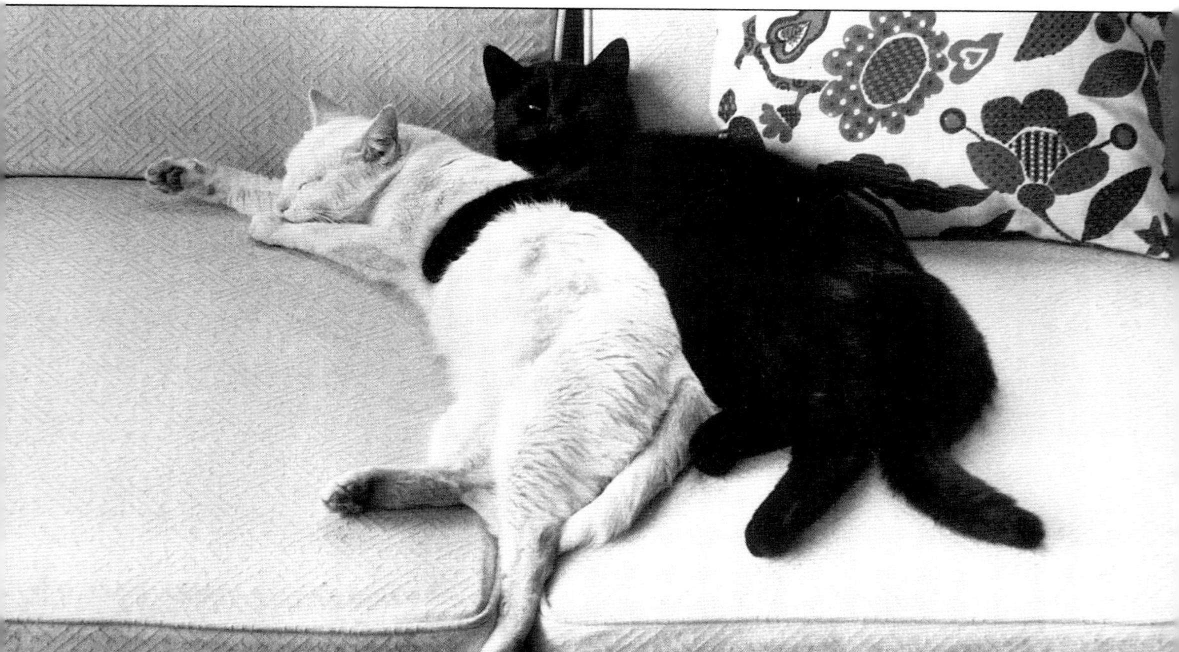

"Hanging On: Catnapping on our couch are Blanche and her son Blackie, who is big and strong but still seems to be a mommy's boy" —March 26, 1983.

Five

And Other Appealing Animals

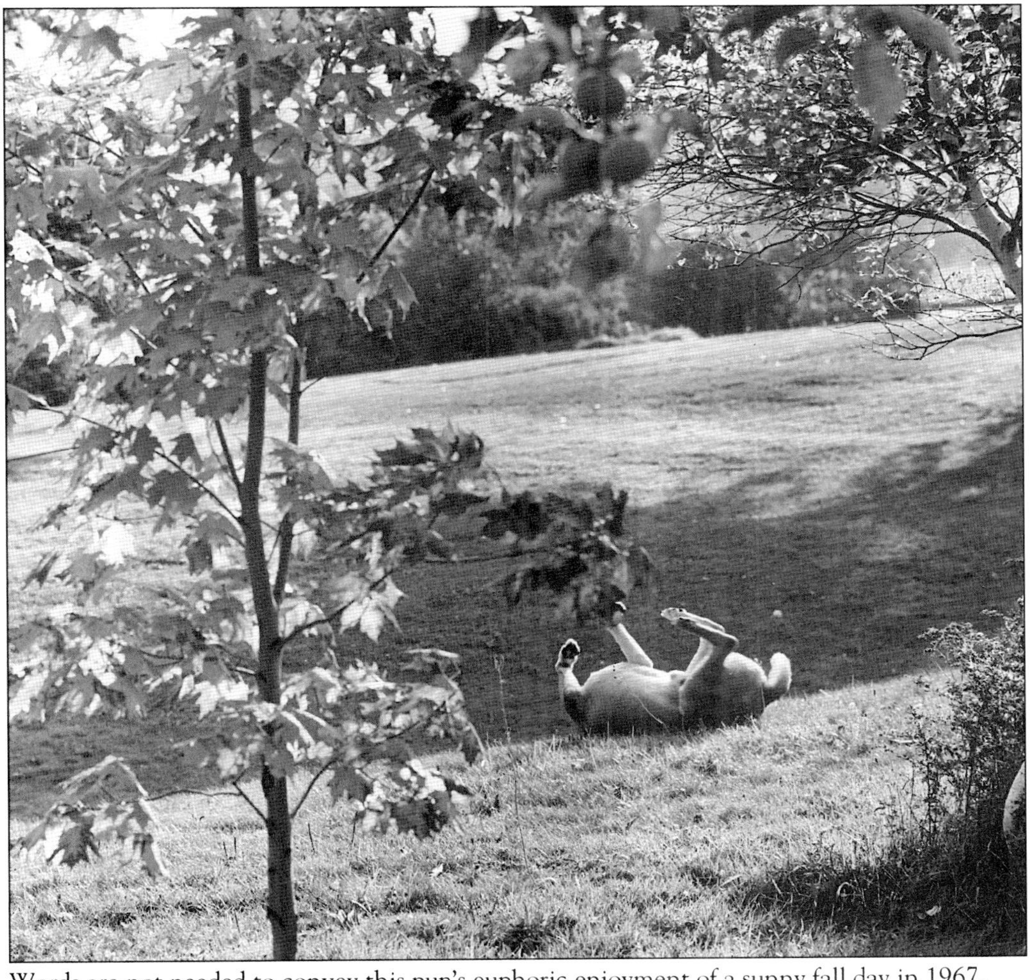

Words are not needed to convey this pup's euphoric enjoyment of a sunny fall day in 1967.

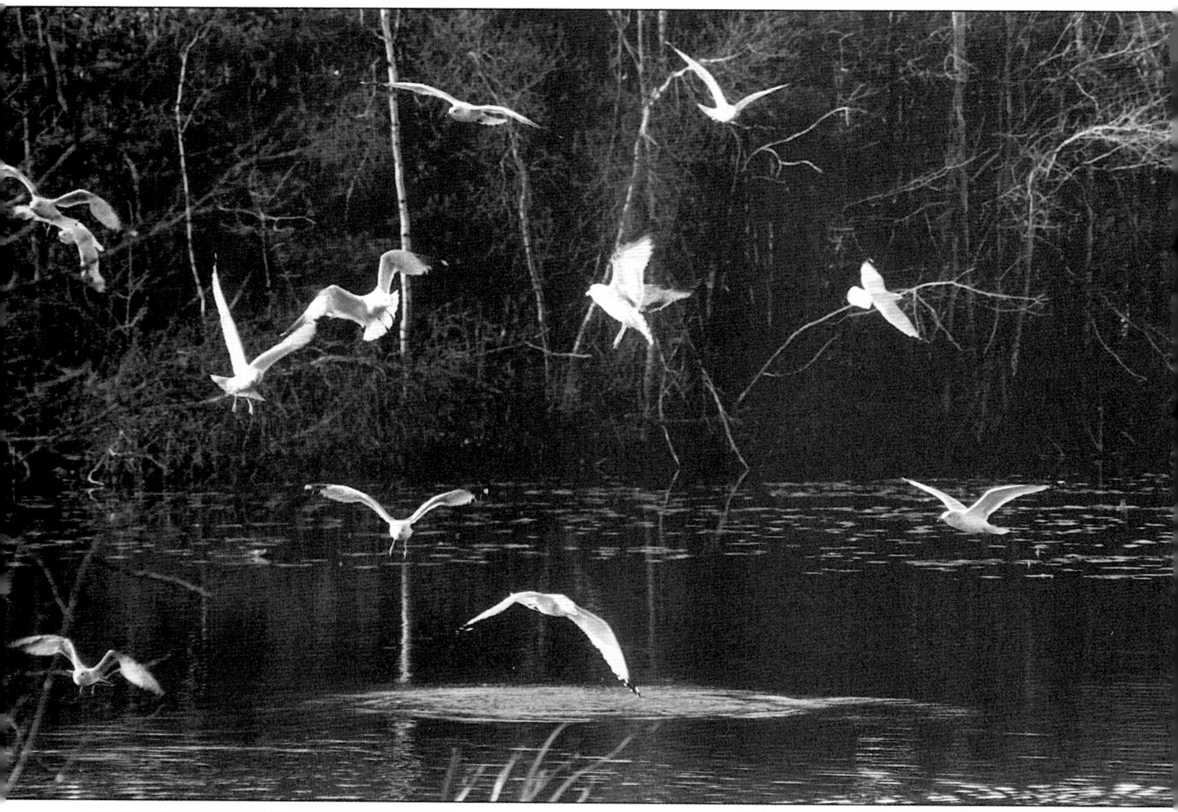

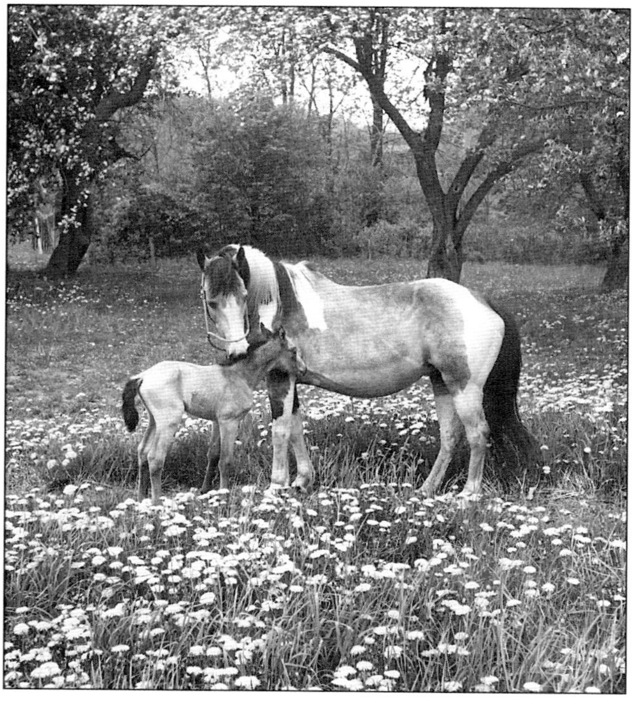

This view of ring-billed gulls hovering over a secluded bay on Onota Lake was one of Tague's last photographs before he died in November 1990.

"Looking ahead to spring becomes a common pastime right about now in the Berkshires where most of us are getting a little tired of heavy clothing, cars not starting, and shocking fuel bills. Spring begins officially in about one month, but it will be at least another month after that before scenes like this one, taken some years back [1960, in fact] in Lenox, will be a possibility" —February 24, 1968.

Gently falling snow, a lone horse, an old apple tree, and an ancient hay rake compose this attractive still life in February 1989. Below, an evenly spaced flock of birds screens a view of trees about to burst into spring foliage in April 1987.

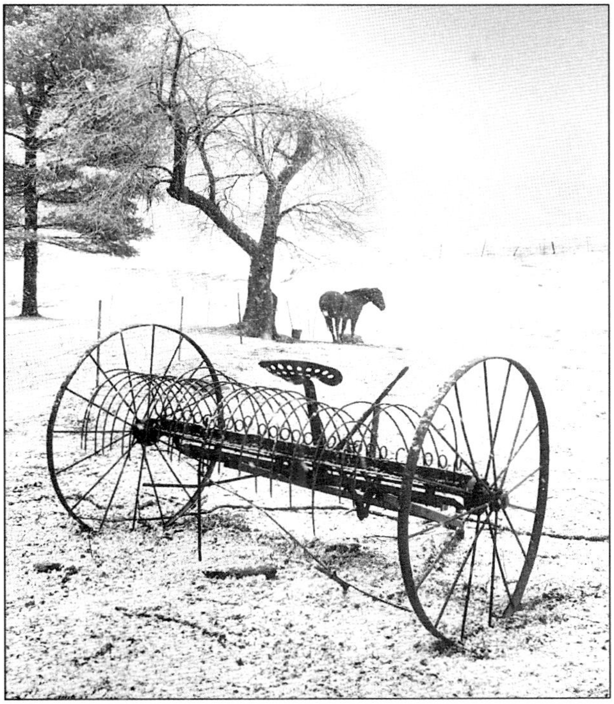

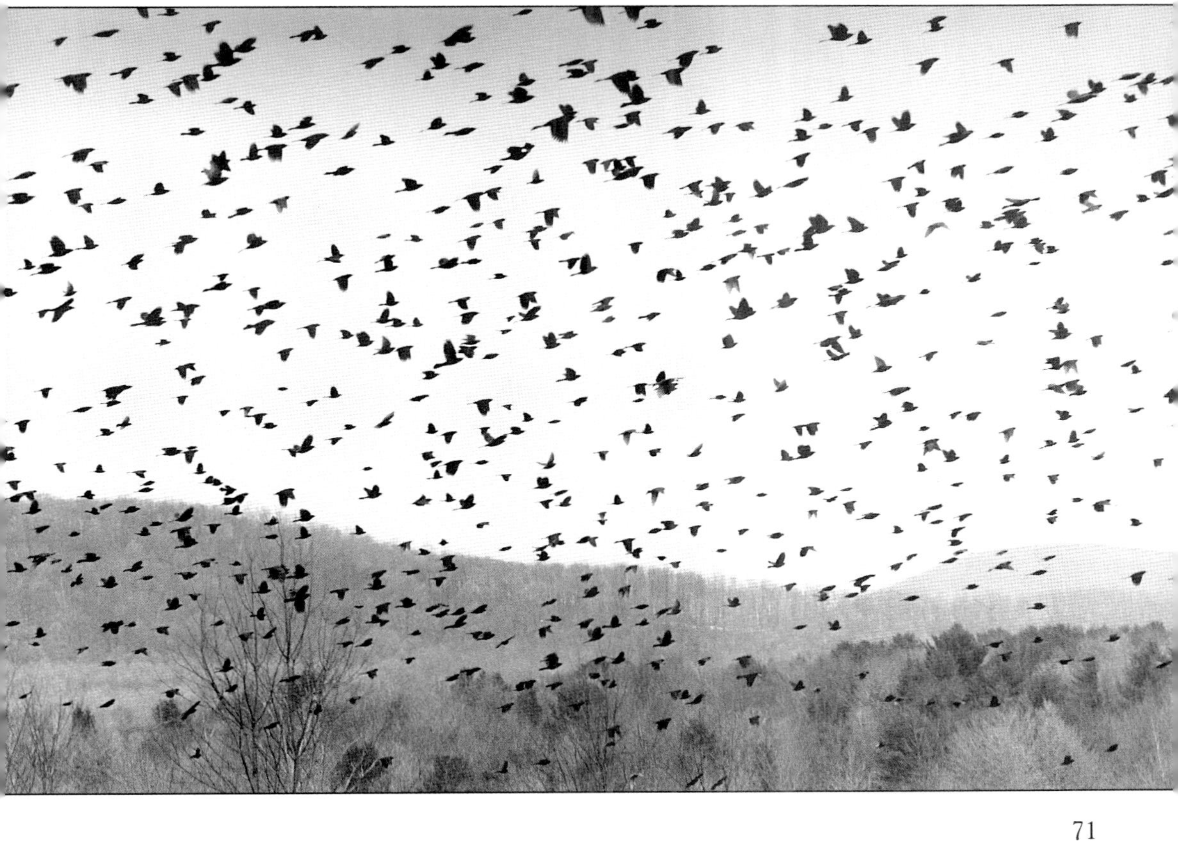

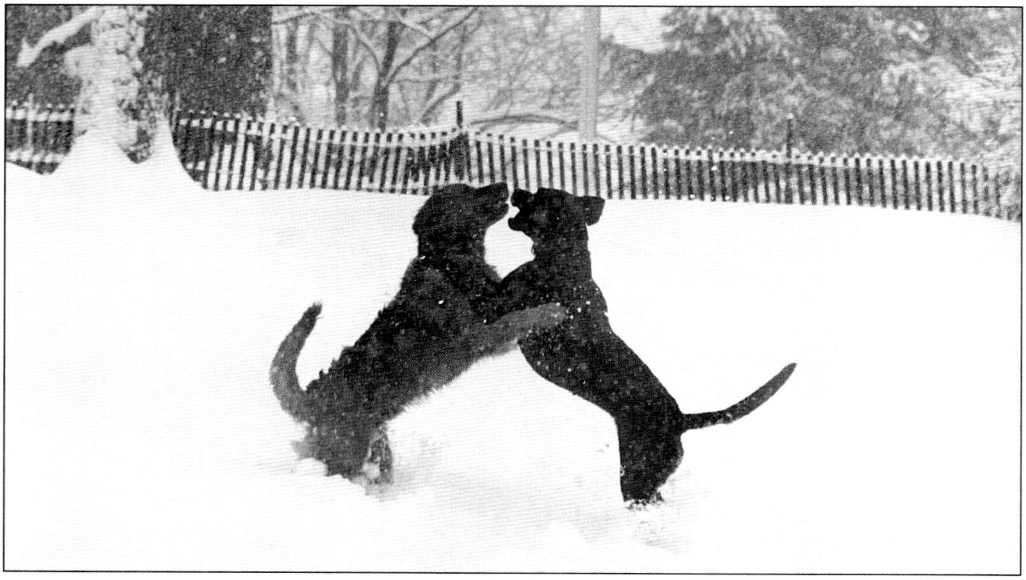

"Reunion: Two dogs exuberantly embrace in Williamstown as if they hadn't seen each other in years. They probably had been separated 10 minutes" —February 7, 1981.

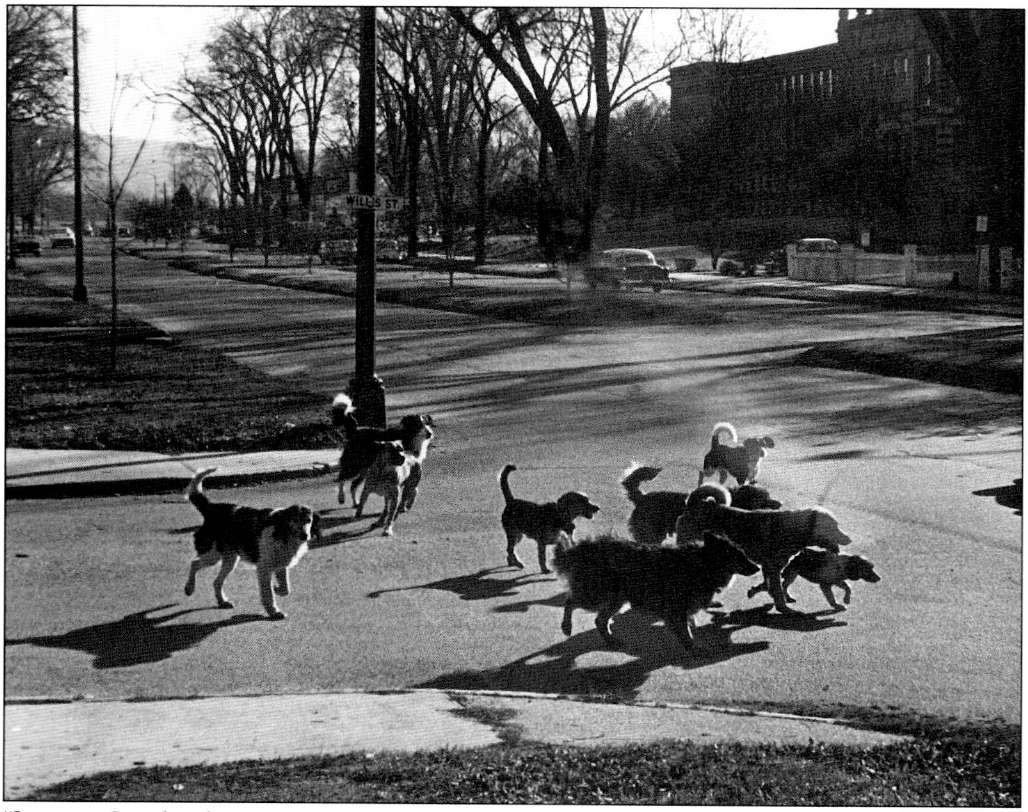

"Joggers: Out for their morning run on East Street were these nine four-footed exercisers in November 1961. Dog-control measures have stopped this" —November 16, 1985.

"Who? A barred owl stares from a tree on the Taconic Trail in Williamstown as if in wonder about the meaning of the intrusion of a human who goes 'click, click' " —February 7, 1981.

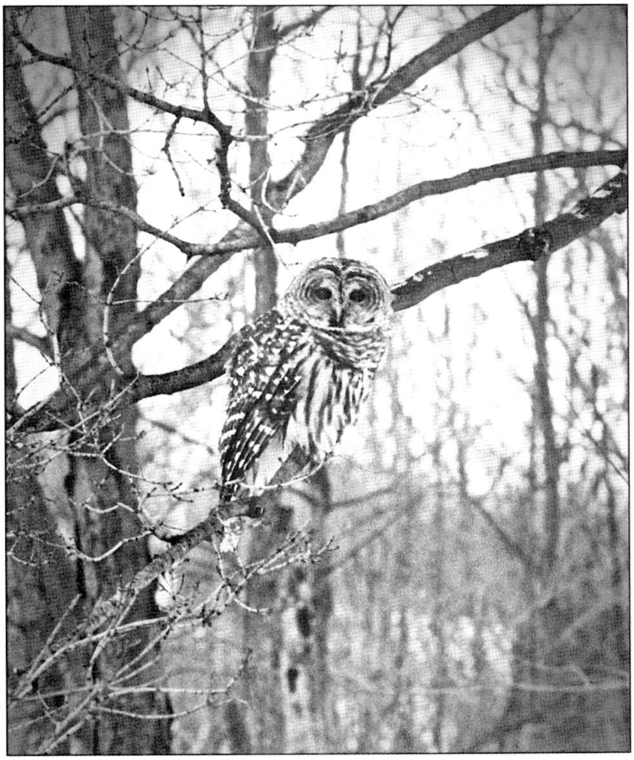

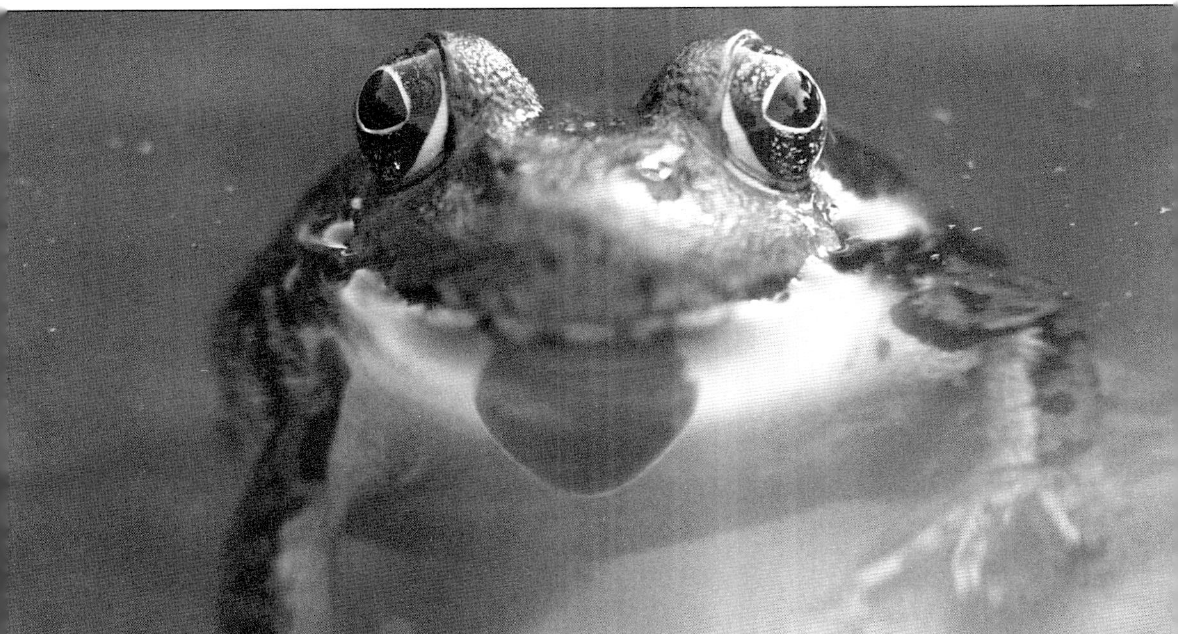

A granddaddy of a bullfrog, at ease in one of thousands of ponds that abound in the precious wetlands of the Berkshires. This picture, accompanied by the title "Greetings from the Berkshires," is one of the best-sellers of Tague's work on postcards.

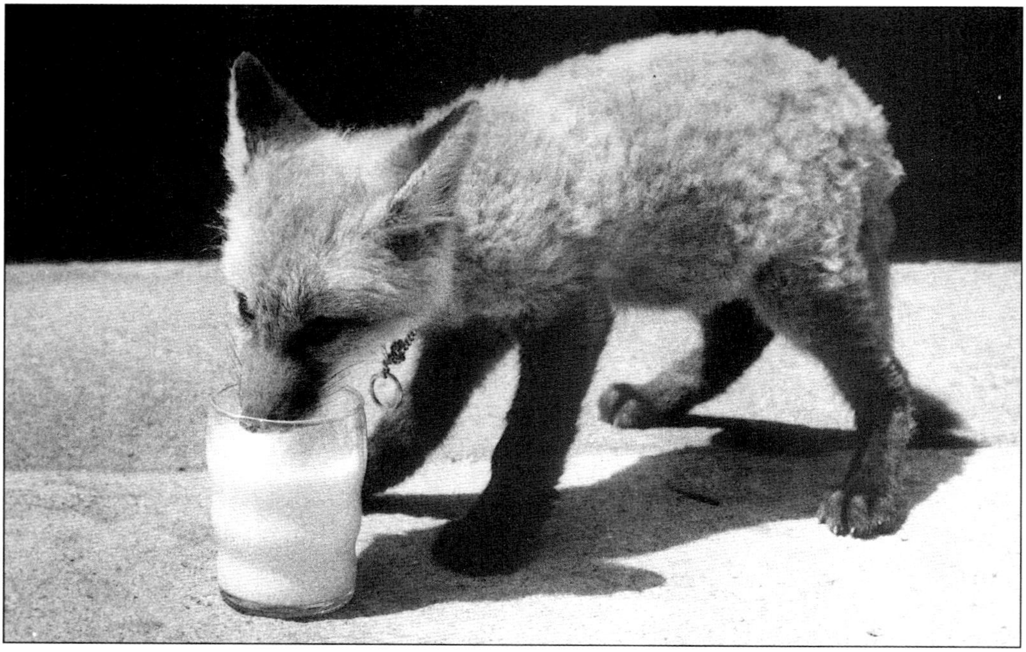

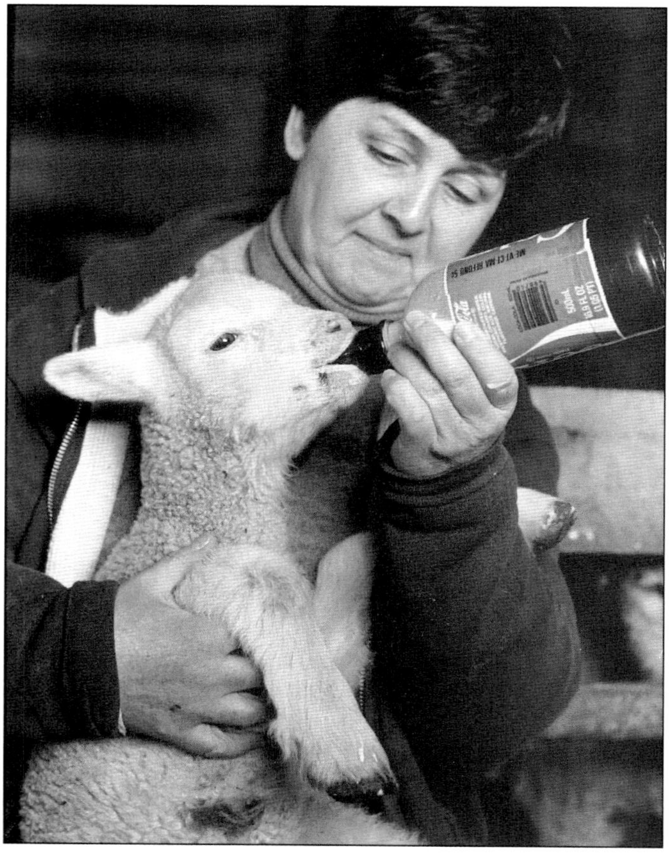

This thirsty fox, two months old, drinks milk outside the old Bridge Lunch, long located over the railroad tracks on Pittsfield's North Street. The fox was given to Murray Kellogg and James O'Neill by a Charlemont woodchopper who found it shortly after it was born and raised it on a milk diet. The photo was published May 26, 1956.

"Lunch time: Recent arrival in the flock at Townry Farm, North Main Street, Lanesboro, is given one of five daily bottle feedings by Barbara Feakes, who with her husband, Clifford, owns the farm. The mother sheep didn't produce enough milk for this lamb and its twin" —December 31, 1983.

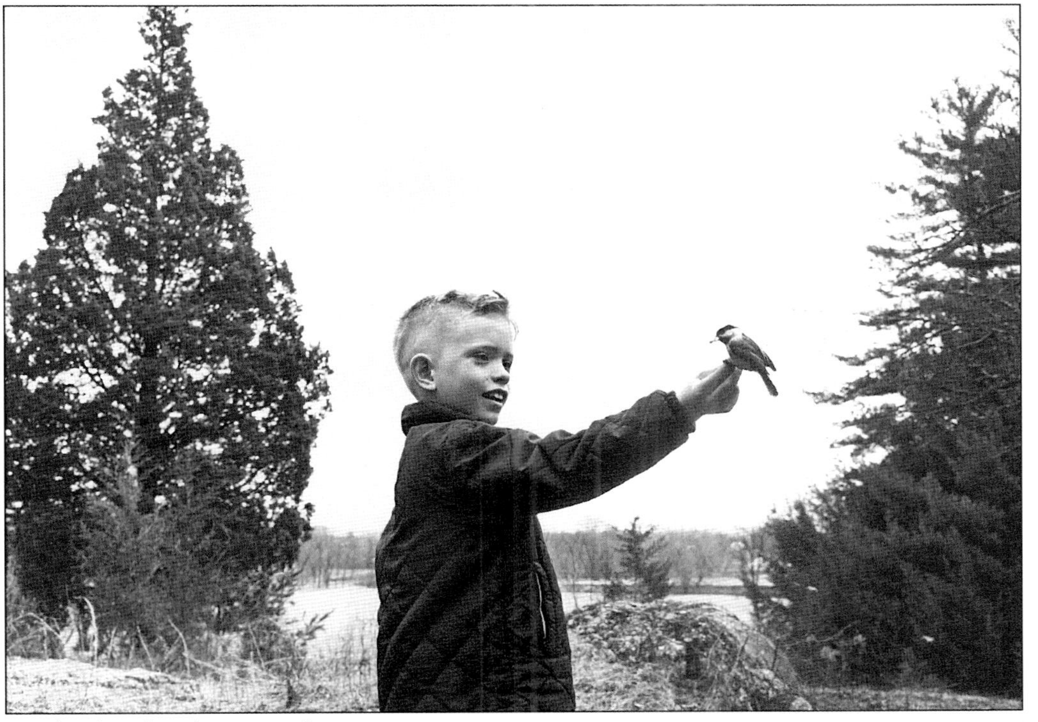

"Bird in hand is always worth two in the bush, particularly at Bartholomew's Cobble. Peter Tague, 8, has attracted a chickadee by offering a sunflower seed. The chickadees there are quite trusting, having been fed like this for some time by warden Howard Bain" —April 17, 1965.

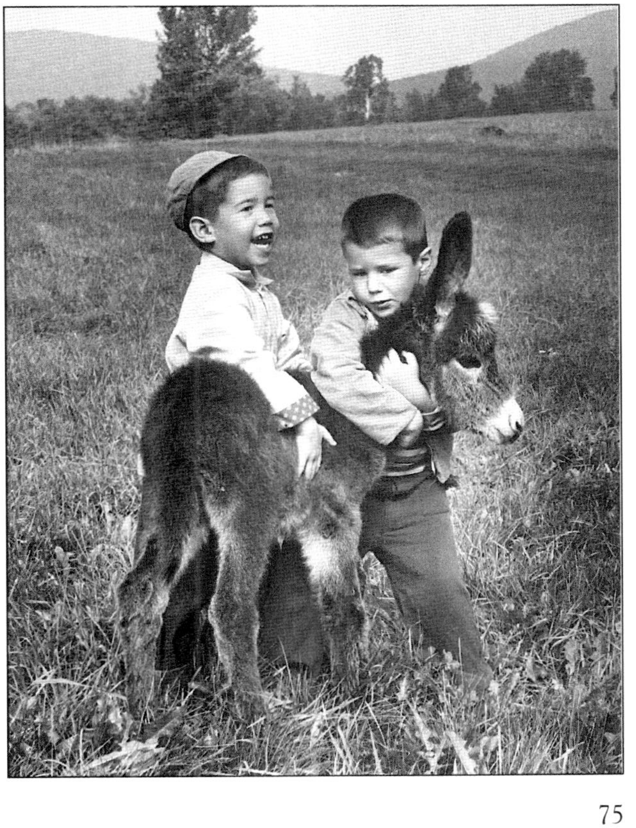

"Clutch play is required to hold back a young burro who would prefer to be romping loose in a field off Churchill Street. This picture was taken exactly 10 years ago this month" —September 20, 1969.

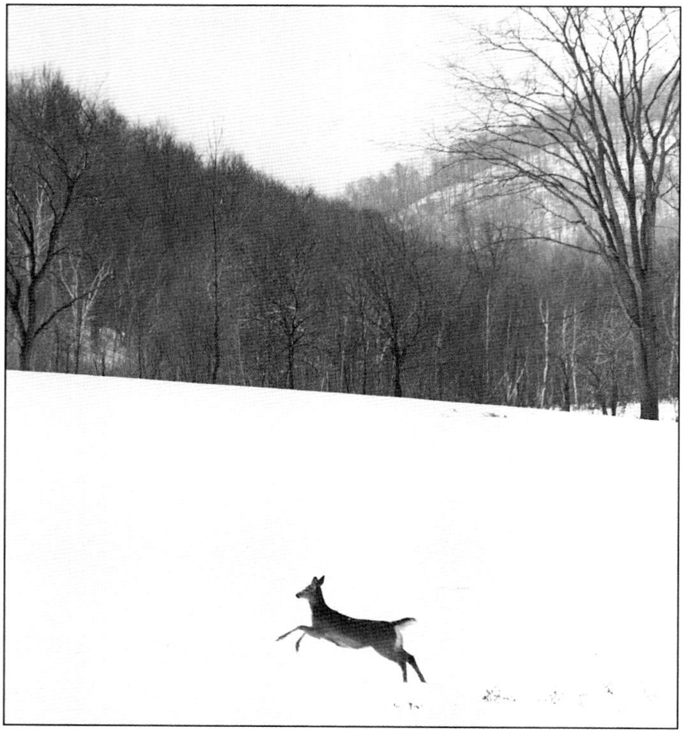

"Springing through a snow-covered field, a deer demonstrates its awareness of a hunter with a camera, namely me. This probably is a buck (antlerless now because deer shed them in January), one that strayed from a herd living in the Mt. Hope Farm area of Williamstown. Deer regularly come out of the woods at this time to feed in open fields where the snow melts quicker" —April 3, 1971.

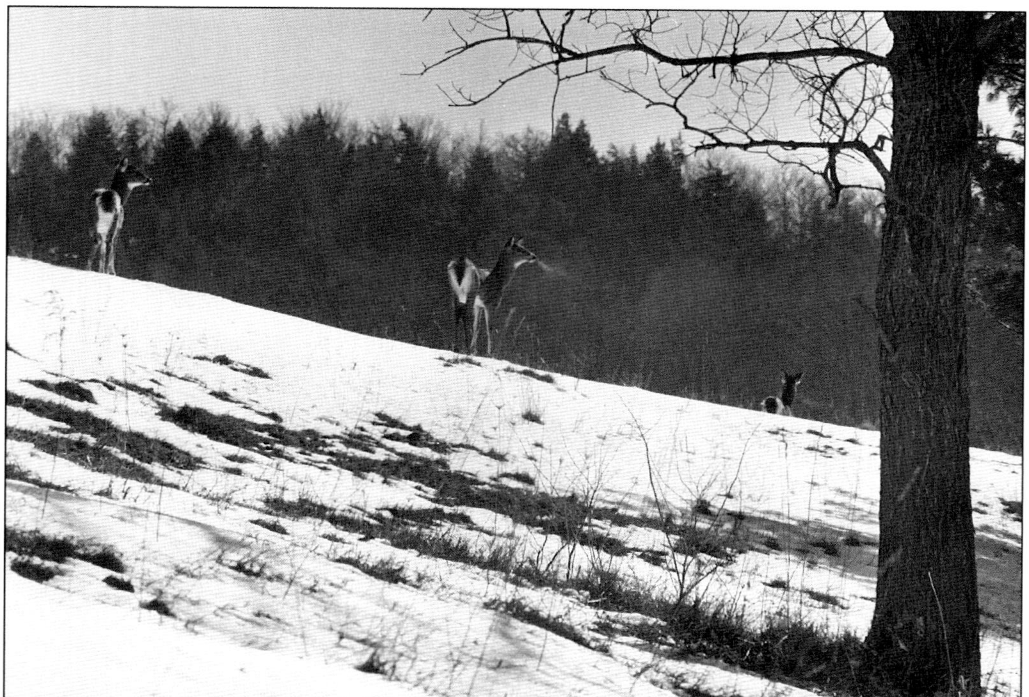

A little tuft of breath is visible from this whitetail's snout on a cold day in Williamstown in March 1971. She was probably emitting a snort on sensing the photographer's approach.

"Outdoorsman and hard-working conservationist Joe Wilk of Cheshire and his dog, Shambi, look over forest land owned by him in Savoy. School superintendent in New Ashford, Cheshire, Lanesboro, and Hancock, he was a leader in the fight to save Greylock" —January 21, 1967.

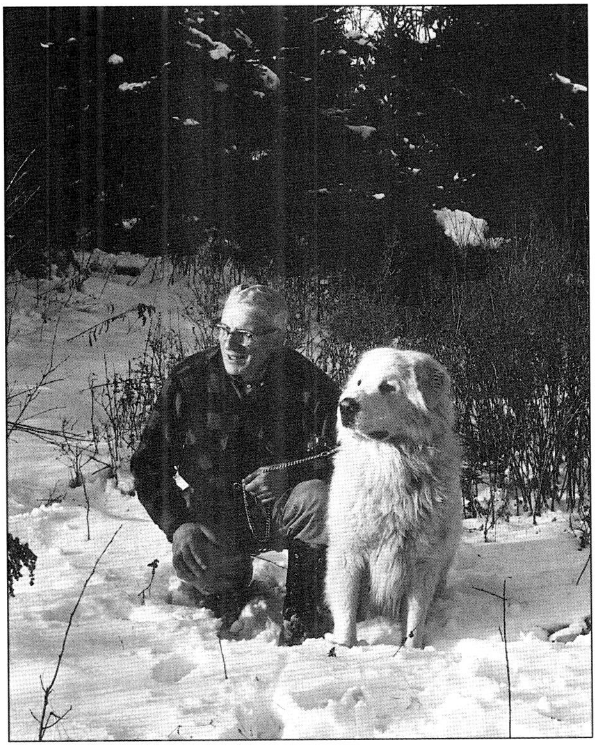

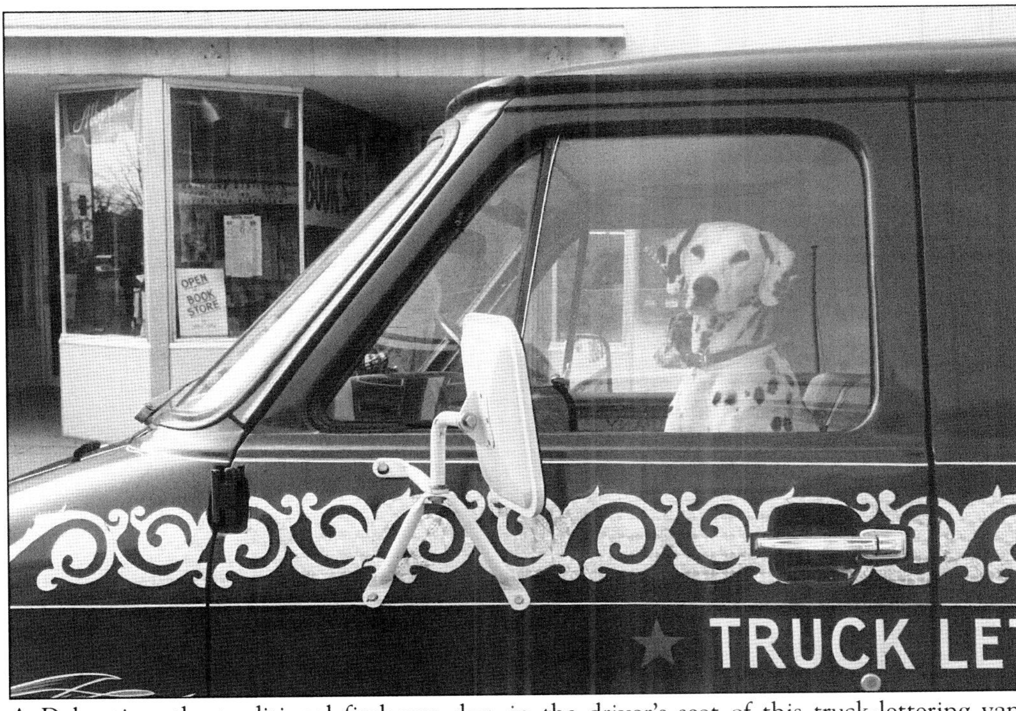

A Dalmatian, the traditional firehouse dog, in the driver's seat of this truck-lettering van, proved an irresistible subject for the photographer.

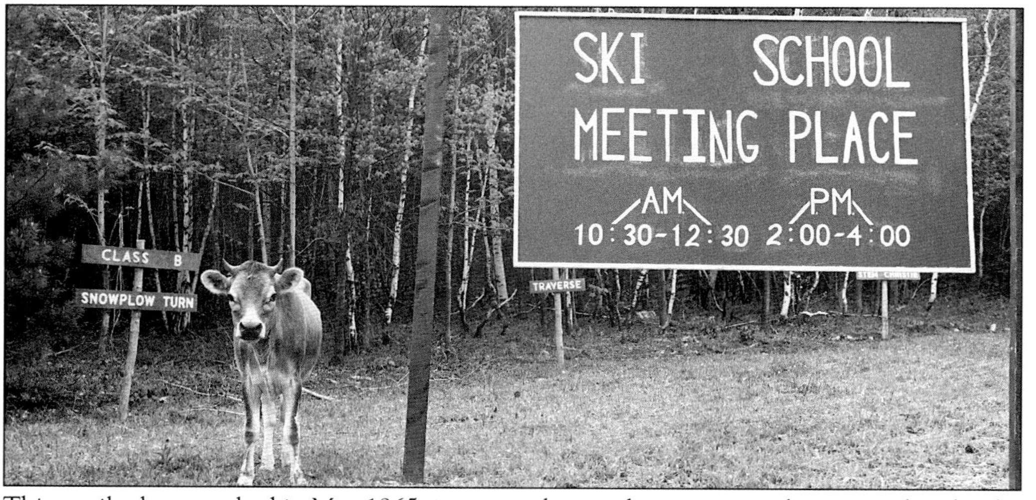

This pupil, photographed in May 1965, is just too late in the season to take part in ski school.

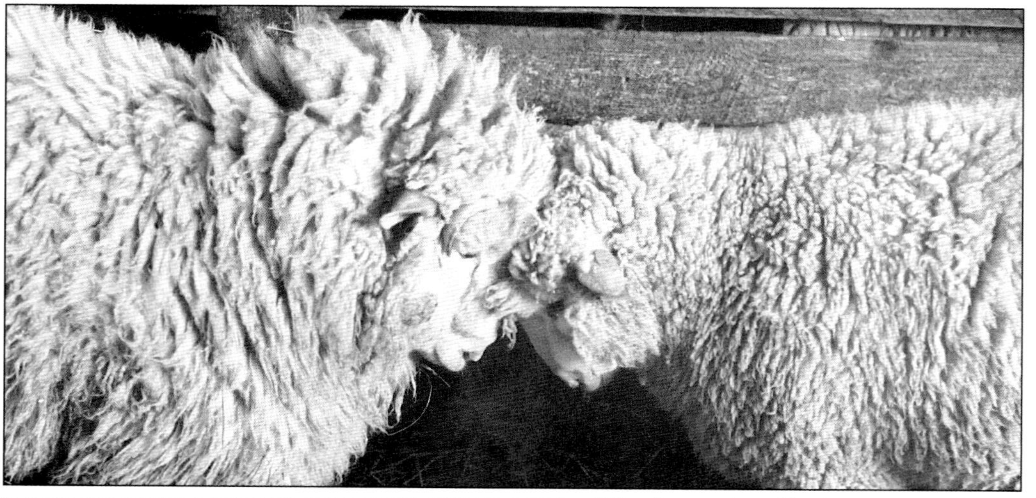

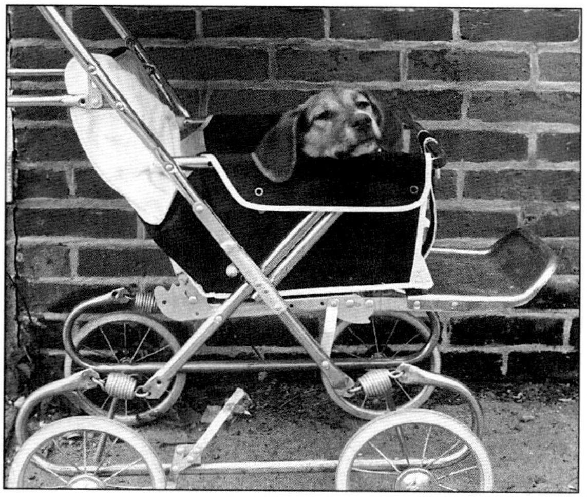

"Confrontation: Having narrowed their positions, originally six feet apart, with a rush and a thud, two rams on the Feakes farm have reached a meeting of the minds. This method is not recommended for humans" —December 31, 1983.

"Hot dog has climbed into baby carriage to get out of sun. We happened to notice this enterprising fellow in Williamstown" —June 30, 1967.

Six

Vocational Pursuits

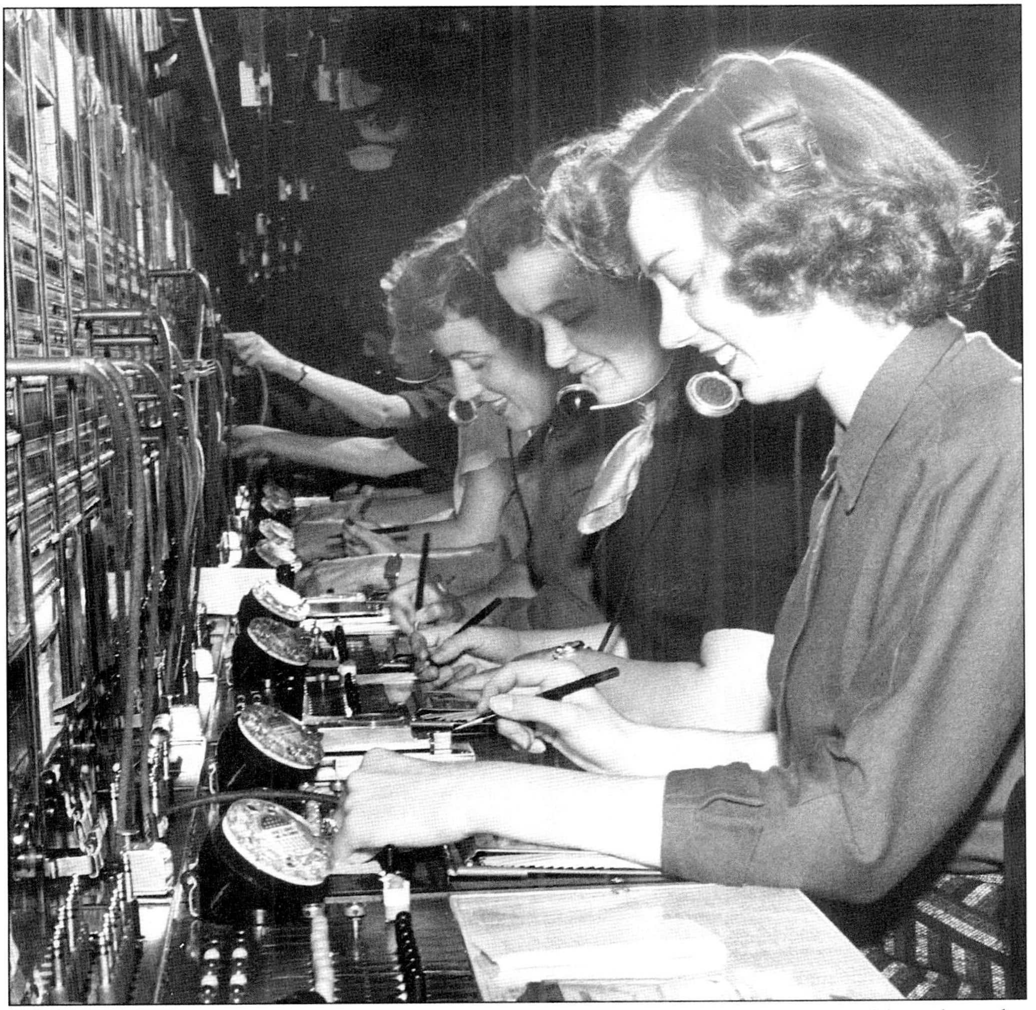

"Before the appearance of computerized equipment, this was how the switchboard at the Pittsfield telephone office looked. Making a long-distance call was a decidedly more human experience then" —November 6, 1982. The date of the original scene was the mid-1950s.

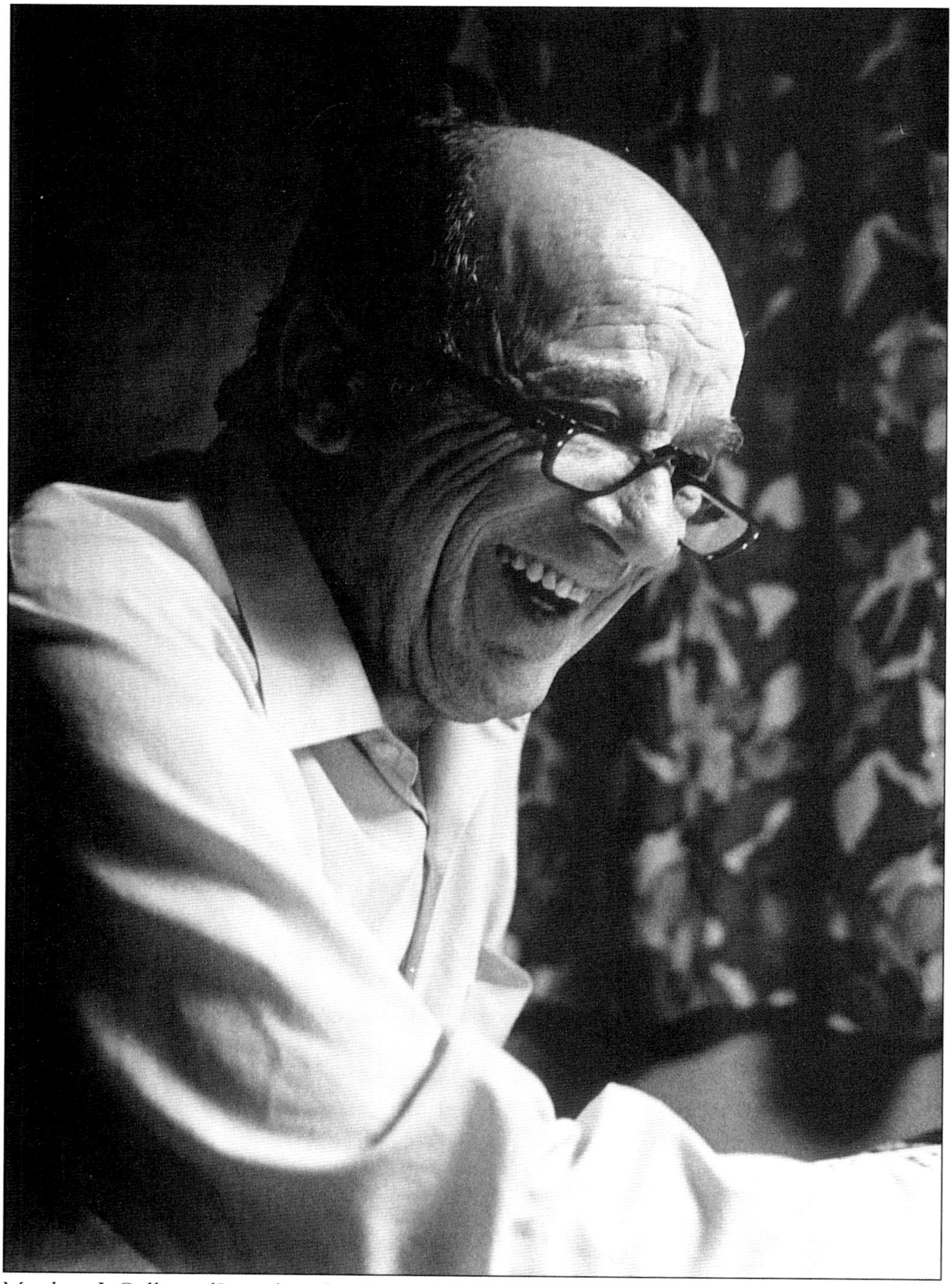

Matthew J. Collins of Lanesboro breaks into a victory smile as he learns that he has won election in November 1972 as the new Berkshire County treasurer. Tague stayed with him that evening to record the moments, sometimes tense but usually jovial, of receiving election returns.

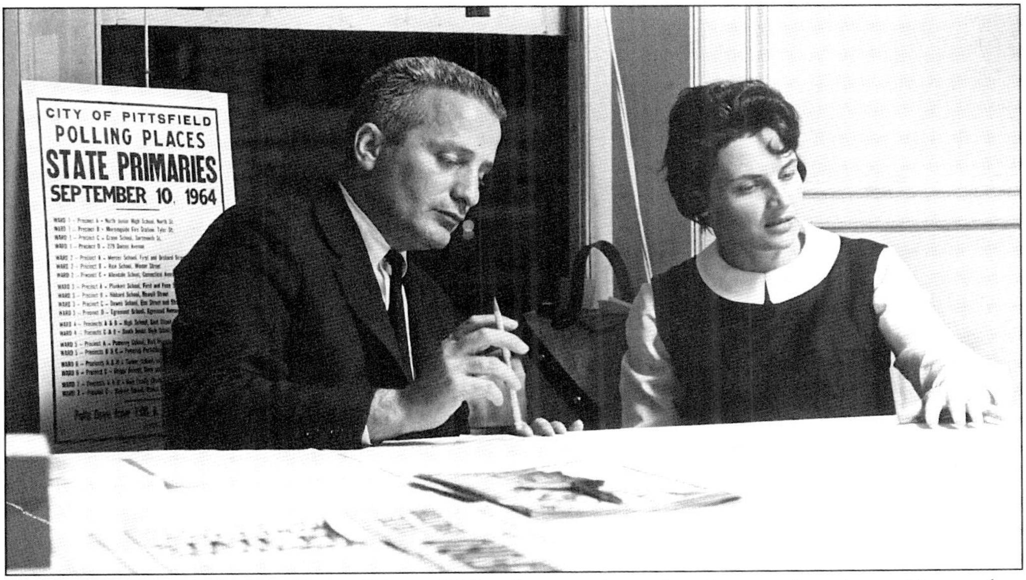

Political figures Andrea and Irene "Batesy" Nuciforo await results of state primaries on September 10, 1964. They were the parents, both now deceased, of Andrea F. Nuciforo Jr., incumbent state senator from Berkshire County.

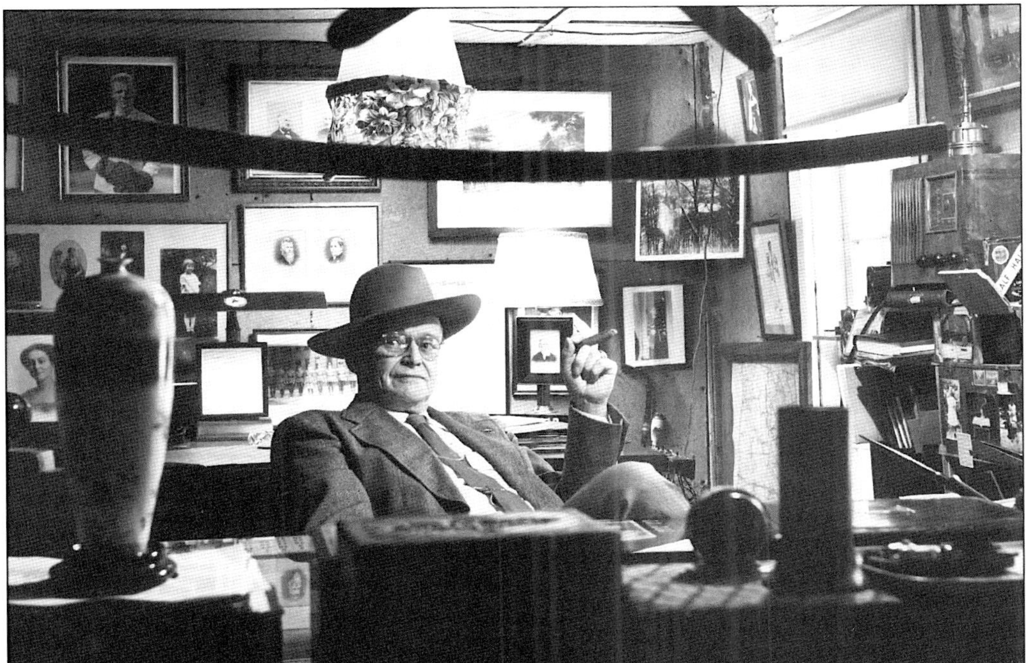

"From the east part of Lee comes the town's highest ranking and most colorful military figure, Lt. Col. William H. Weingar, USA retired, who wouldn't look natural without the cowboy hat he wears incessantly. Born in East Lee, he has lived in the same house all his life. He was 75 last Saturday. His Army career began in 1898 and ended in 1945. An enthusiastic student of history, he is currently working on the history of his home town" —April 2, 1955.

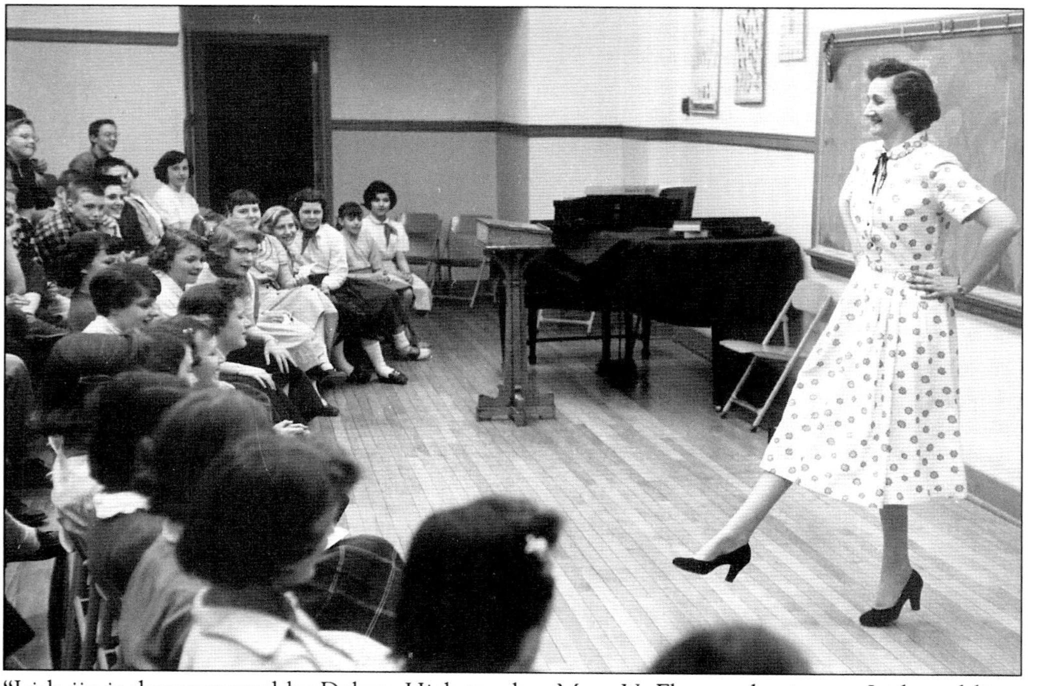

"Irish jig is demonstrated by Dalton High teacher Mary V. Flynn, who is very Irish and lives on Shamrock Street in Stockbridge. She's teaching the jig to her class on the day before St. Patrick's Day. Moments before, she spoke on Irish achievements" —March 19, 1955.

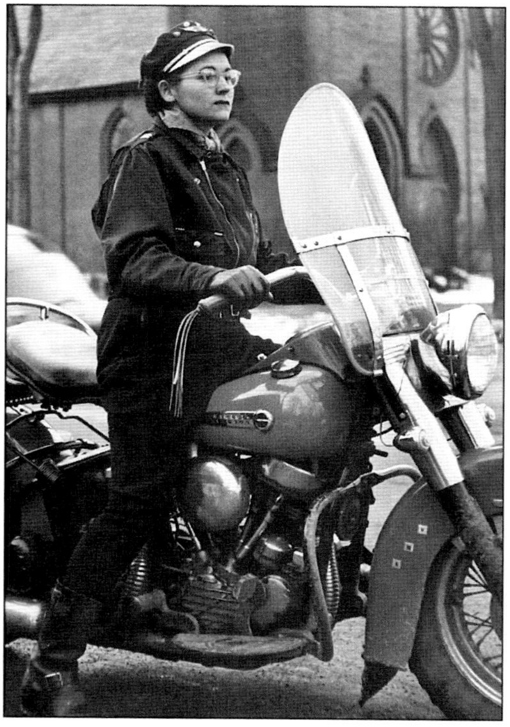

"Motorcycle lover: Miss Alice M. Godfrey, 23, of Henderson Road, Williamstown, is so enthusiastic about cycling that she drives all year round despite the Berkshire weather. She is not adamant about taking friends riding with her" —March 21, 1953.

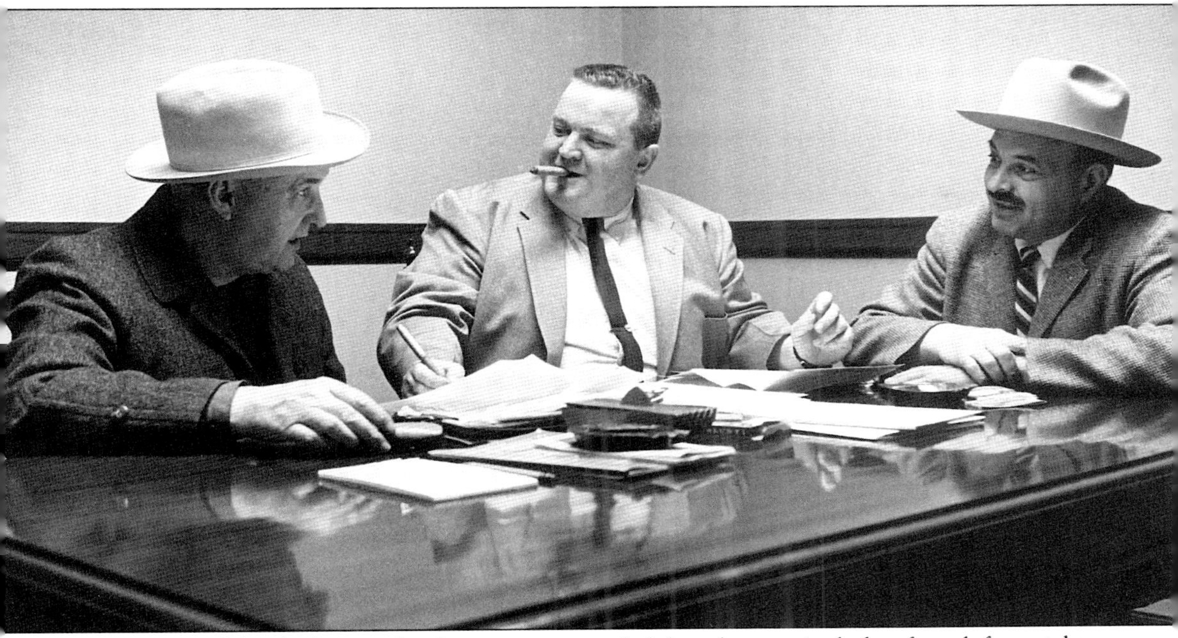

The nature of the deal arrived at here is not recorded, but the cast includes, from left to right, James Aloysius McCabe (a horse fancier and realtor), George Crane, and Izzy Goodman, all well-known figures in the community. The date is April of 1962.

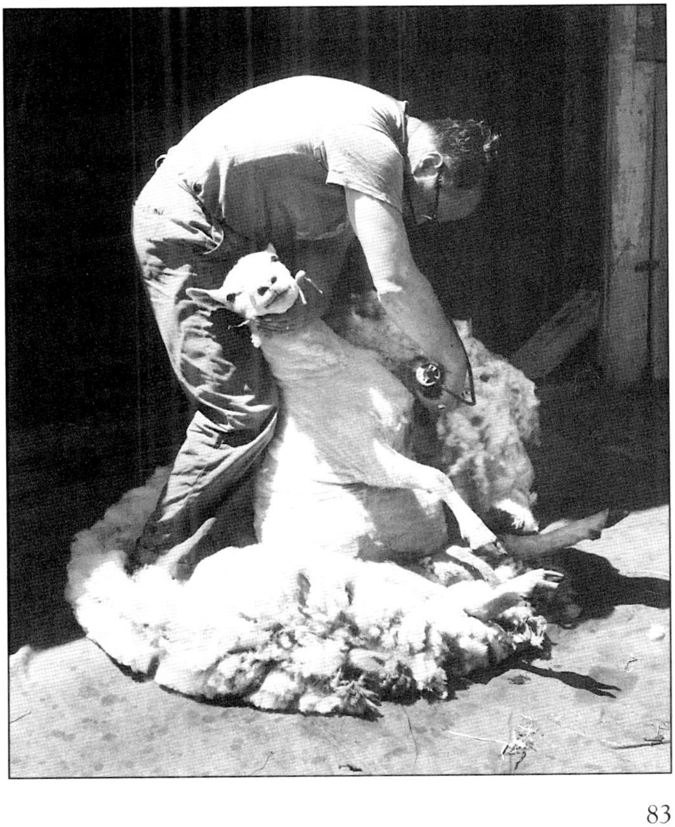

"Disrobing of sheep by 4-H agent Robert Hall in 1958 gave the sheep the feeling that he'd been clipped, if not fleeced. Later, his feeling changed to one of shear pleasure" —September 20, 1969.

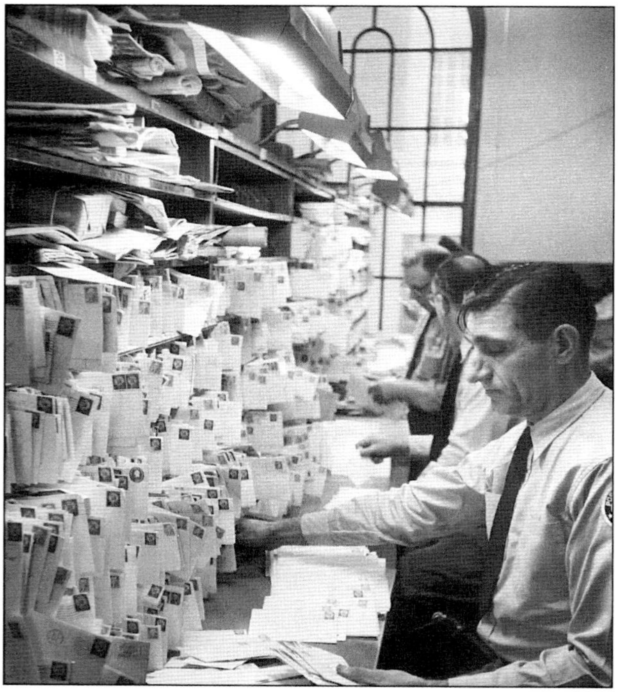

Two pictures from a series on how busy Pittsfield Post Office workers were in December of 1956.

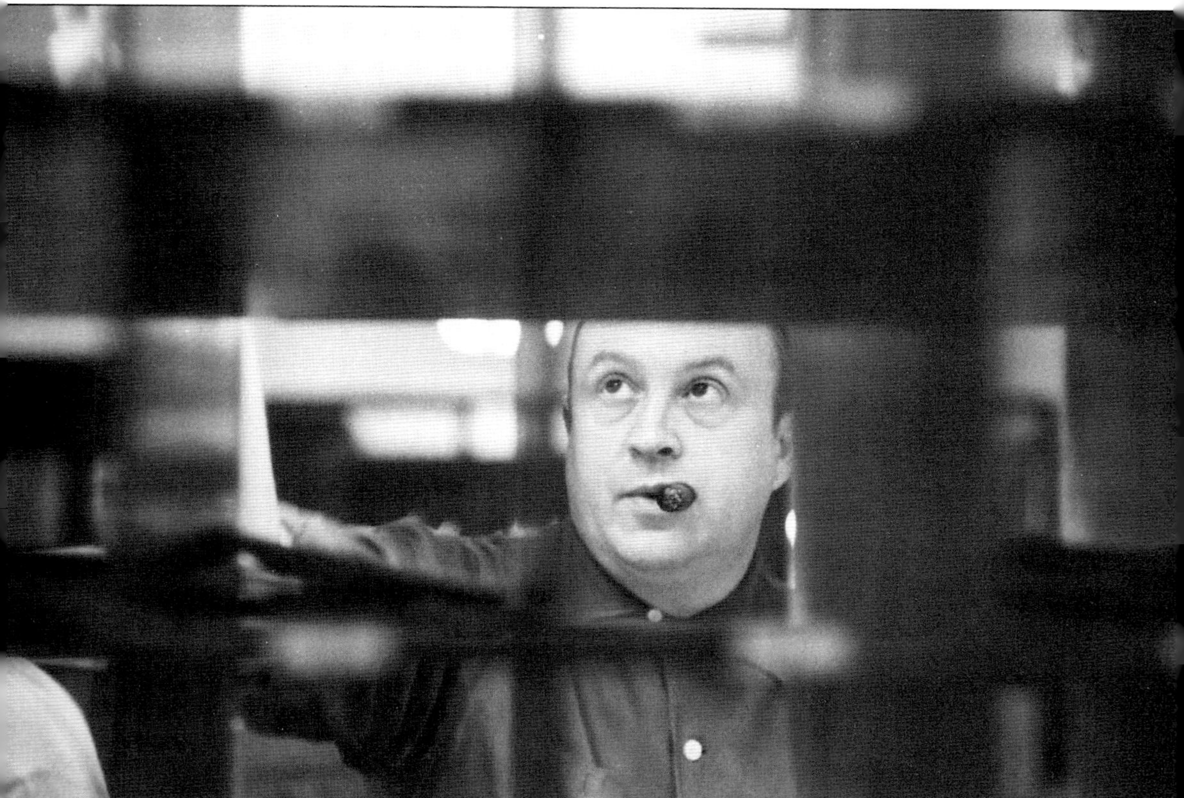

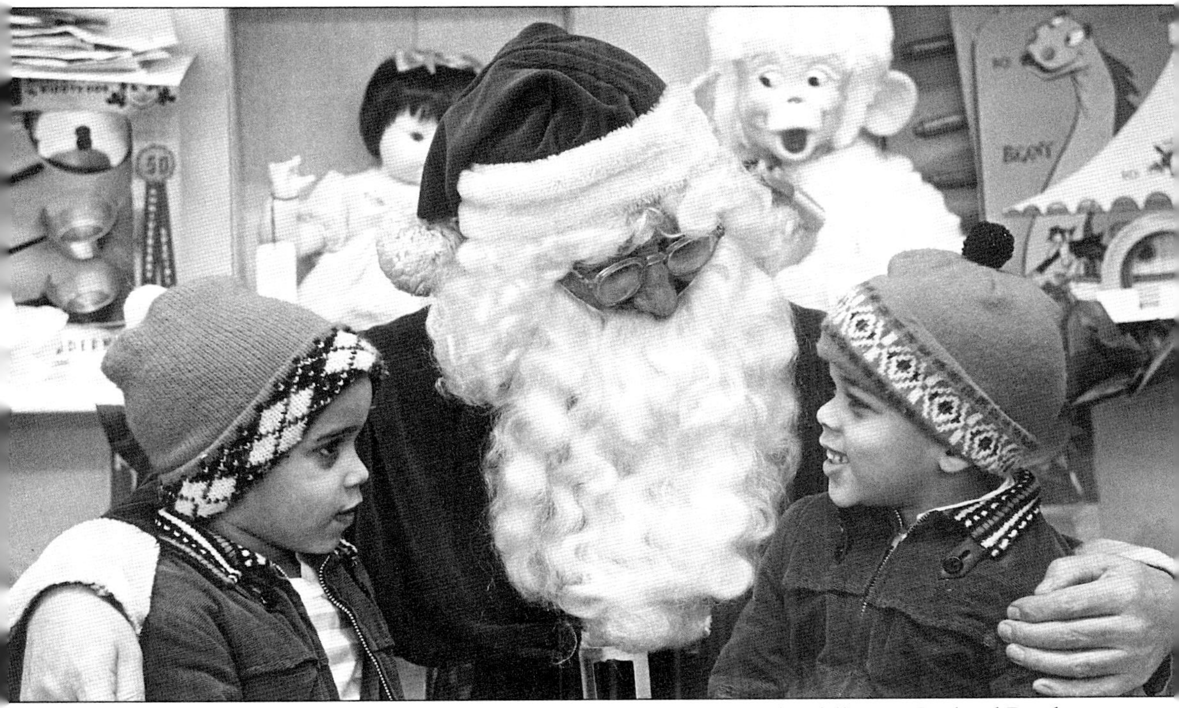

The vocation of a Santa Claus is a short-lived one each year, but this fellow at England Brothers in December of 1962 appeared to be successfully persuading a couple of believers.

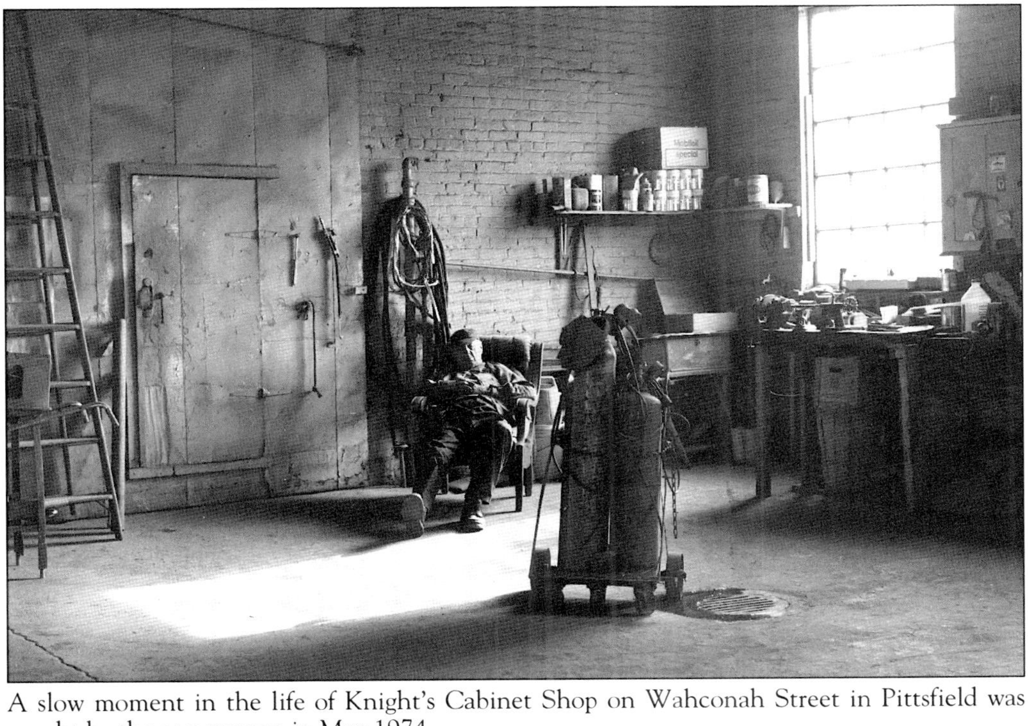

A slow moment in the life of Knight's Cabinet Shop on Wahconah Street in Pittsfield was caught by the cameraman in May 1974.

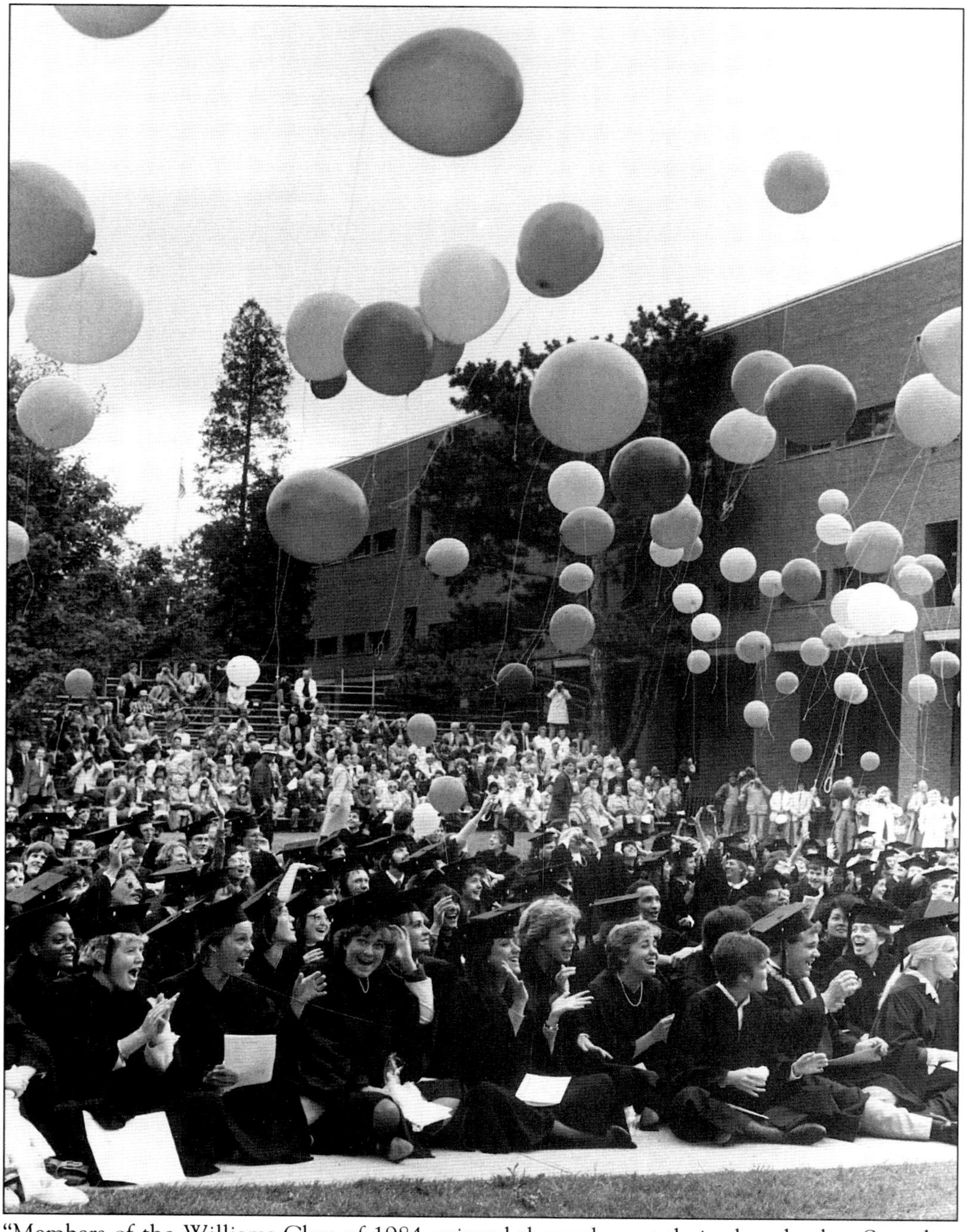

"Members of the Williams Class of 1984 enjoyed themselves at their class day last Saturday. Activities included such lighthearted traditions as the ivy planting and dropping of the class watch from atop the college chapel. Here they are releasing their balloons, signifying nothing in particular" —June 9, 1984.

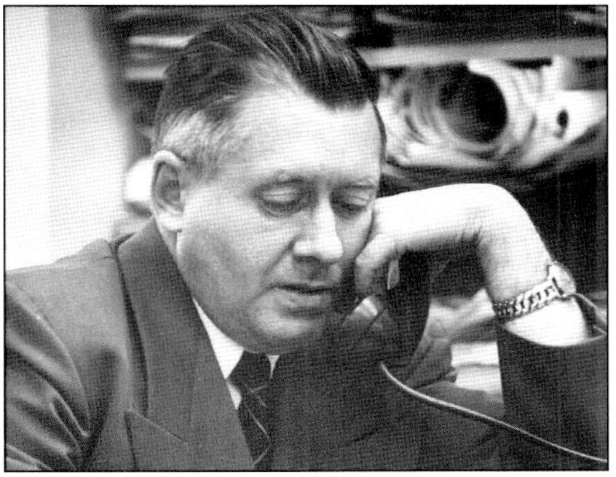

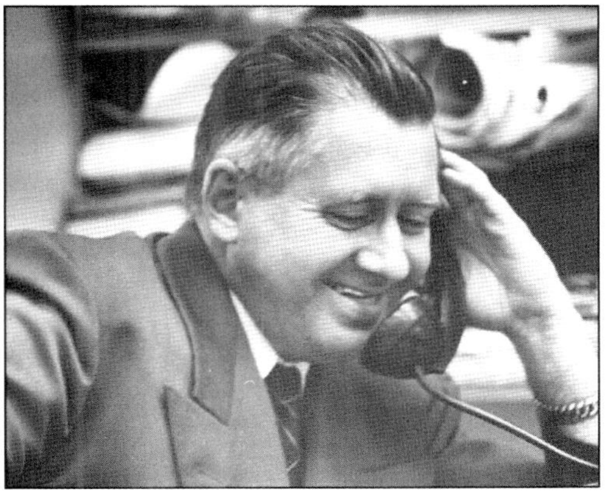

Roger O'Gara, longtime sports editor of *The Berkshire Eagle*, is captured on film by his colleague during a phone conversation in the early 1960s.

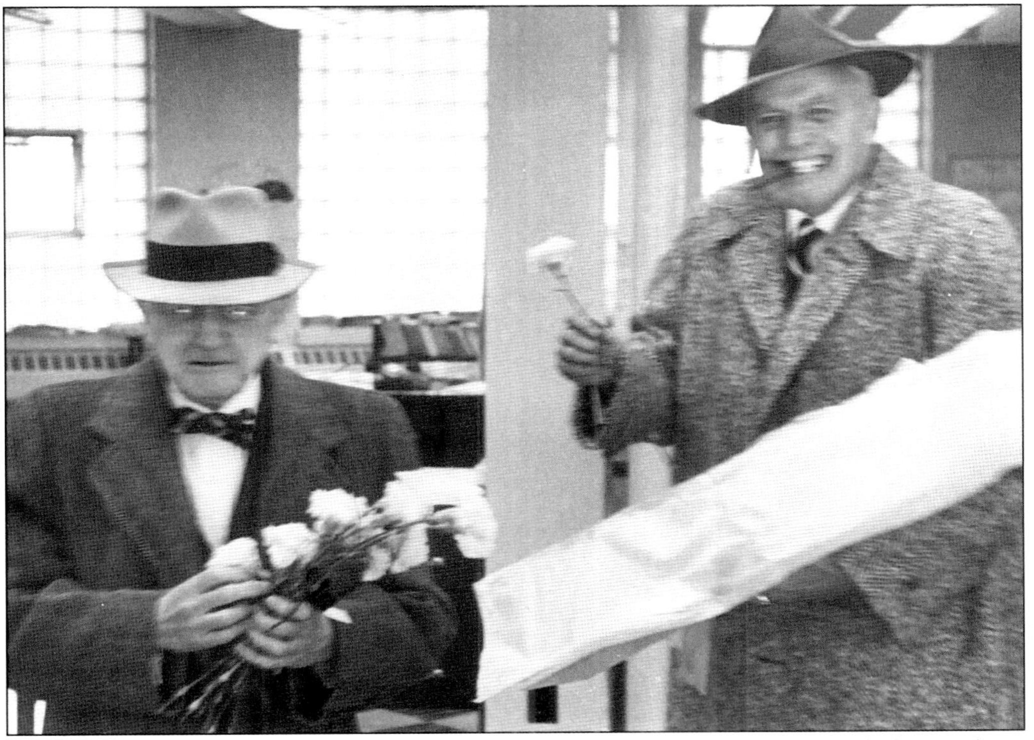

Roger H. Wellington, right, whose vocation was usually that of an undertaker, and whose politics were very Republican, couldn't conceal his glee in 1952 when Gen. Dwight D. Eisenhower defeated Adlai E. Stevenson. He brought flowers to the Stevenson-leaning *Eagle* staff out of "condolence."

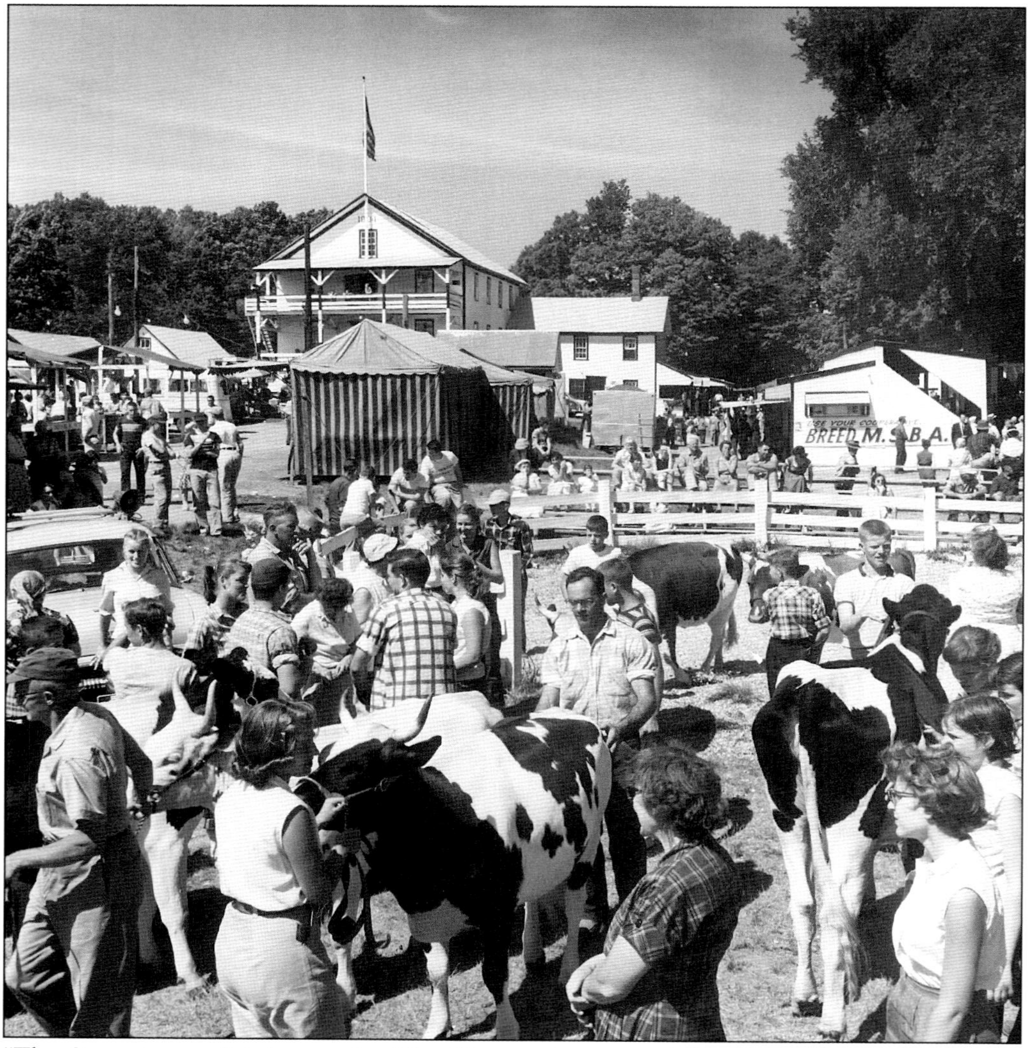

"The Cummington Fair has retained for 69 years the cowsy, folksy flavor of a bona fide, non-pari-mutuel country fair. Its livestock show, produce exhibits and ox drawing contests were concluded last Sunday and will run again next year, without the assistance of Boston promoters or horse racing" —August 31, 1957.

Seven

A Diversity of Trees

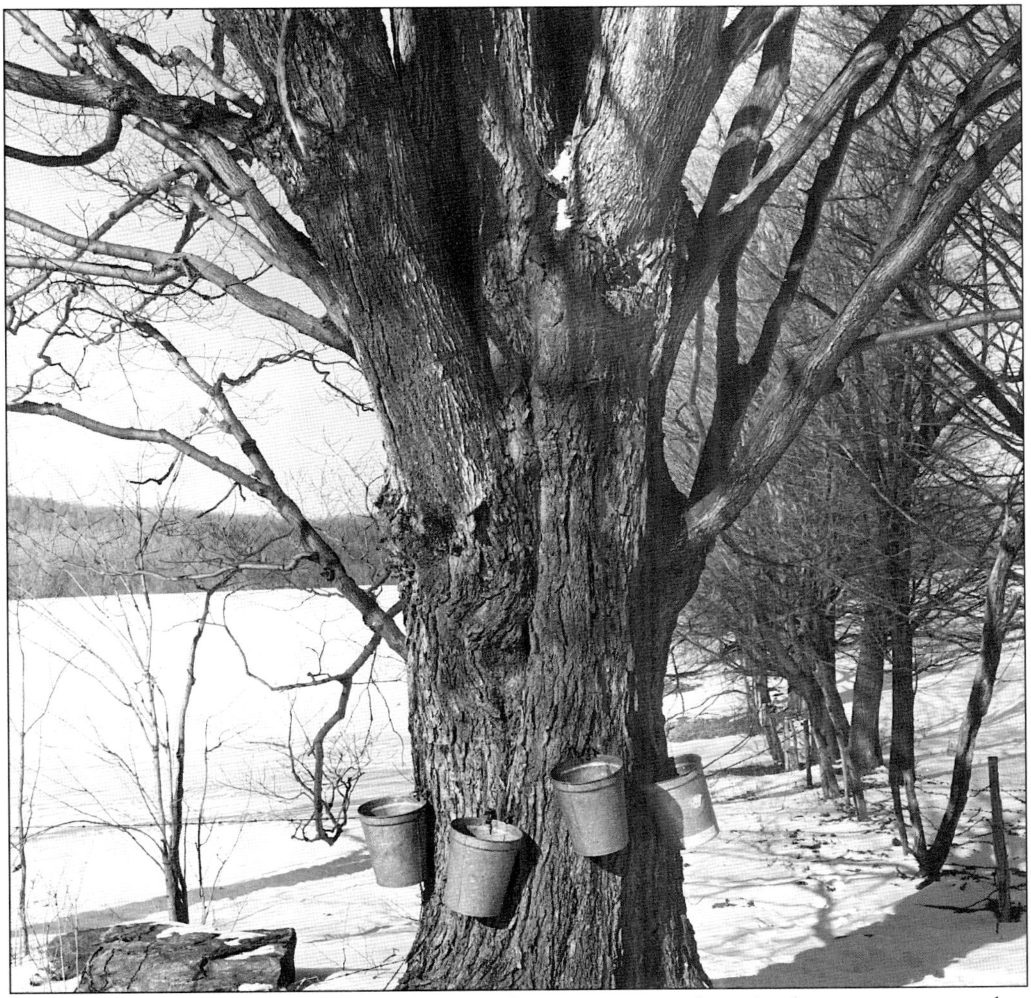

"Sweet sign that spring can't be far away is the appearance of sap buckets on sugar maples. These are on a street in Lanesboro" —March 9, 1968.

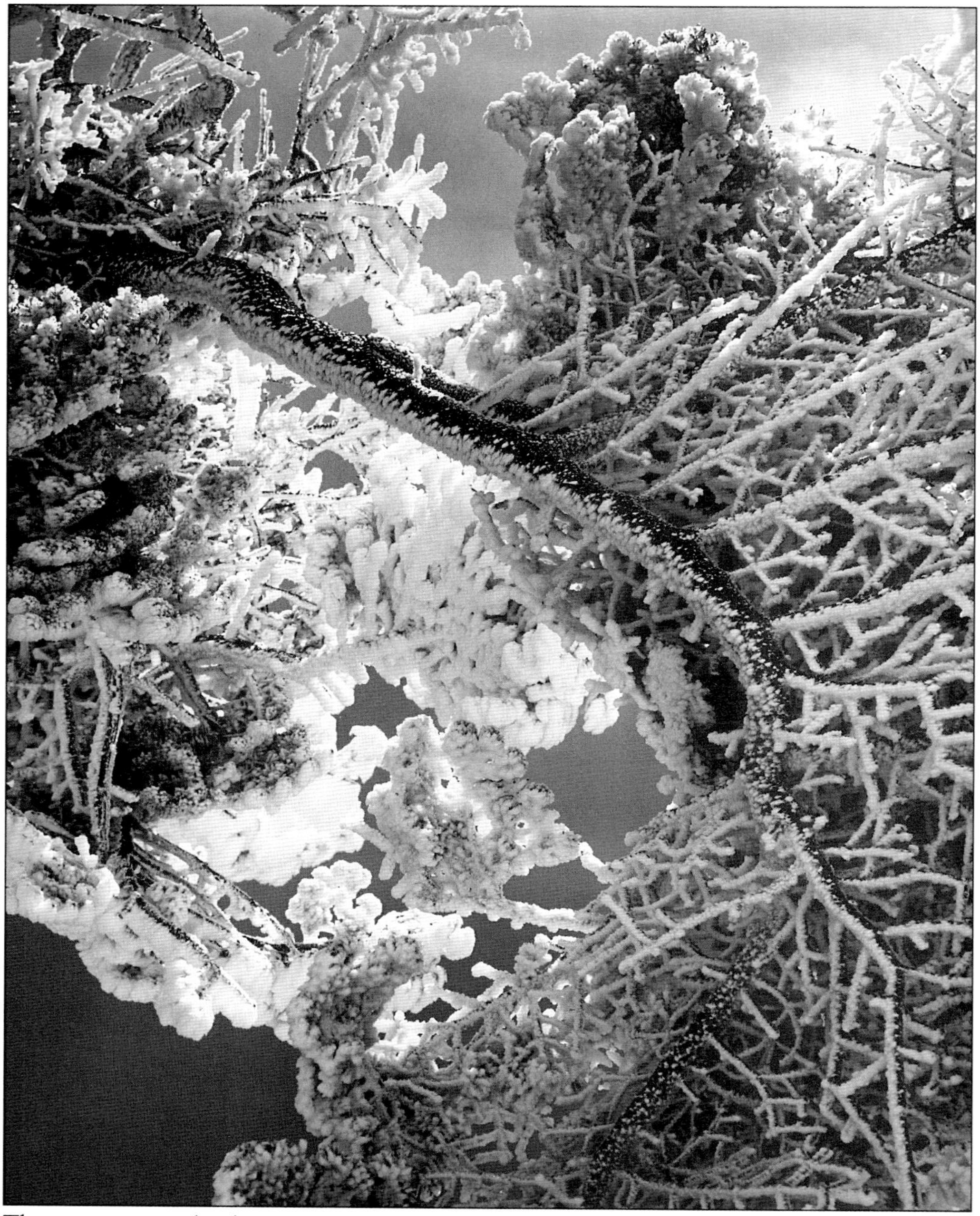

The most spectacular designs trees can provide are when they're coated with snow and rime ice. This was a view on top of Greylock in late October 1960.

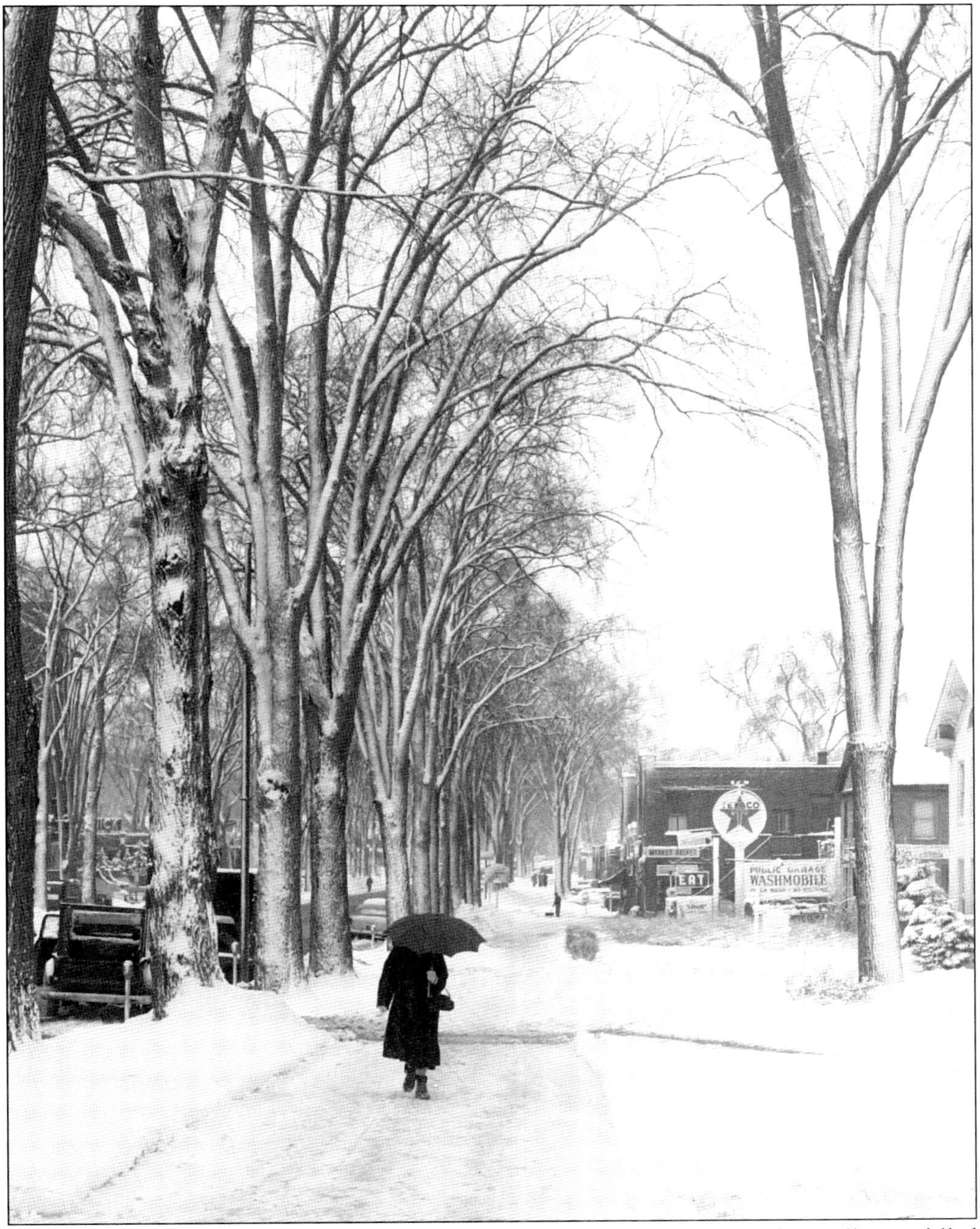

"Twenty-five years ago, South Street was graced by a row of magnificent elms. All were felled by a major aesthetic disaster, Dutch elm disease" —January 29, 1983. The original picture was taken about 1958.

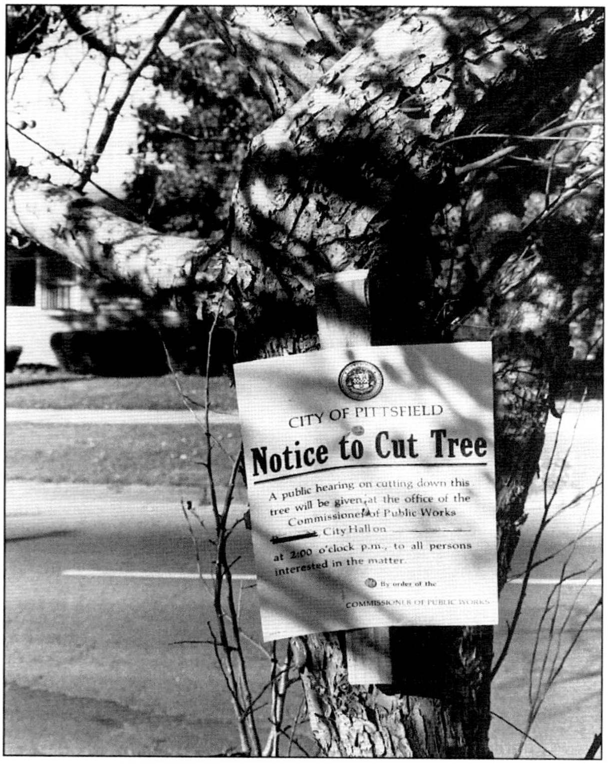

These were common scenes in the 1980s when Pittsfield's abundant elms were in the process of demolition. The house is located on Newell Street.

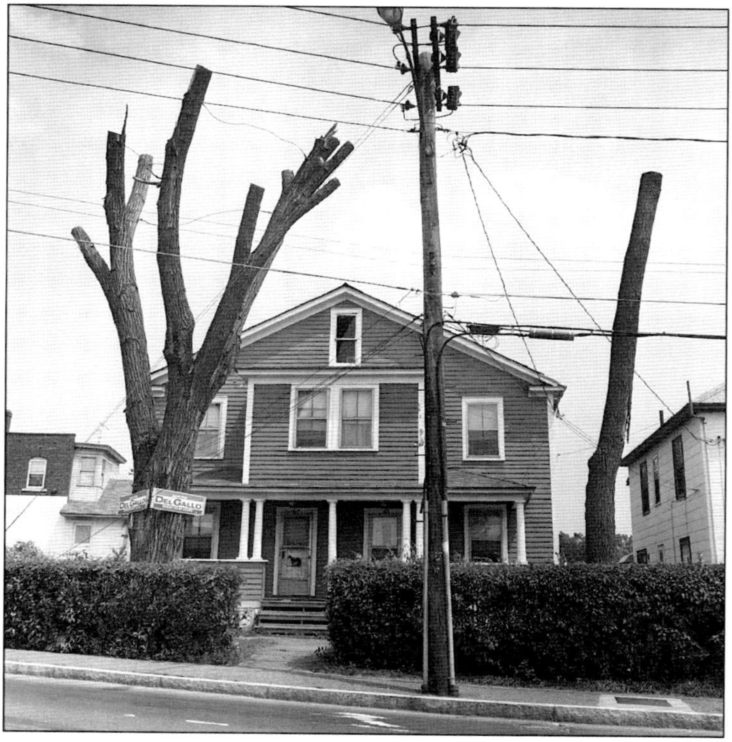

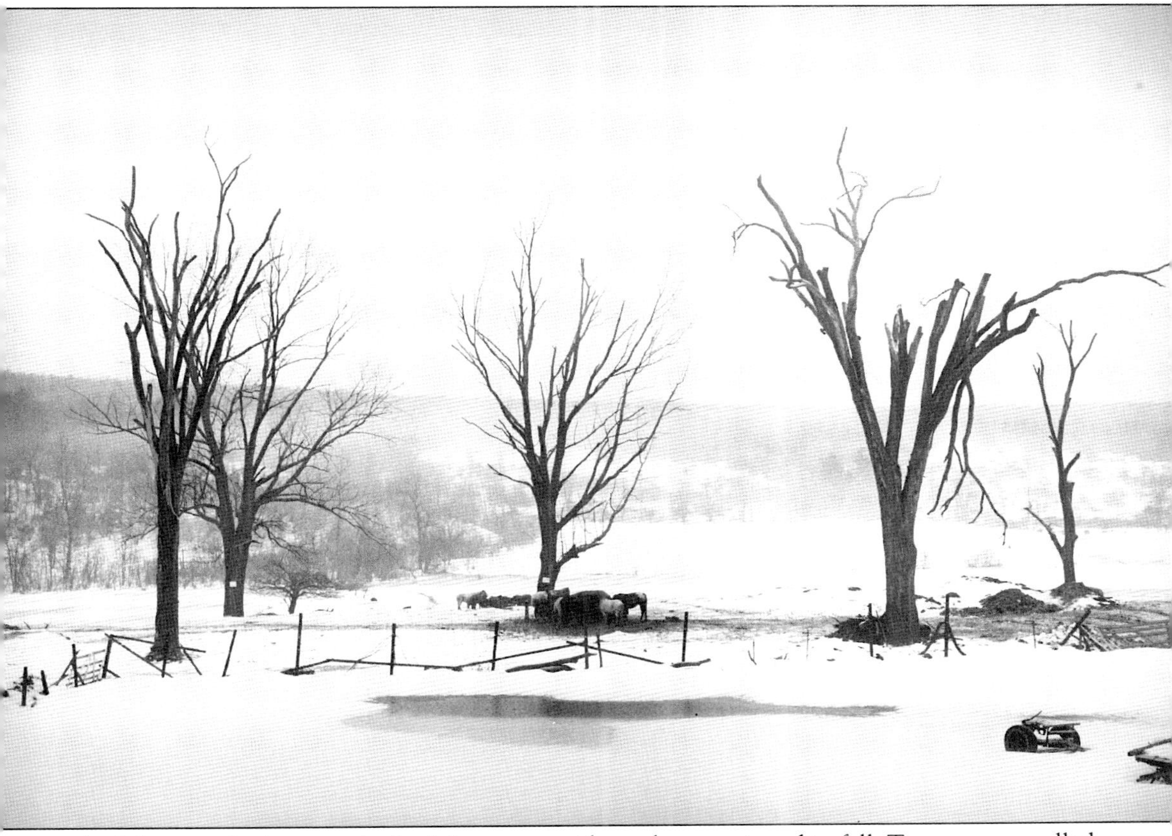

And this was the frequent look of the countryside as elms continued to fall. Tague was appalled by the loss, and his camera often went into action to make a visual record, at least, of the phenomenon.

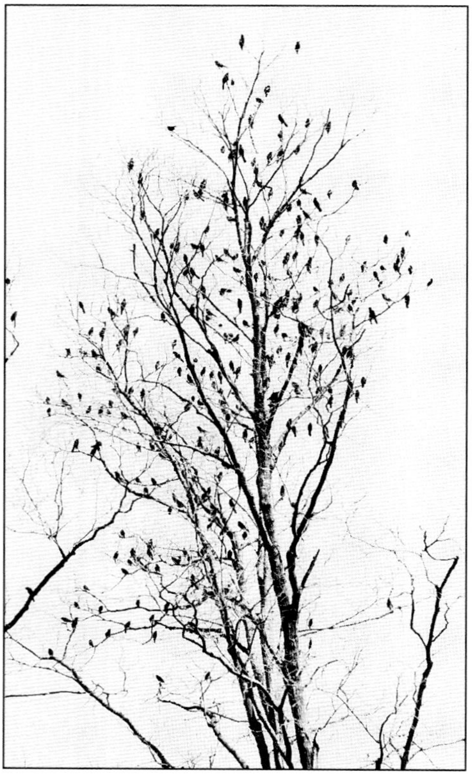

Early spring offers so much visual appeal—the return of birds and the promise of warmer times. You can almost feel these young ash trees soaking up the sun.

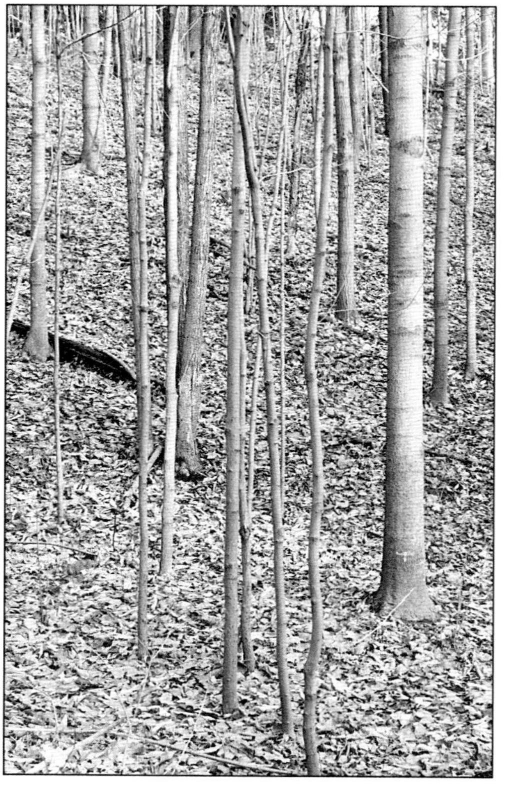

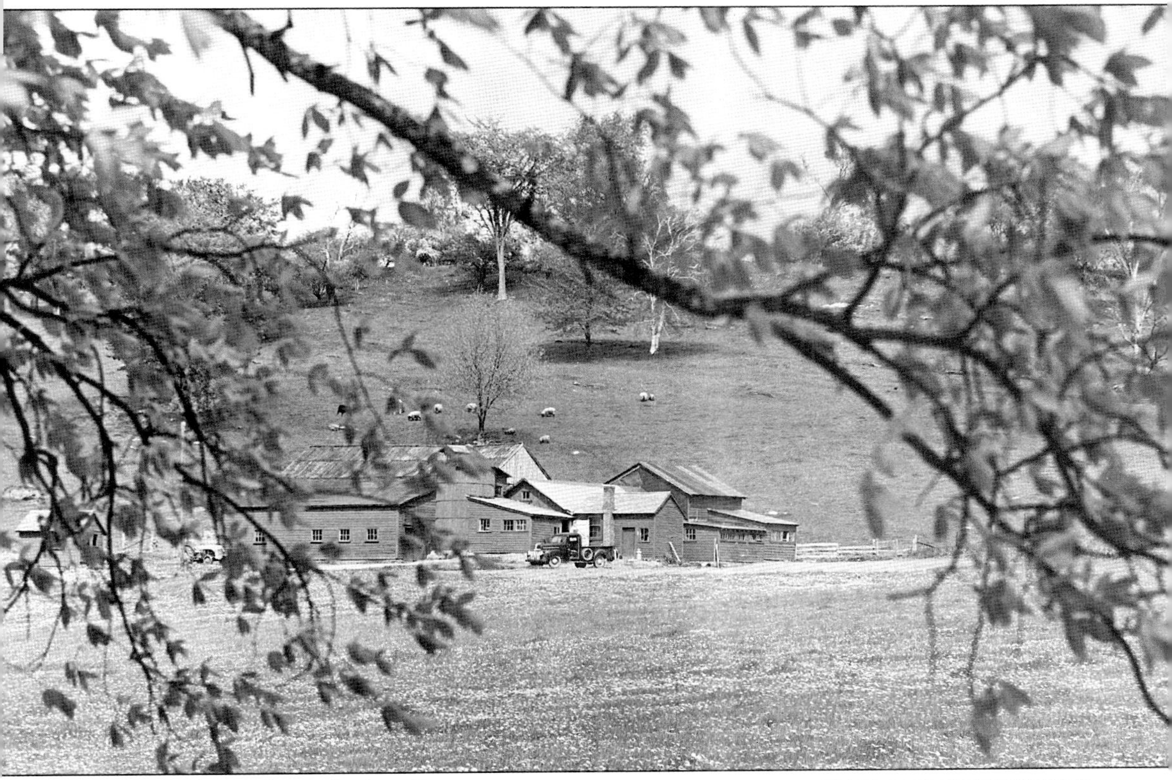

Finally the leaves burst forth, offering still new kinds of visual delight. This farm was in South Williamstown in 1961, and the beech were on the Mt. Greylock State Reservation.

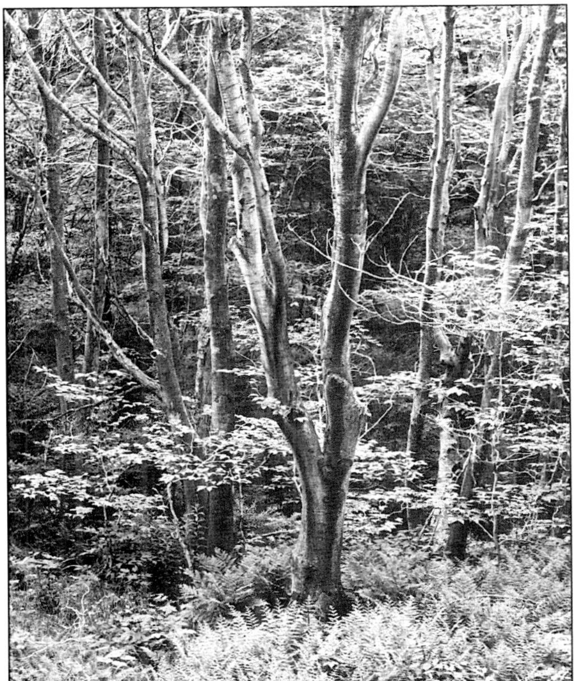

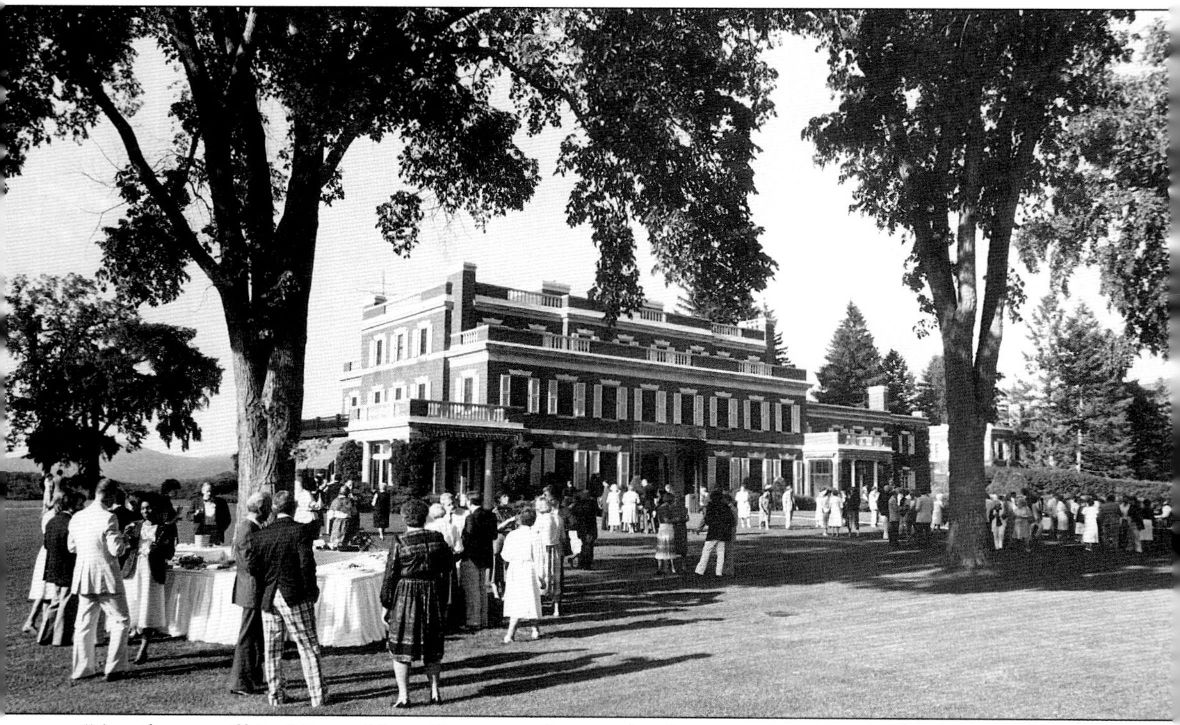

"An elegant affair: Mount Hope Farm was the storybook setting for a farewell party given by the Williams College faculty for outgoing President John E. Chandler and his wife, Florence. The weather was gorgeous and a fine time was had by all" —June 1, 1985. Mentioned elsewhere on the page were the spectacular elms which had somehow escaped the disease.

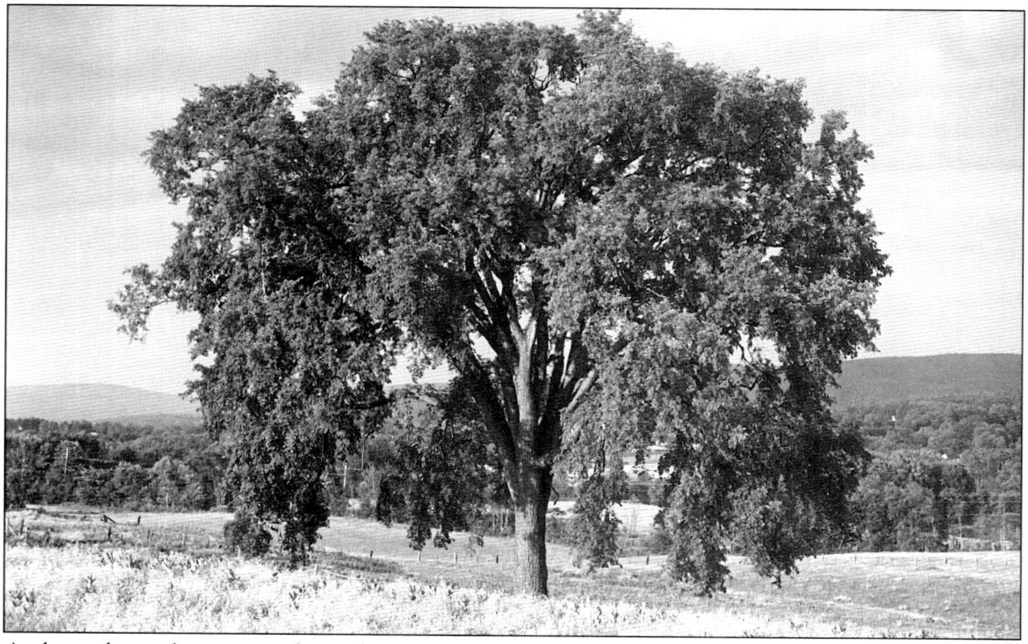

A classic lone elm, pictured in a field in Pittsfield in 1981.

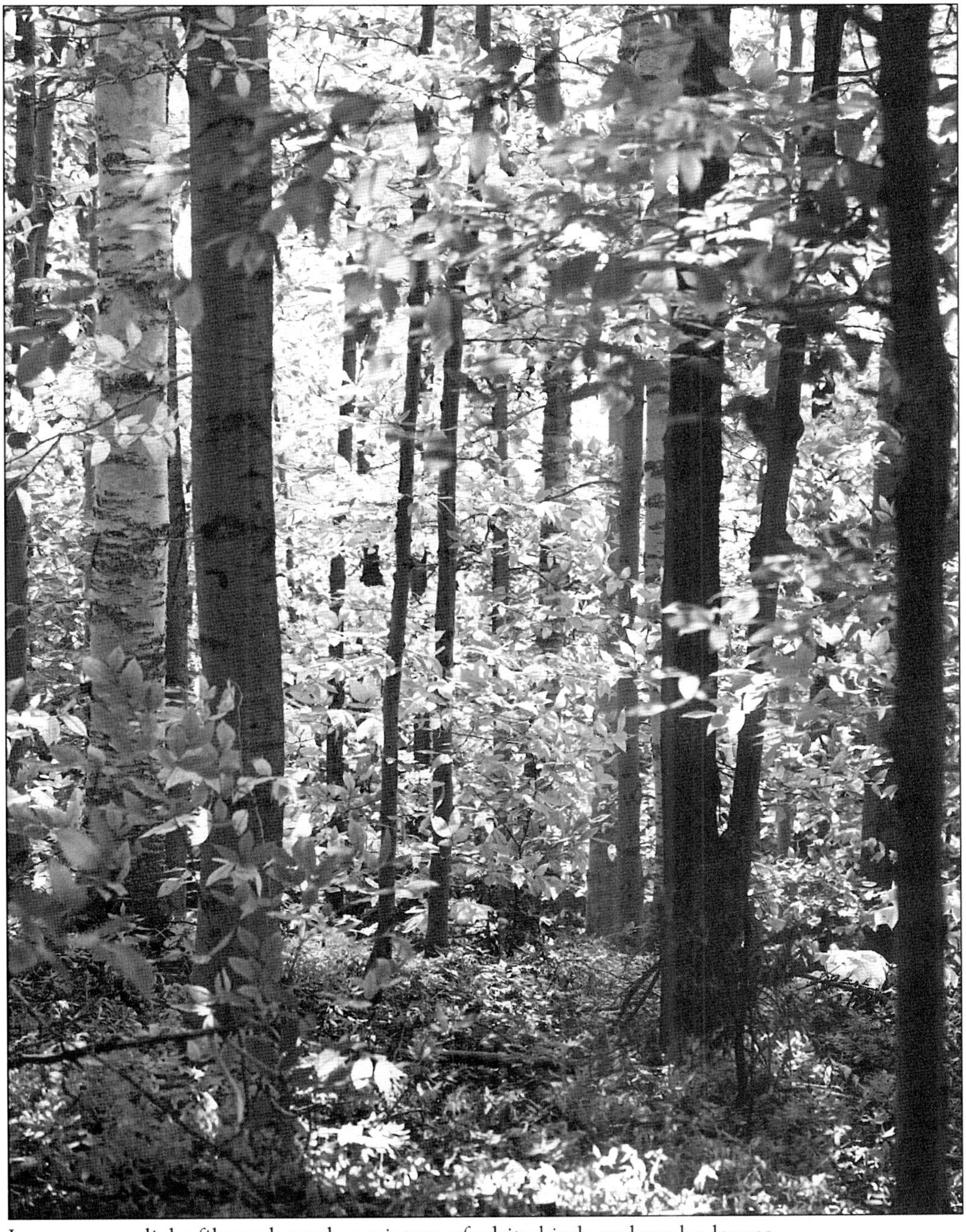

Late summer light filters through a mixture of white birch and poplar leaves.

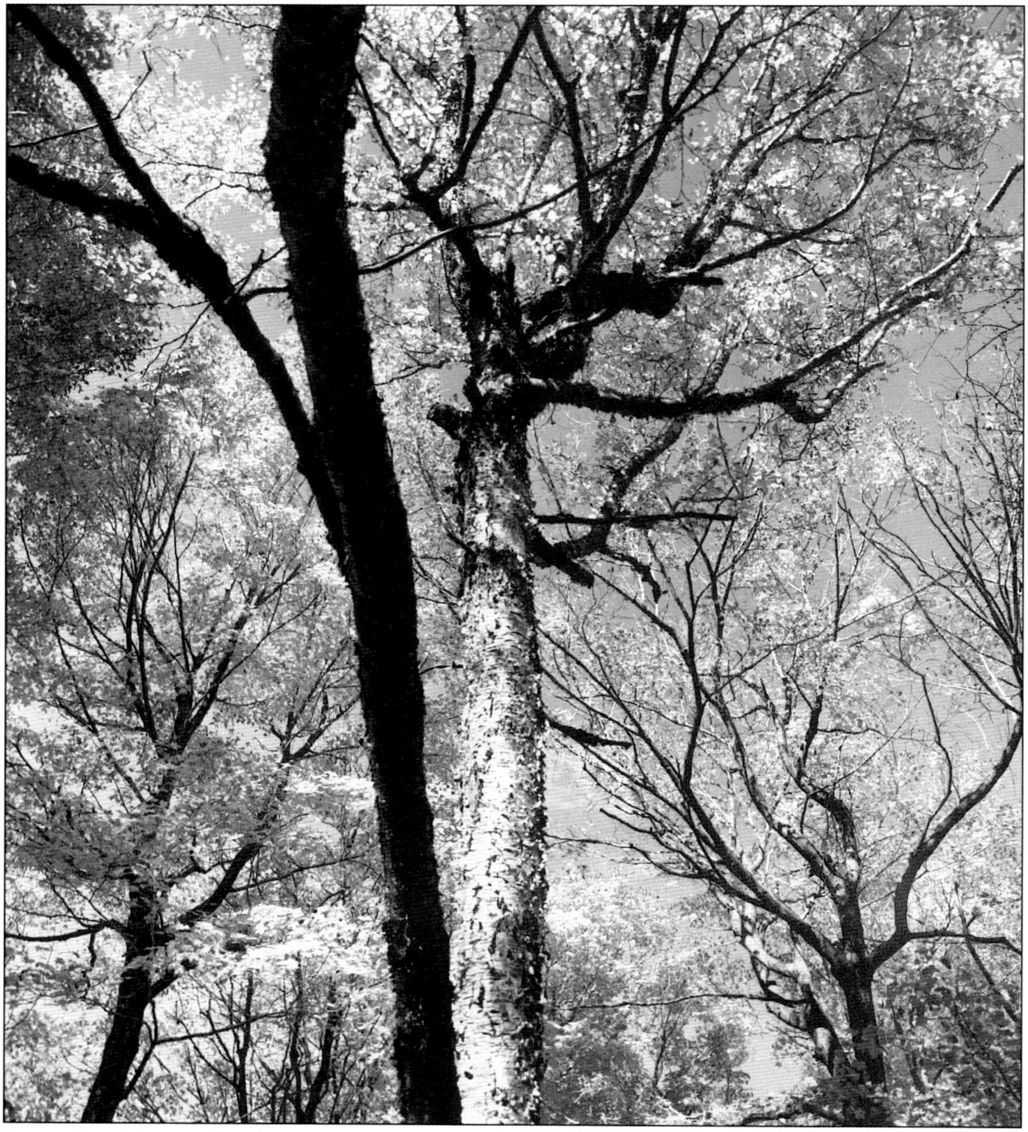

Tague had the knack of capturing the essential characteristics of trees in black and white. This photo fully appreciates the virtues of the yellow birch.

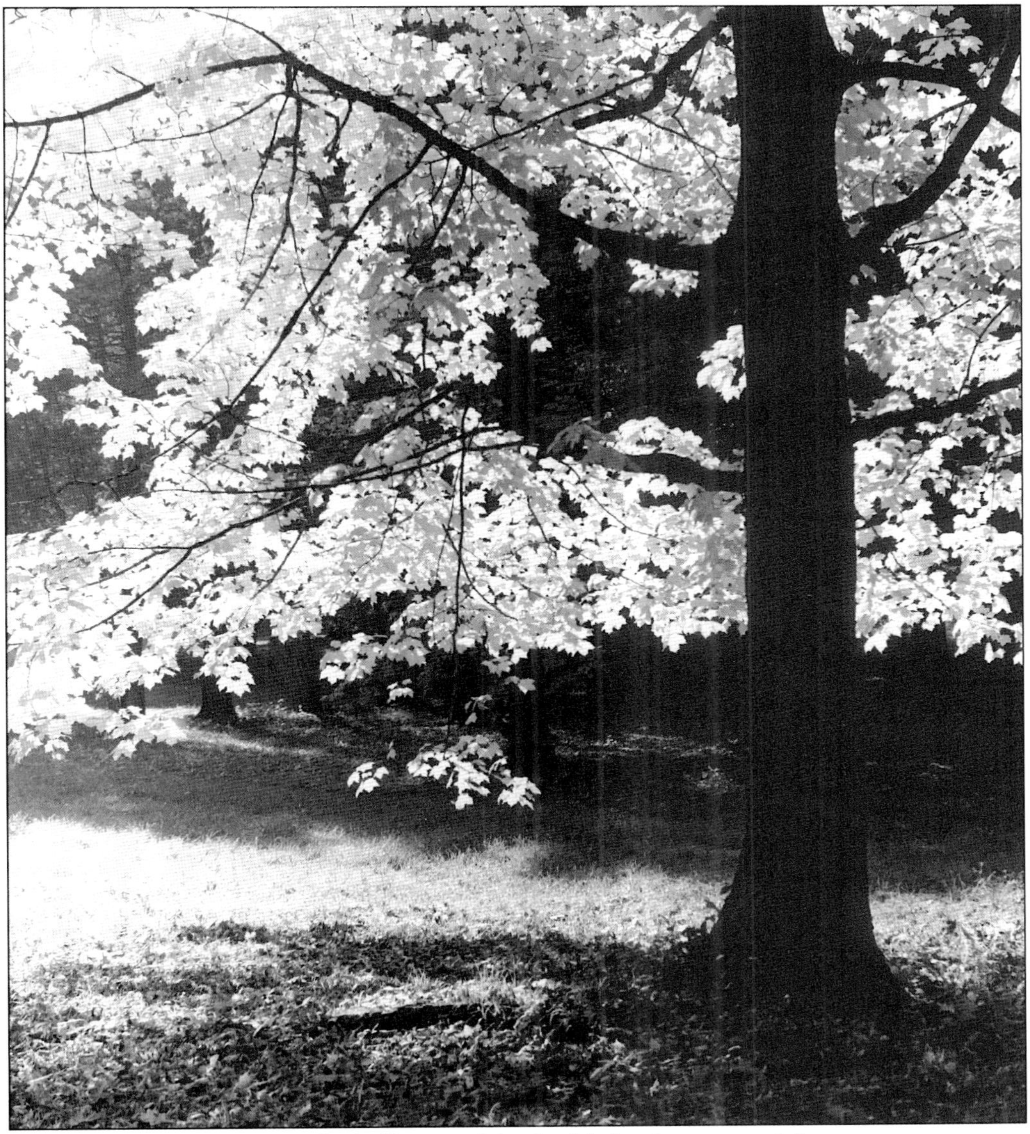

Who needs color to convey the brilliance of this backlighted sugar maple?

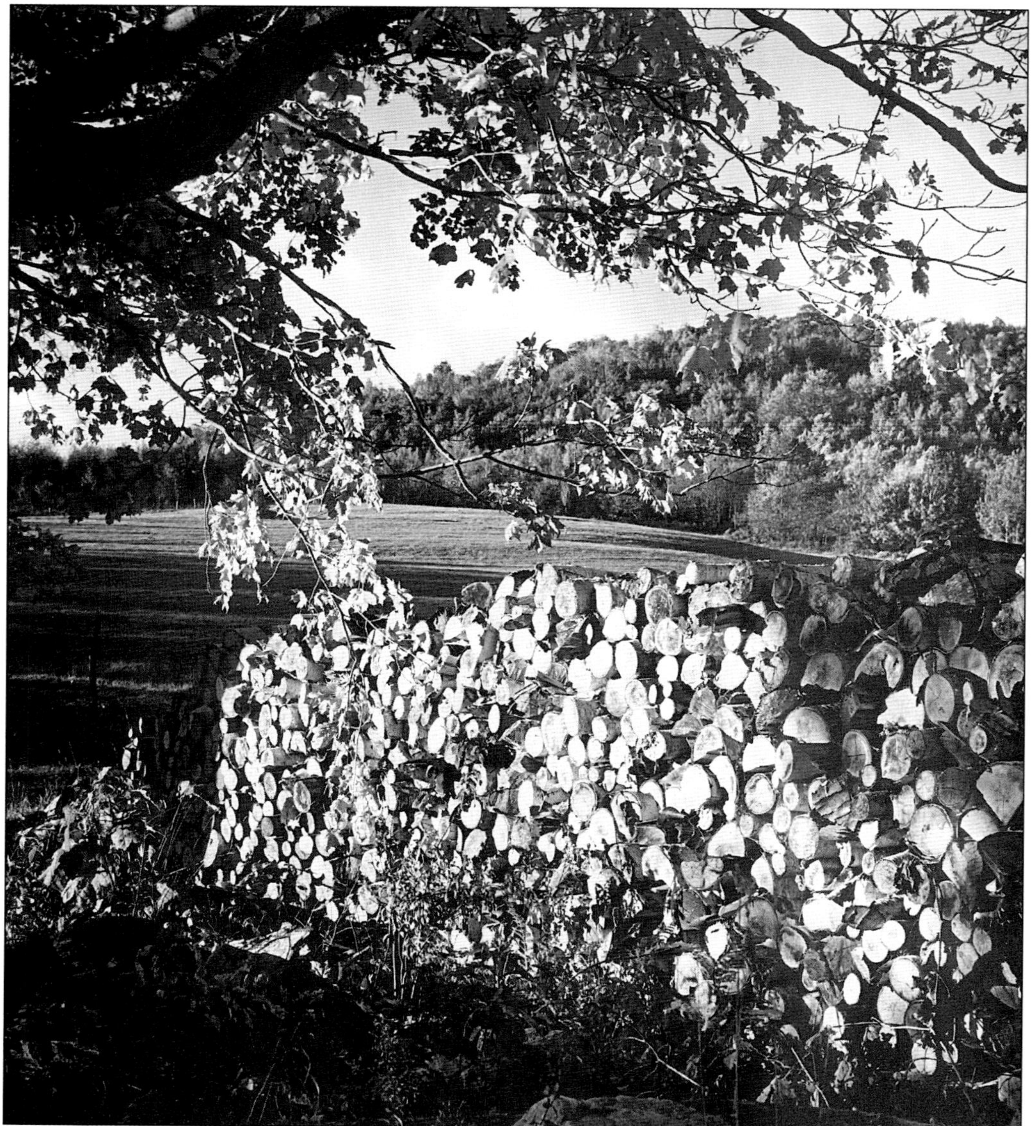

This is an October view of a maple-shaded woodpile ready for the coming season.

Eight

Watery Views

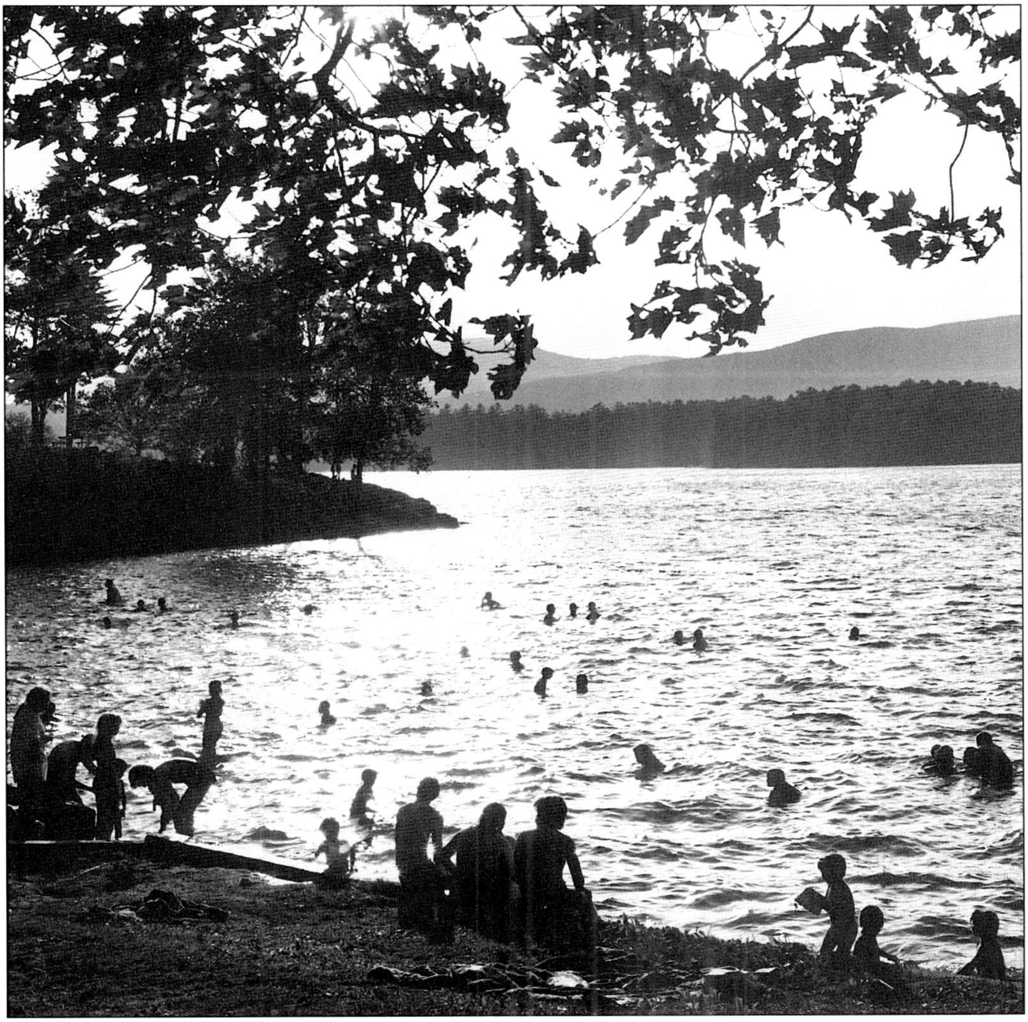

"Antidote: Glittering refreshingly in the late afternoon sun, the waters of the public bathing beach at Onota Lake are studded with swimmers enjoying a respite from this week's heat wave" —July 11, 1981.

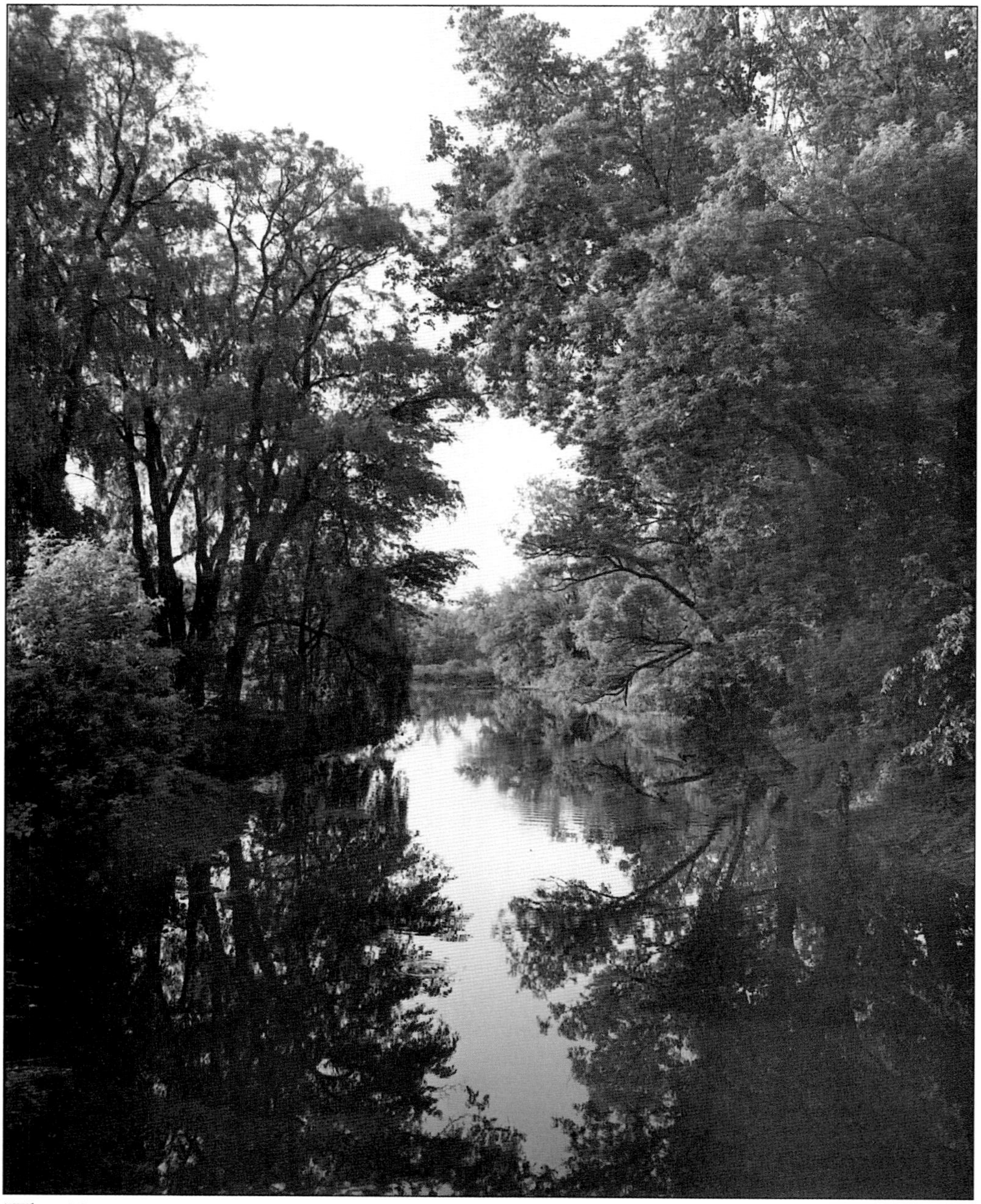

"The Housatonic: Looking north from the Linden Street bridge, one sees a surprisingly picturesque view of the west branch of the Housatonic River. Many people, no doubt, have crossed the bridge without noticing the beauty nearby" —June 14, 1980.

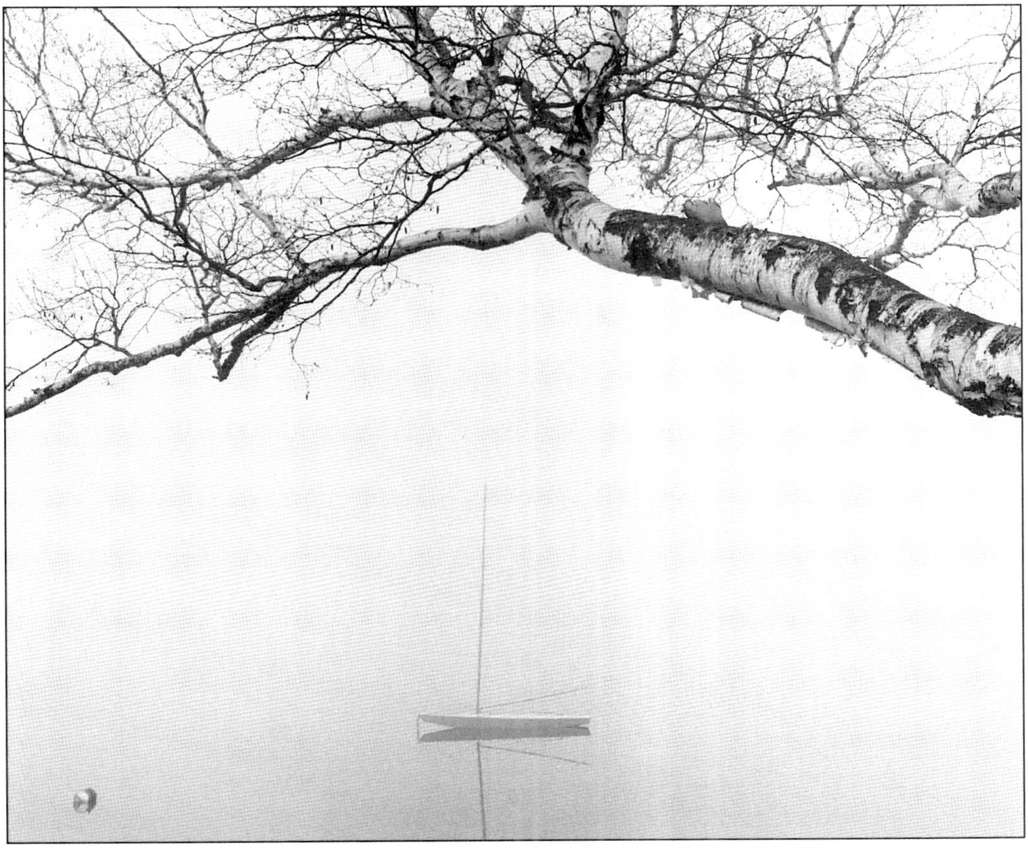

A subtle variation in grays marks this view of a white birch and a small sailboat.

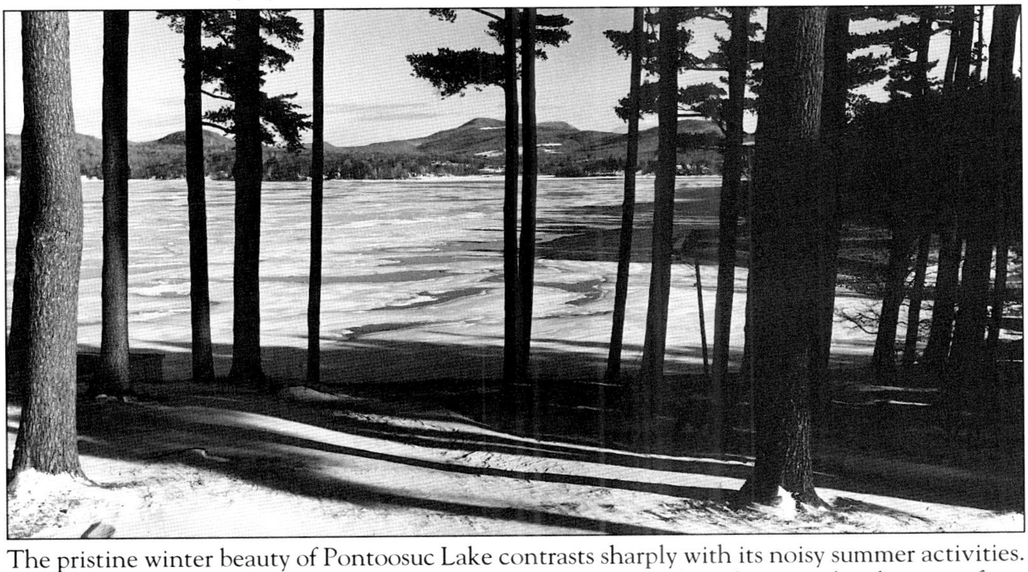

The pristine winter beauty of Pontoosuc Lake contrasts sharply with its noisy summer activities. Mount Greylock, the highest point in Massachusetts at 3,491 feet above sea level, is seen from the picnic area at the south end of the lake.

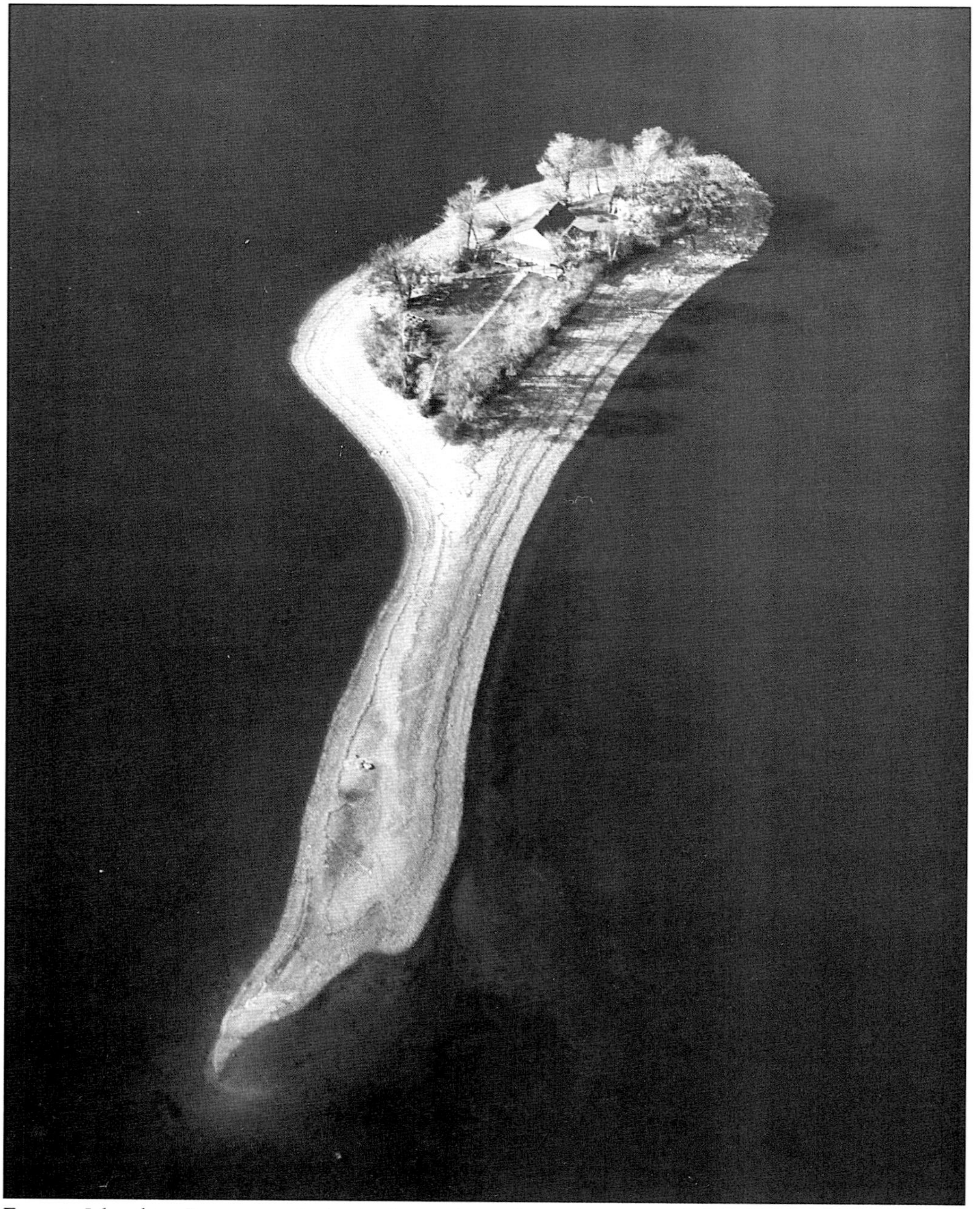

Francis Island in Pontoosuc Lake is shown here from the air in November 1961. The house on the island was the Tagues' residence for a time in the early 1950s. Later abandoned, it was burned by vandals.

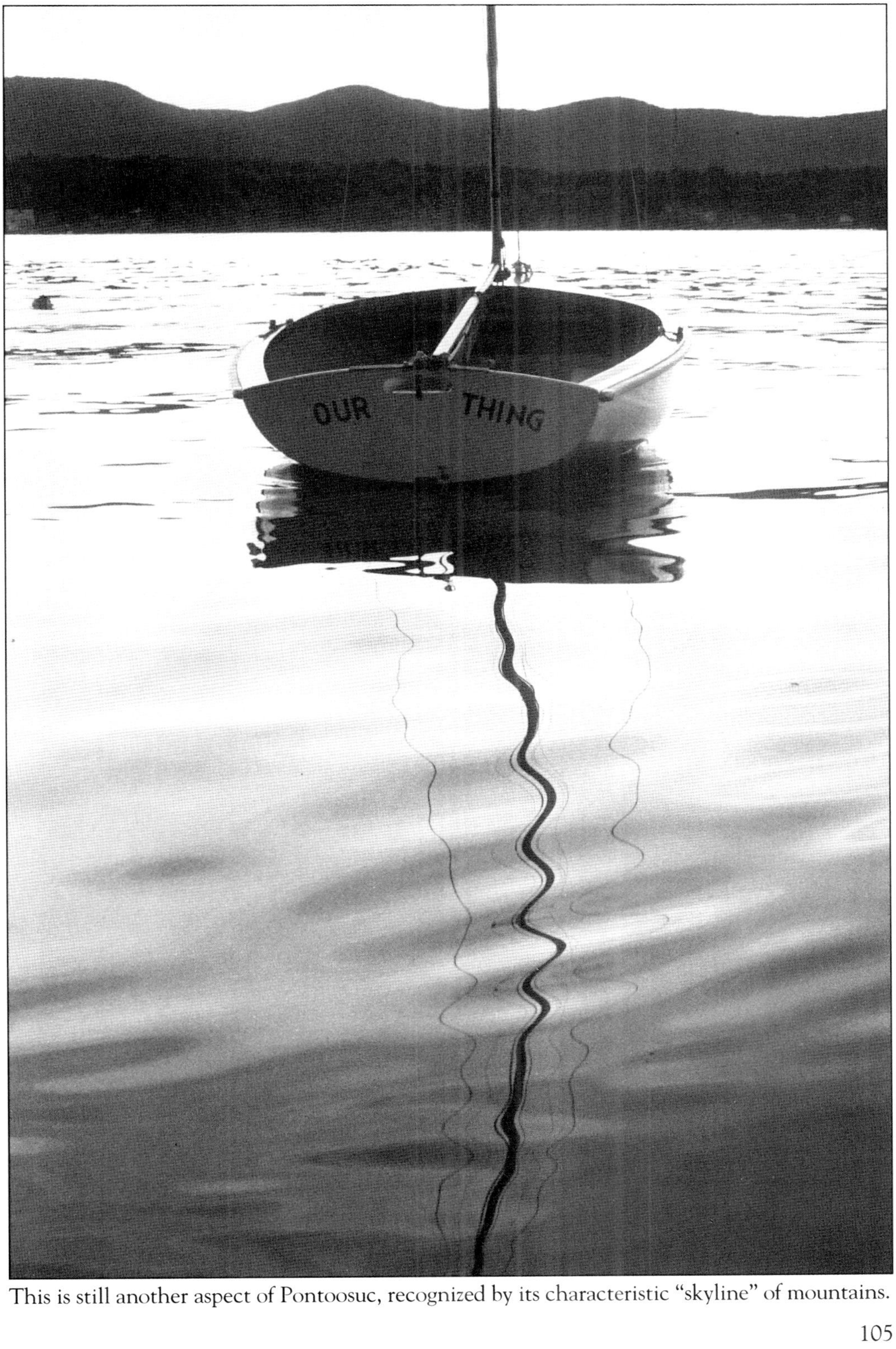

This is still another aspect of Pontoosuc, recognized by its characteristic "skyline" of mountains.

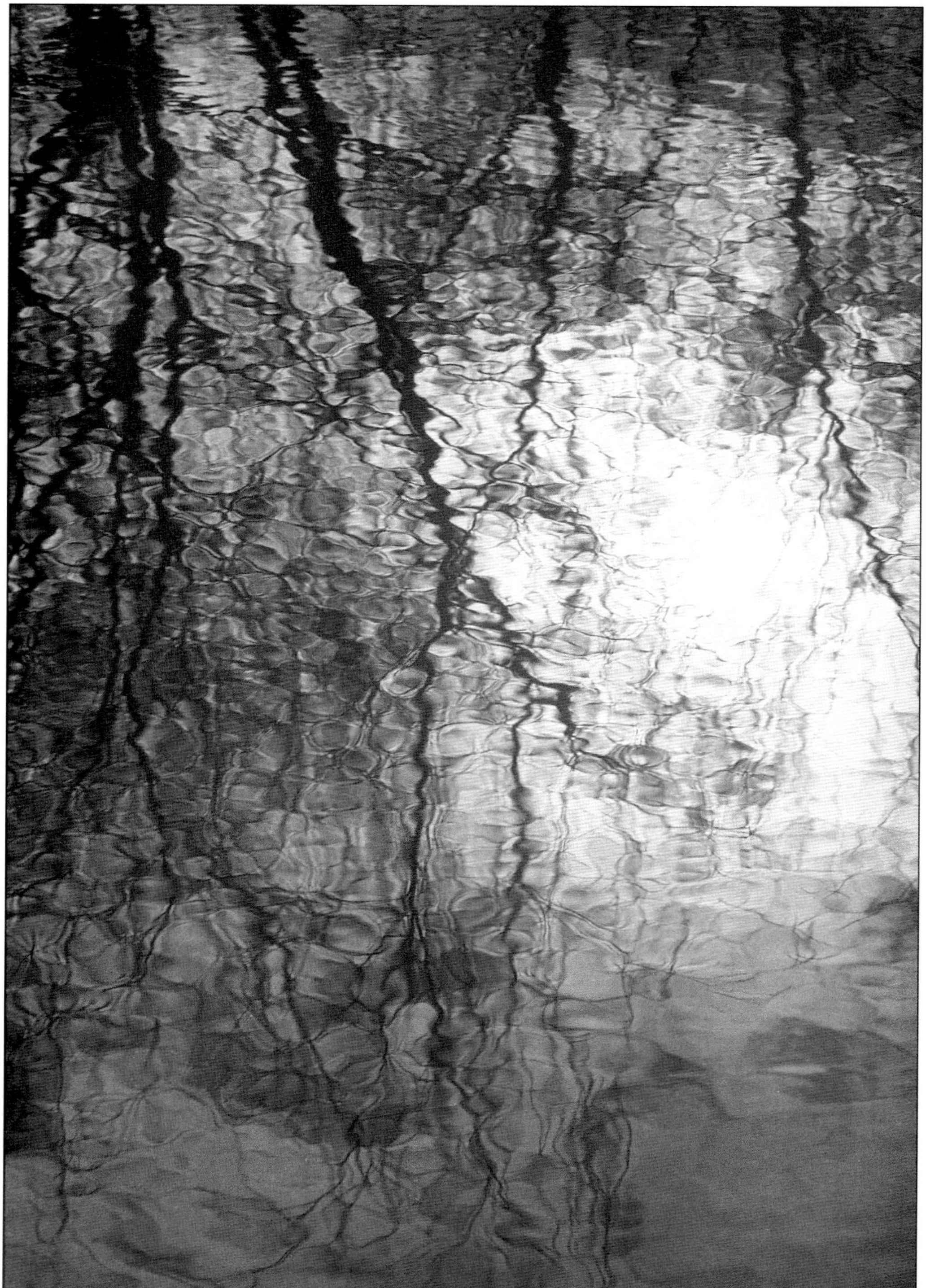

No explanation is needed.

Nine

Dwindling Agricultural Scenes

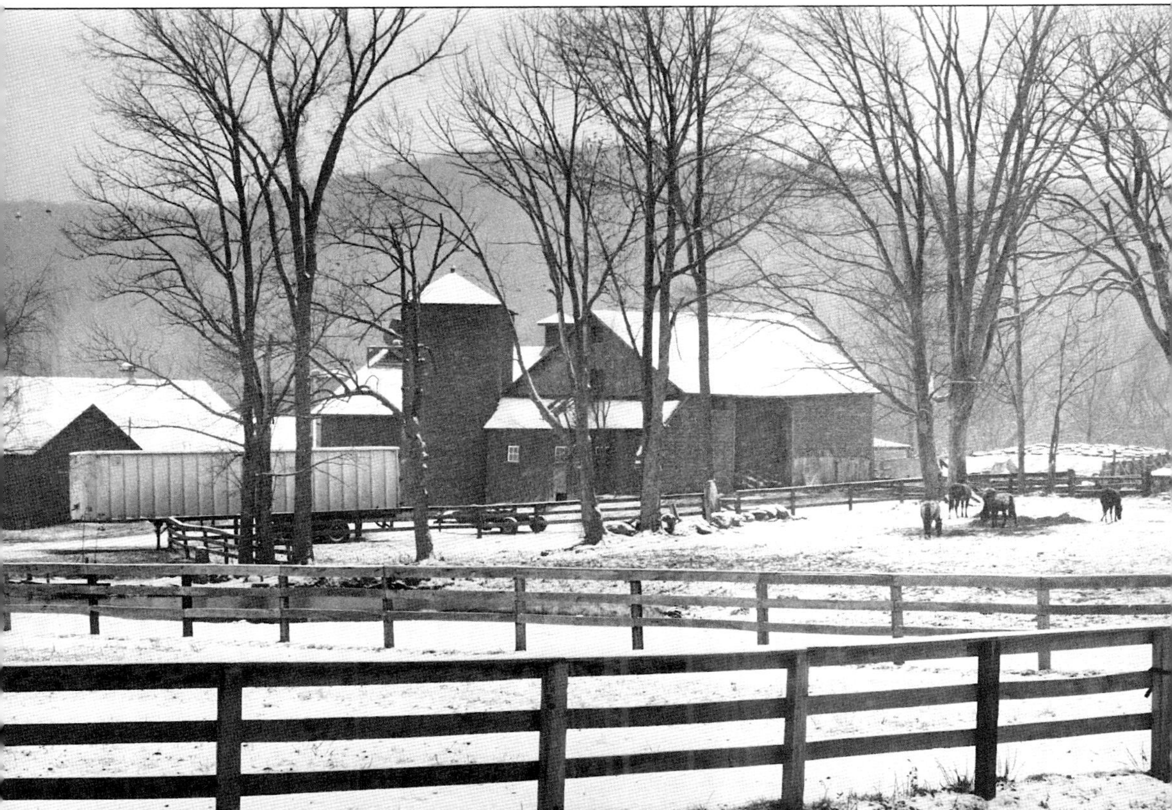

"Farmscape: A touch of white brings out the planes and lines that make up the look of a farm. Though impermanent, snow is an art medium" —November 25, 1978. The subject is the Wirtes farm in Lanesboro.

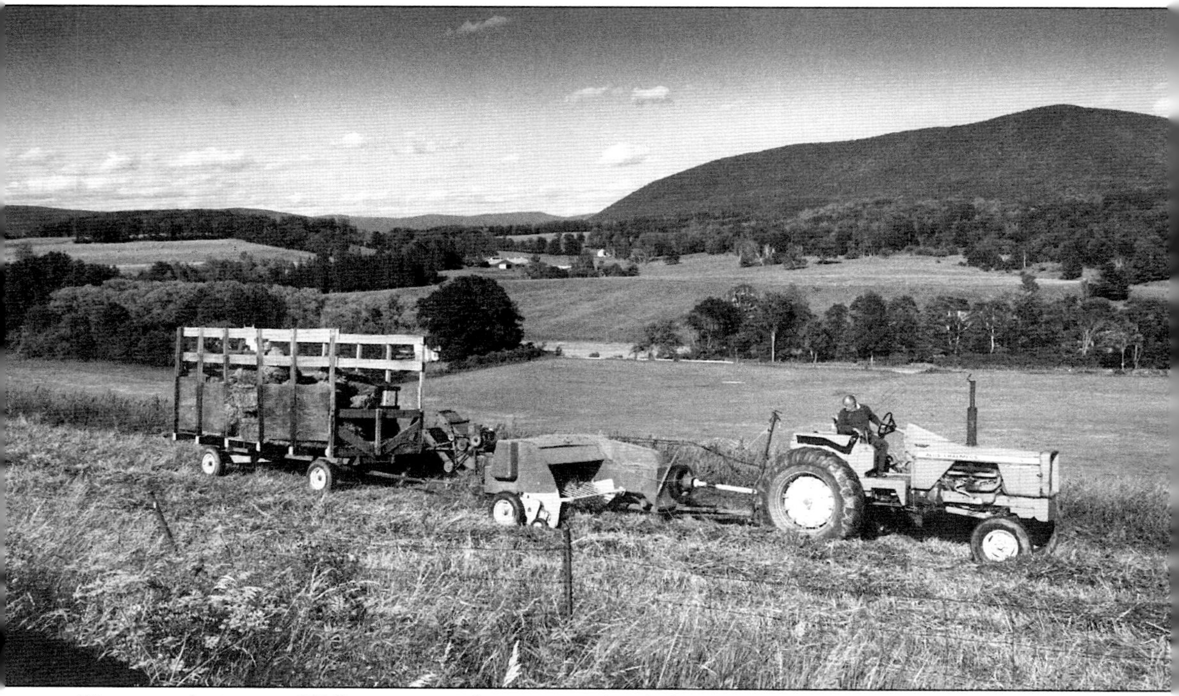

Two grand views in Williamstown of important (and also picturesque) functions in the process of haying: baling, above, and tedding, or the spreading out of the hay to dry, below.

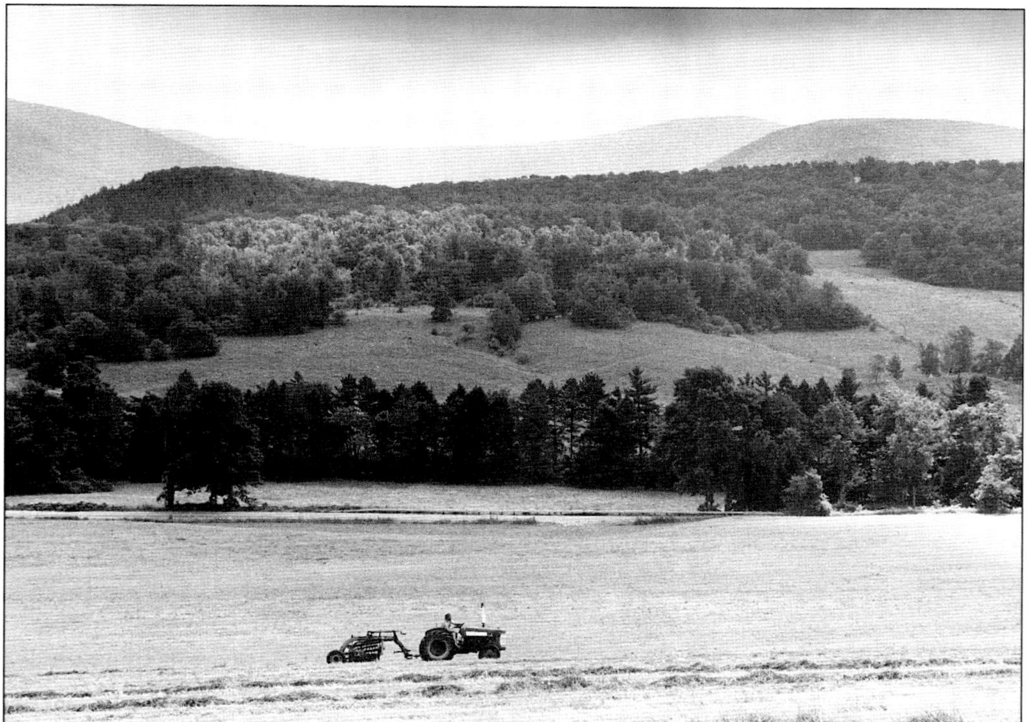

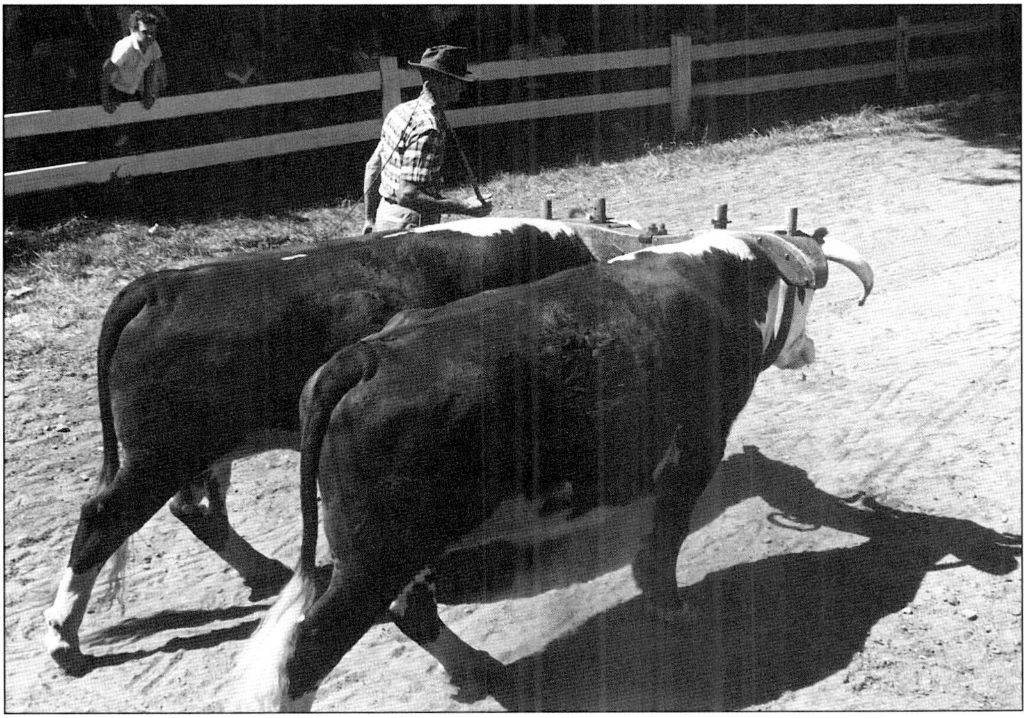

Two pictures of large animals at the Barrington Fair were both taken in the late 1950s: leading a team of oxen, and sharing some shuteye with the cows.

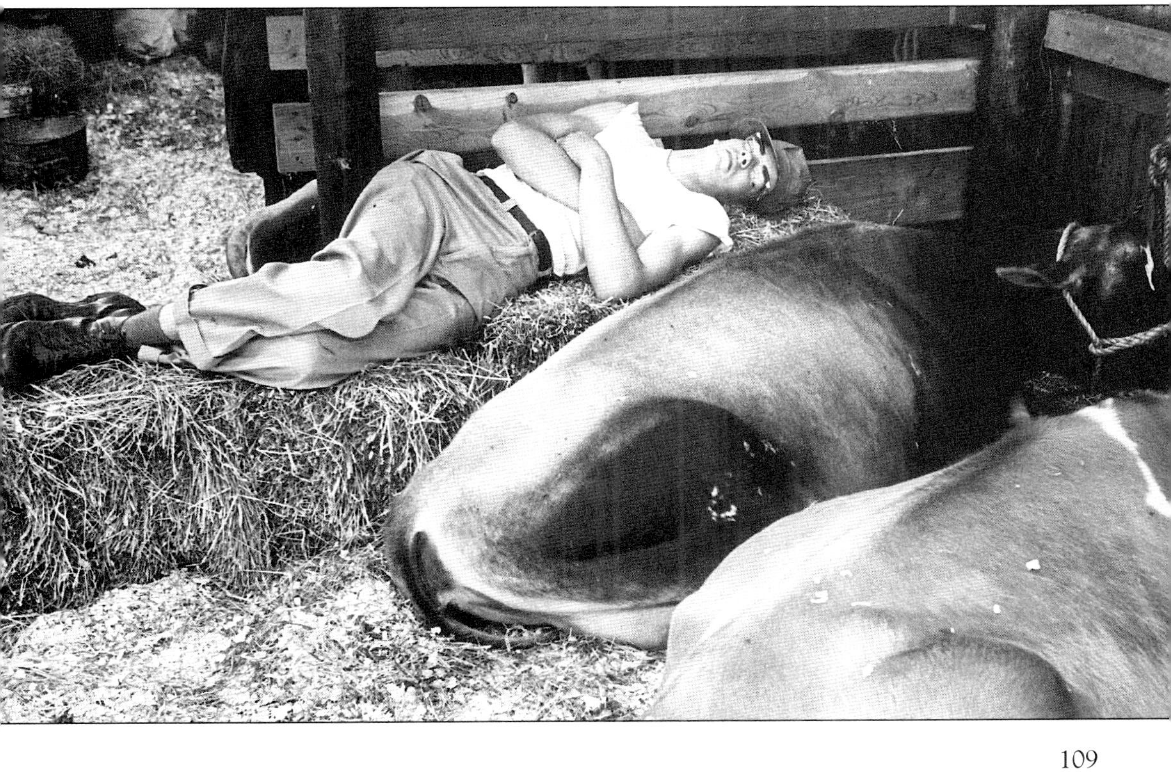

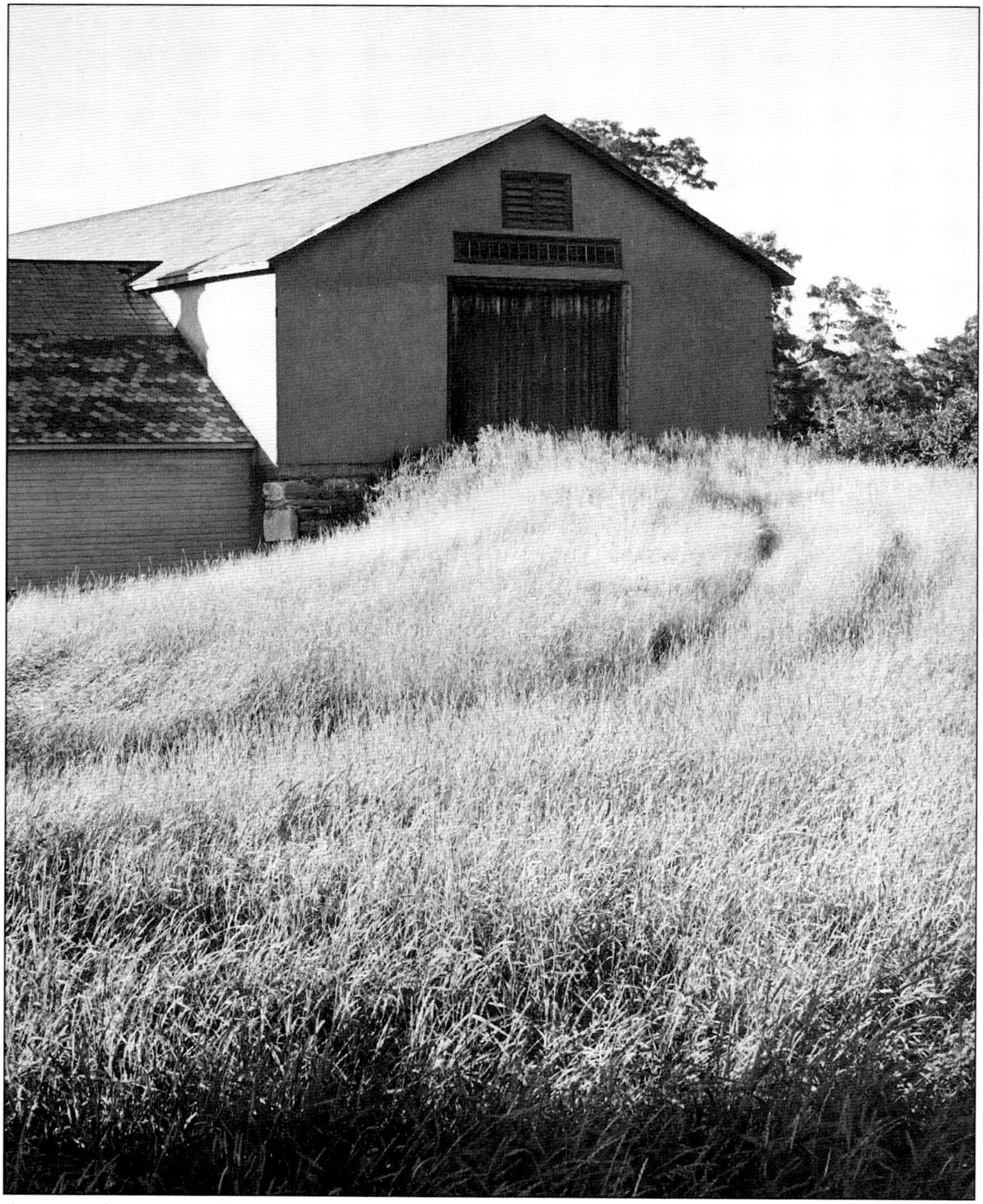

An appealing view of a once-working barn, photographed in July 1971 at the Hancock Shaker Village.

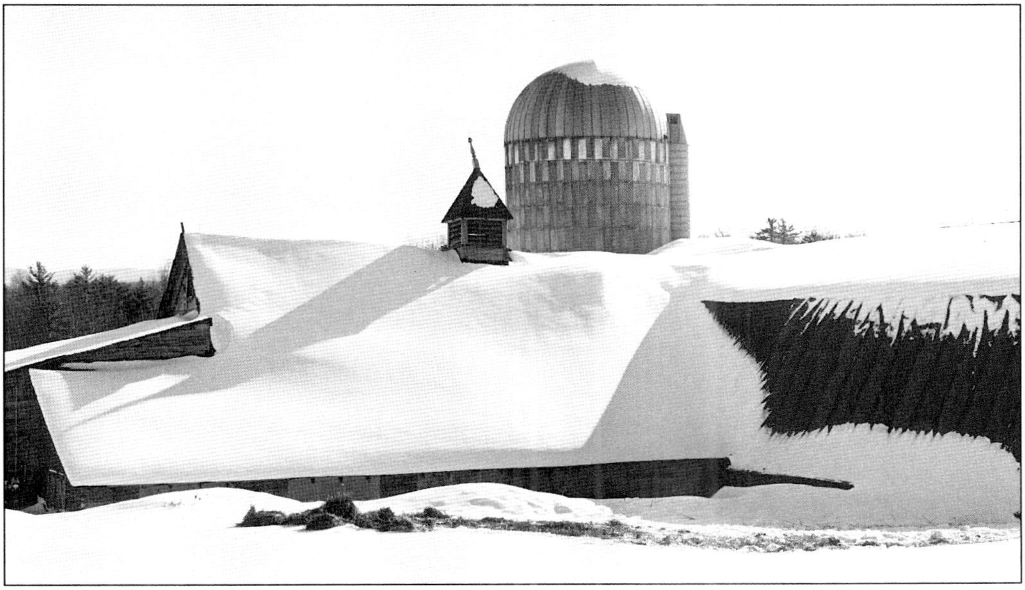

Two pictures that suggest how sturdy New England barns need to withstand vicissitudes of the weather.

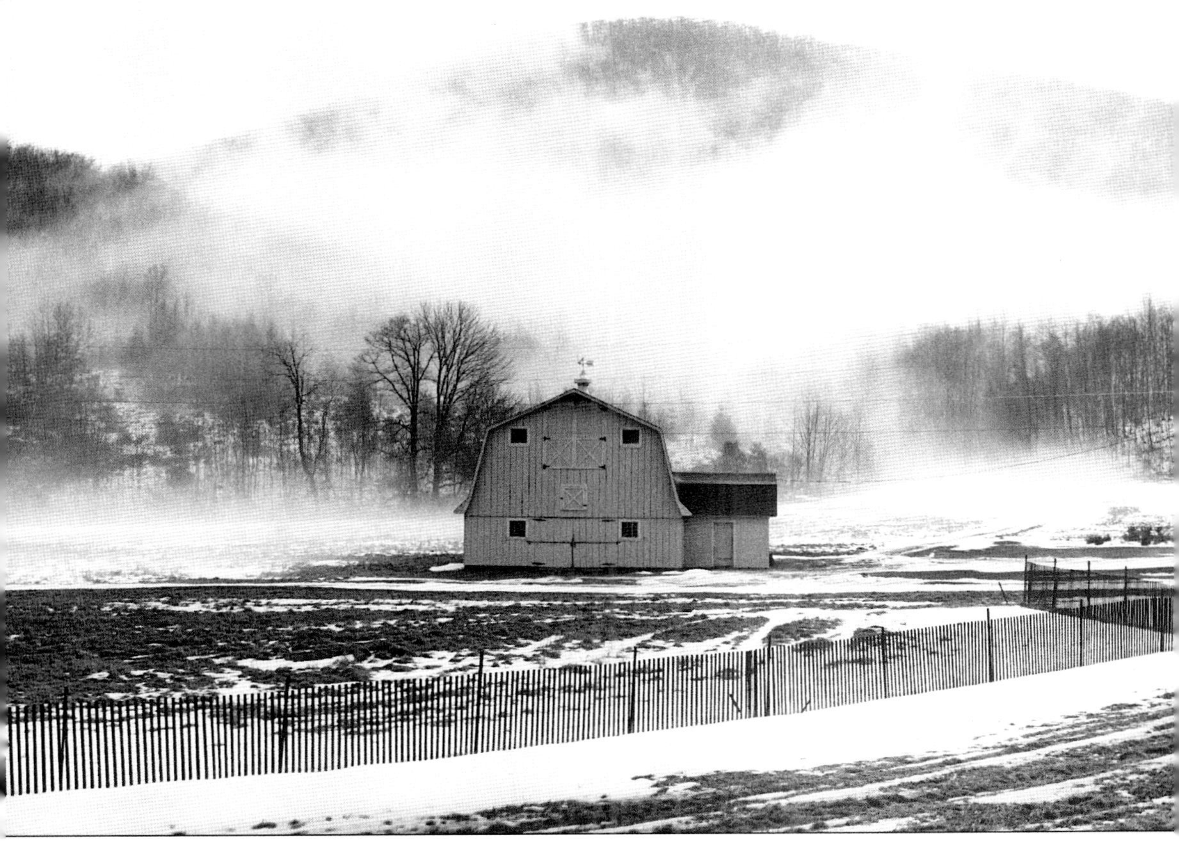

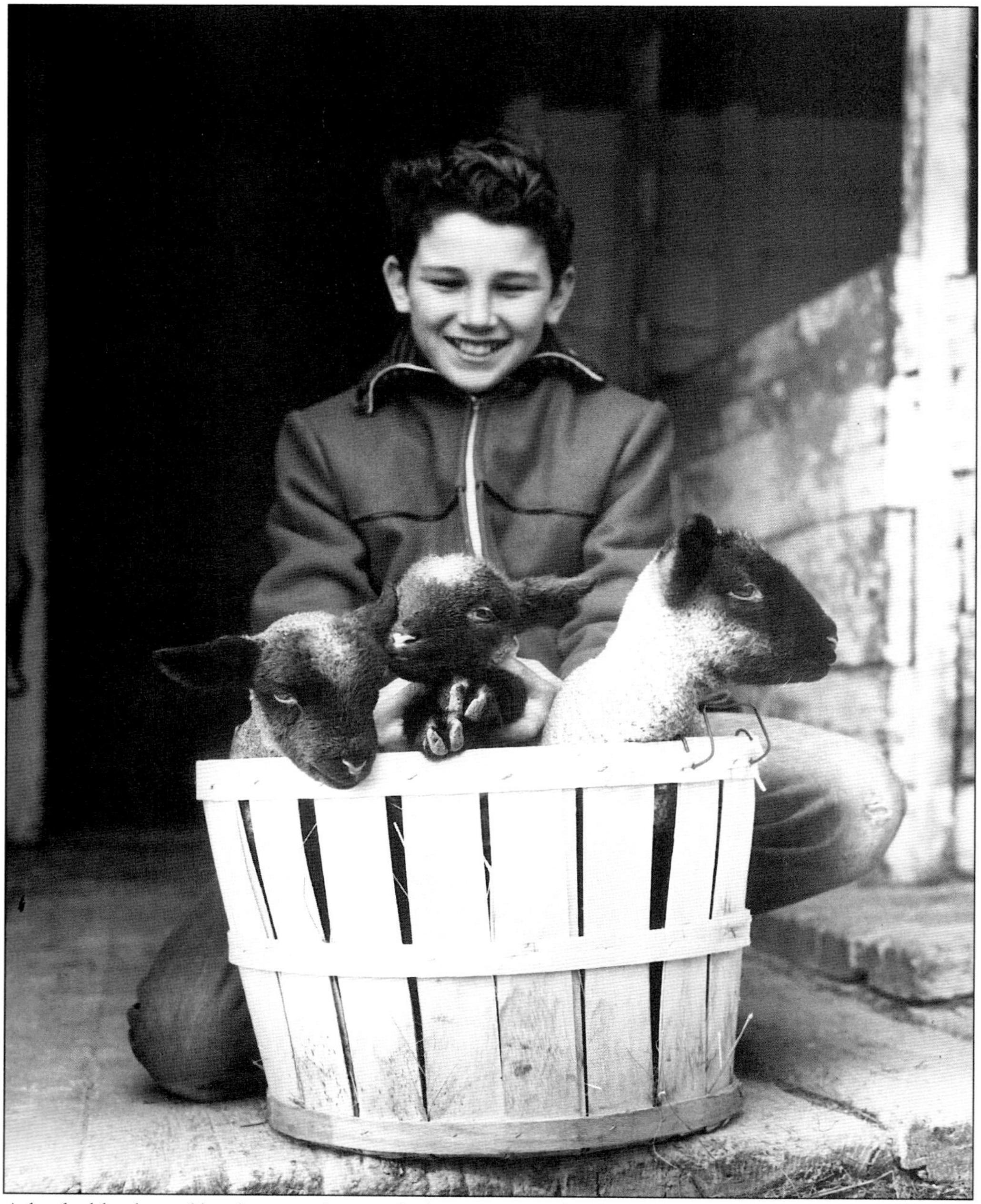

A bushel basket of lambs gets plenty of admiration in this photo taken in March 1959.

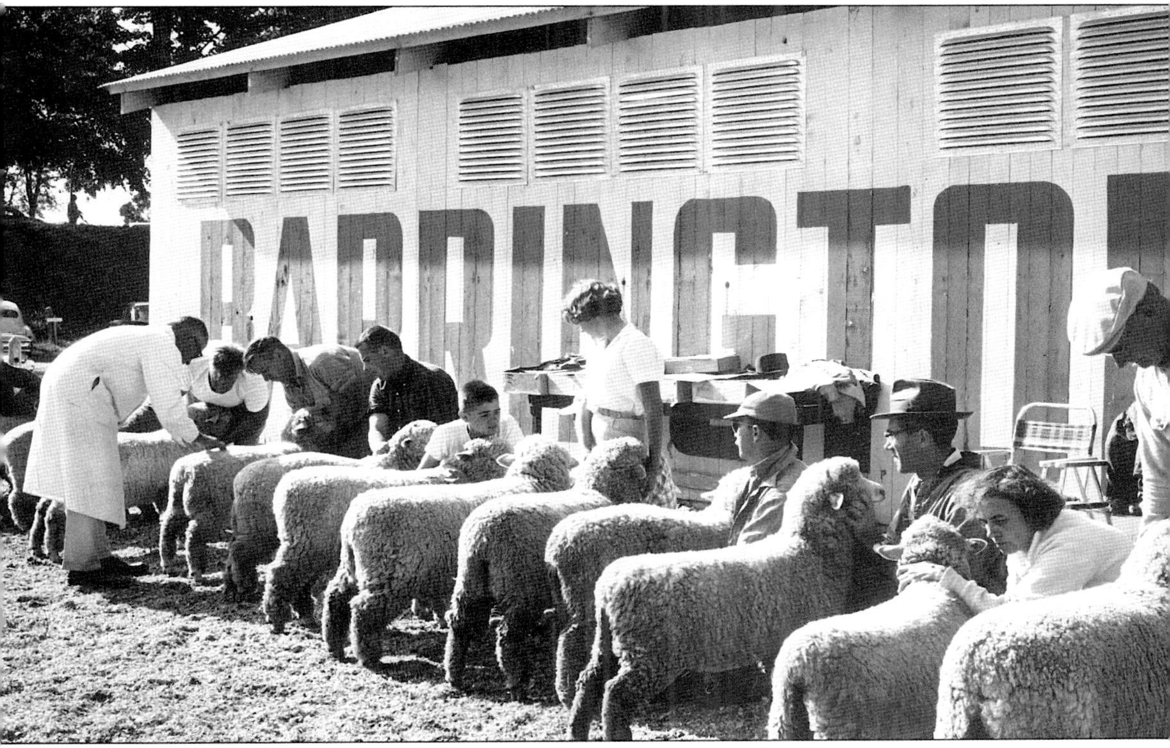

Above, sheep to be shown are lined up for inspection at the Barrington Fairgrounds in September 1959. Below, these gentle beasts always provide a pastoral setting for a photographer with aesthetic instincts.

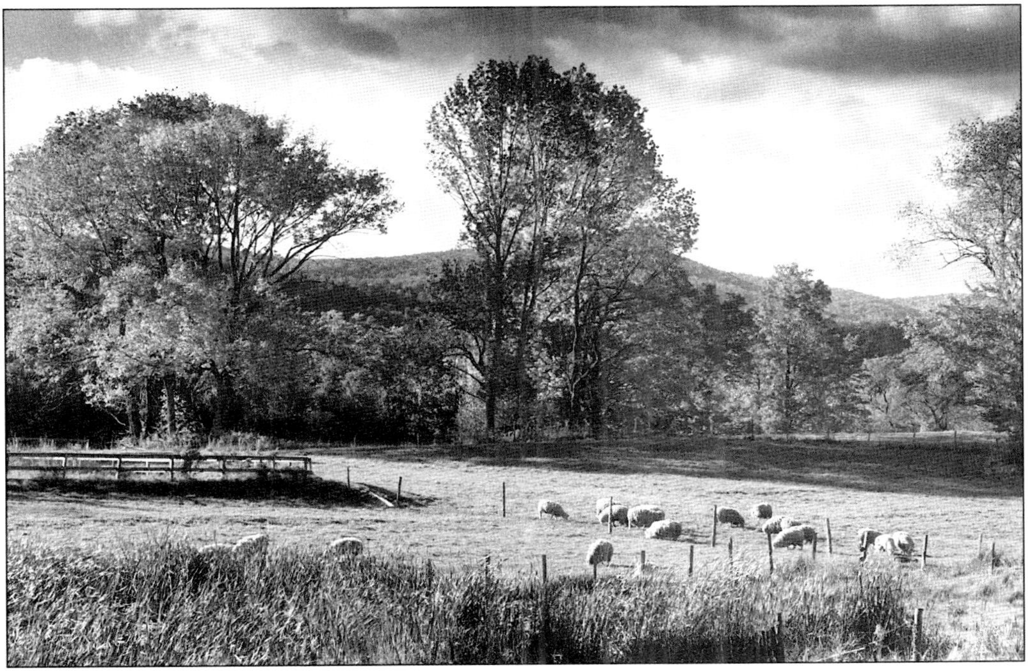

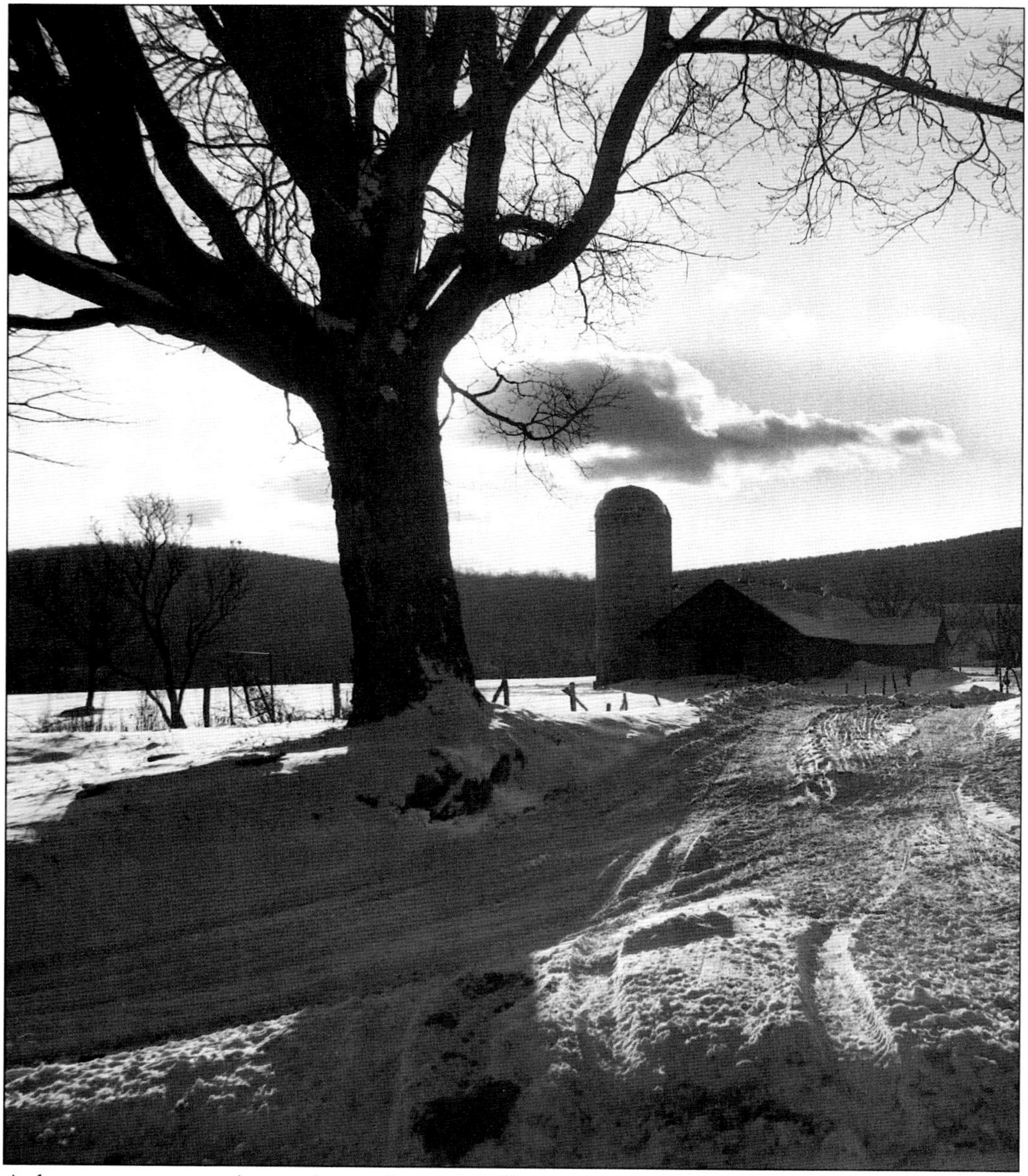
A dormant sugar maple stands guard over a well-worn snow-covered farm road.

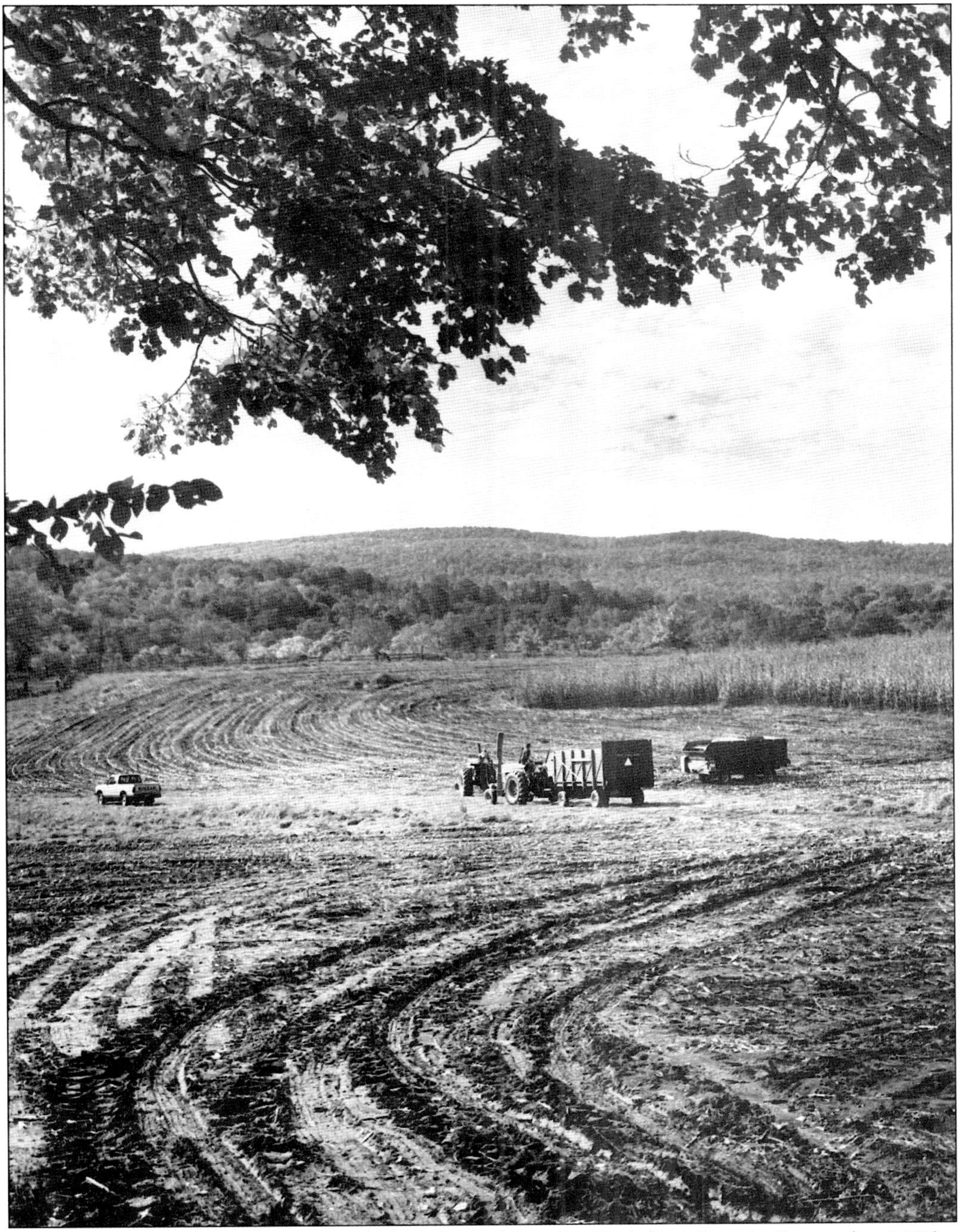

Cutting corn and converting it to silage is the task on this Berkshire farm in September 1986.

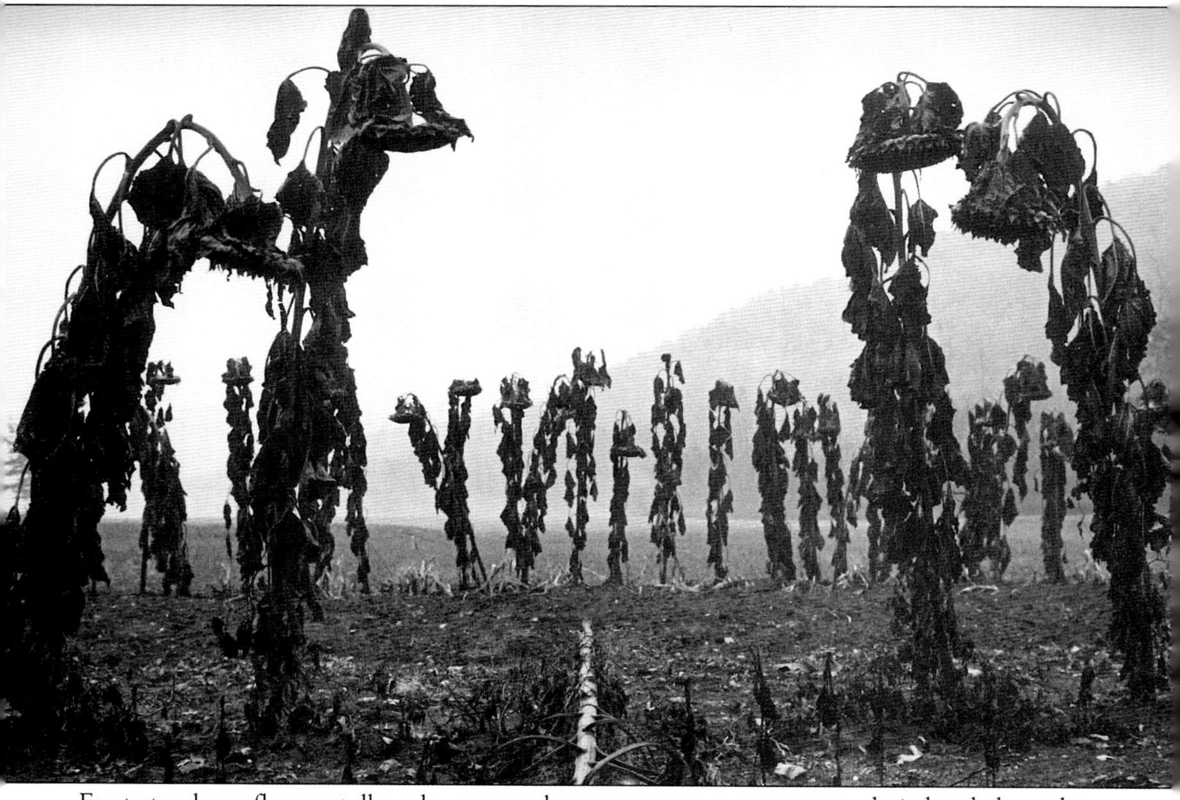

Frost-struck sunflower stalks take on an almost grotesque appearance, their heads bowed in apparent mourning.

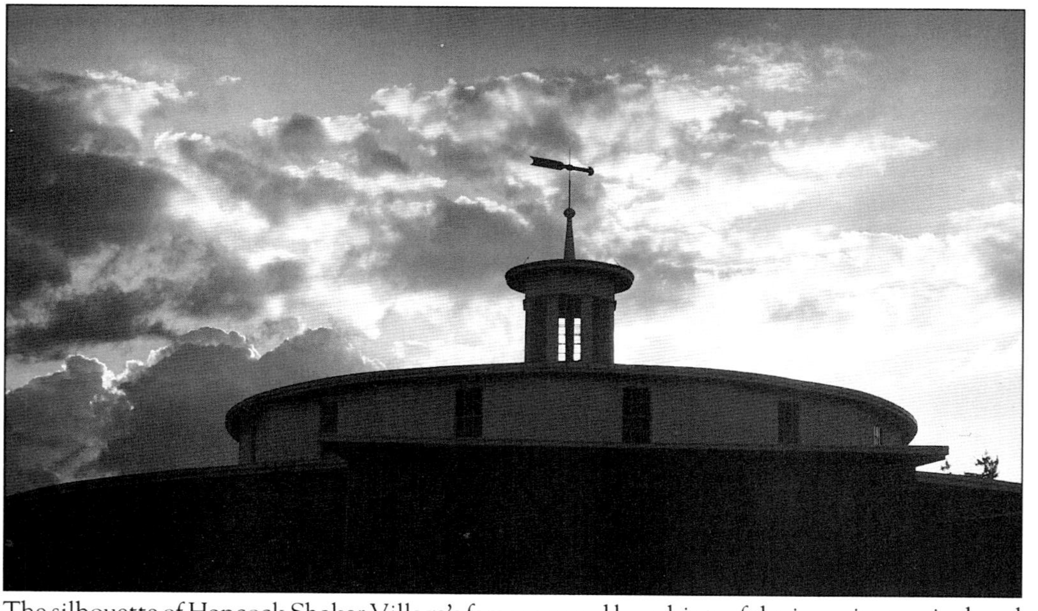

The silhouette of Hancock Shaker Village's famous round barn hints of the ingenious agricultural uses which this building fulfilled in the distant past.

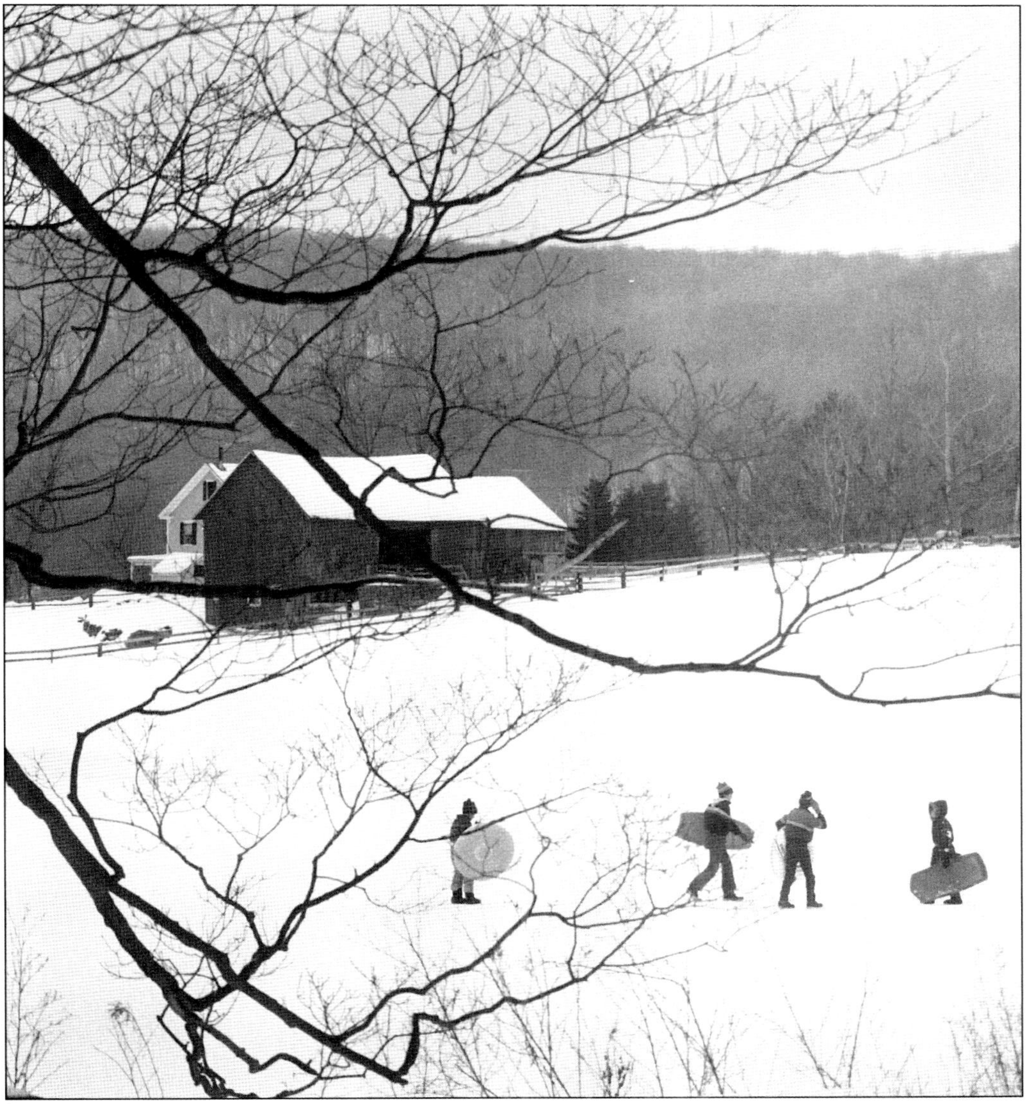

A farmyard can also be used for fun, as these youngsters are doing with their sleds and sliding dishes.

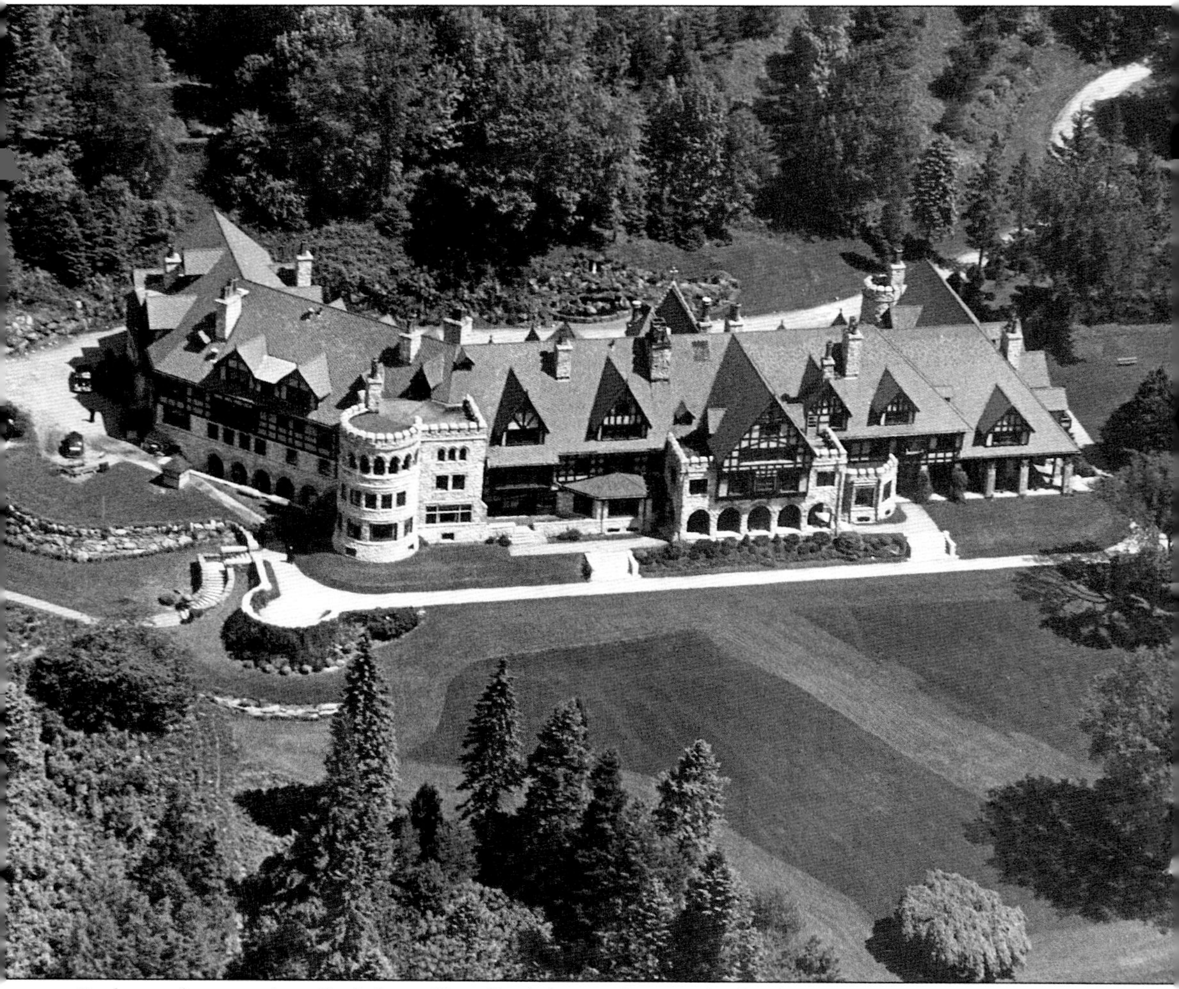

Perhaps the grandest Berkshire "farm" of them all was Shadowbrook in Stockbridge, a 100-room mansion on a spread of 900 acres built in 1894 by Anson Phelps Stokes. Tague took this aerial picture of it in the summer of 1952. It burned in March 1956.

Ten

Silly Signs

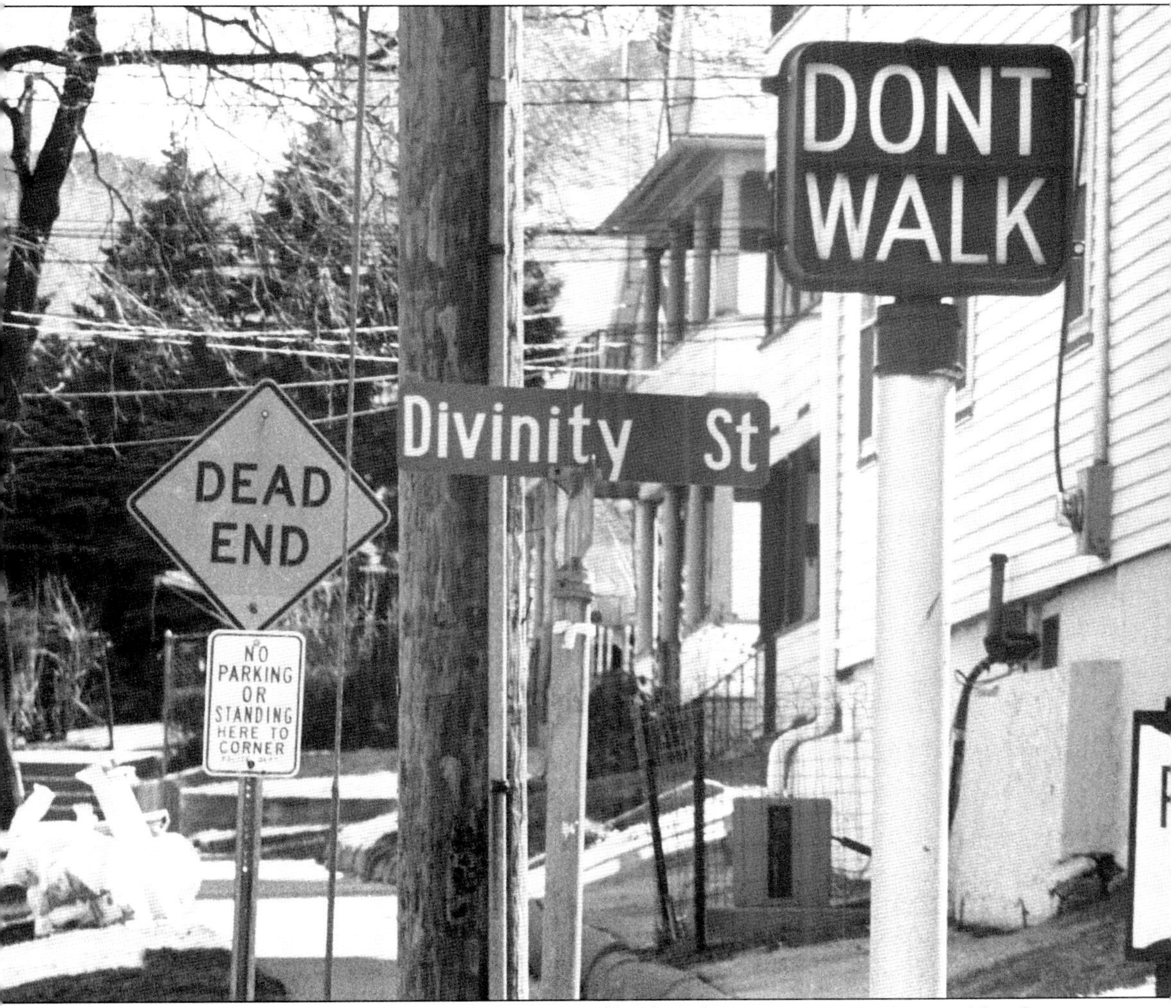

Tague's sense of humor was provoked by especially absurd juxtapositions of signs, like this one with theological overtones.

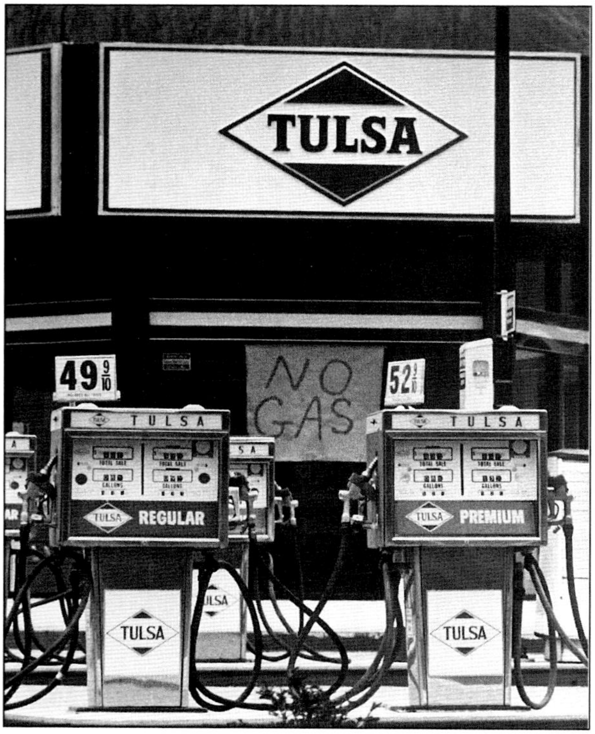

Both the prices per gallon and the "no gas" sign evoke memories of the brief but bewildering gas shortage of January 1974 when there was a crimp in the international supply pipeline.

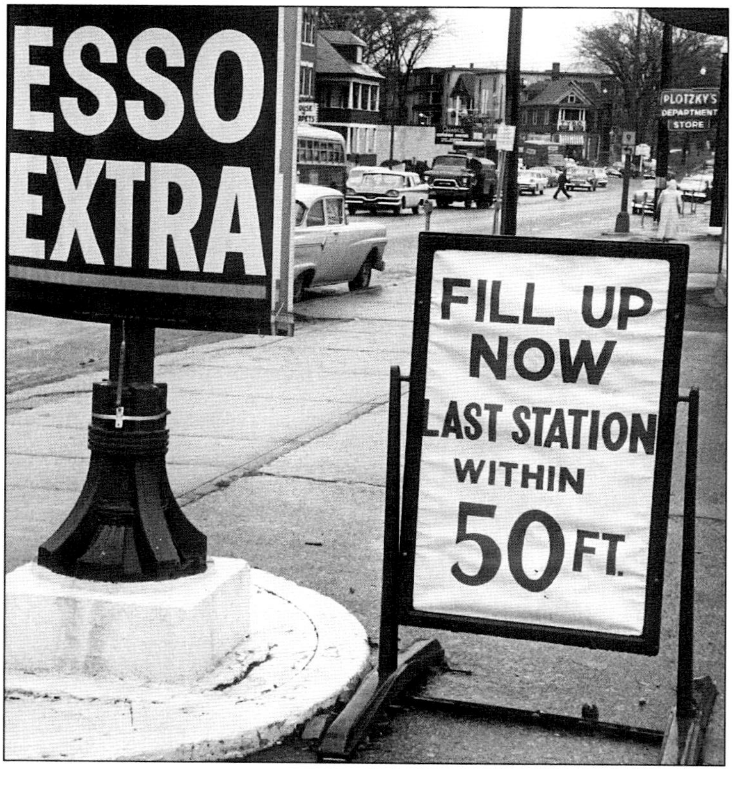

It was October 1958, well before "Esso" was transformed to "Exxon," and this sign was and is just incomprehensible.

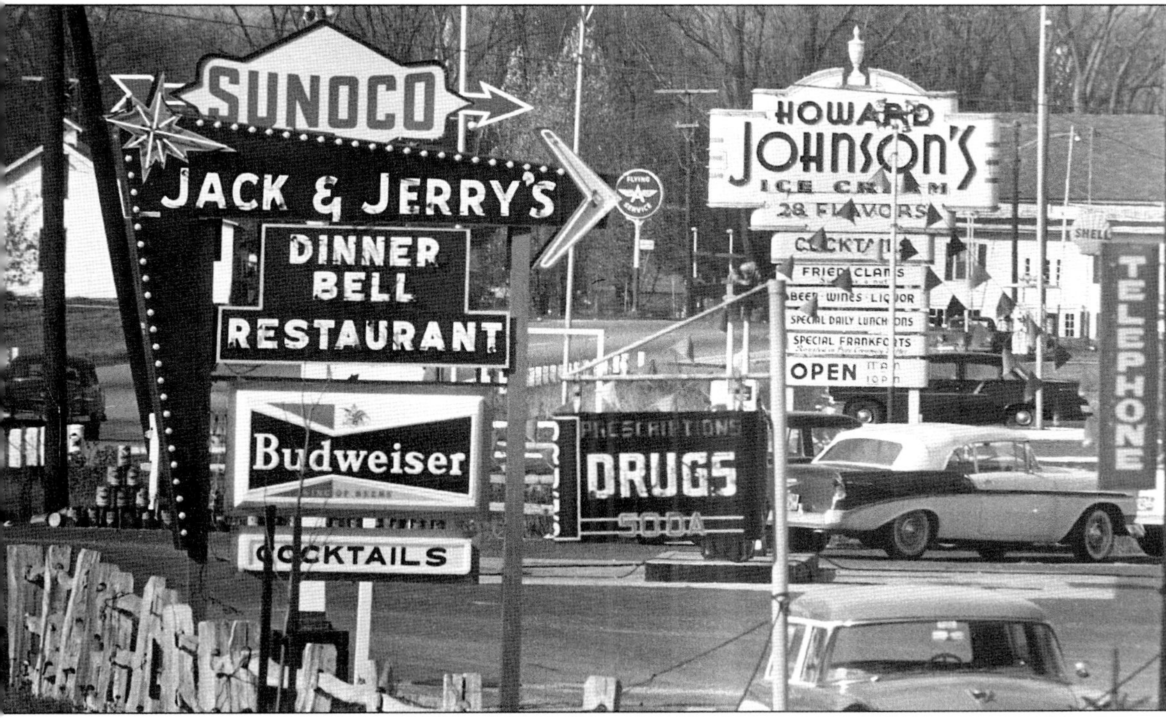

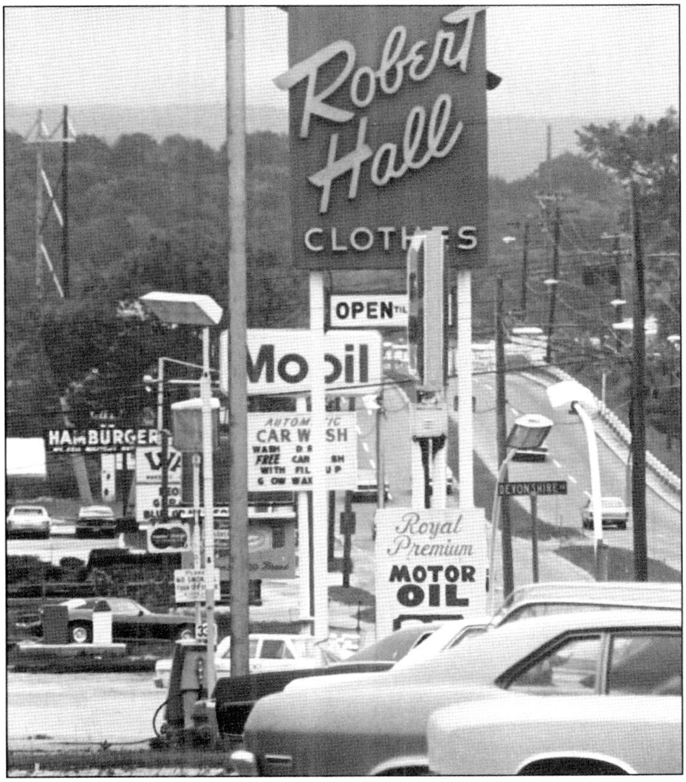

"Berkshire sign blight" was a favorite of target of Tague's, and he was capable of interpreting them starkly, as these two scenes demonstrate. The picture above was taken in the late 1950s along Route 2 on the Williamstown-North Adams Road.

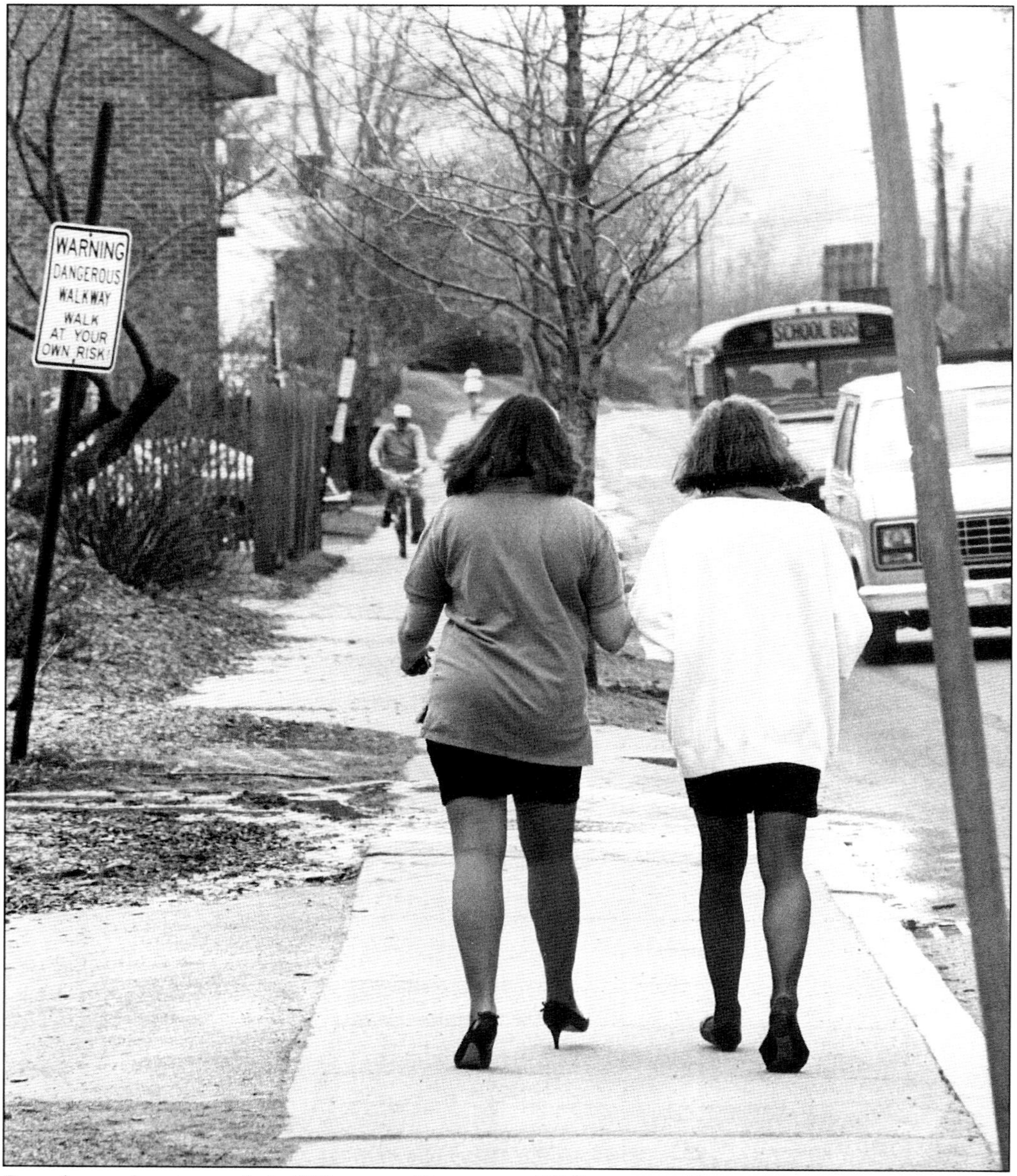

Somehow, the sign at left, "Warning: Dangerous Walkway. Walk at your own risk!" is an apt one for these North Adams coeds with their short-short skirts and pointy heels.

Eleven

Togetherness

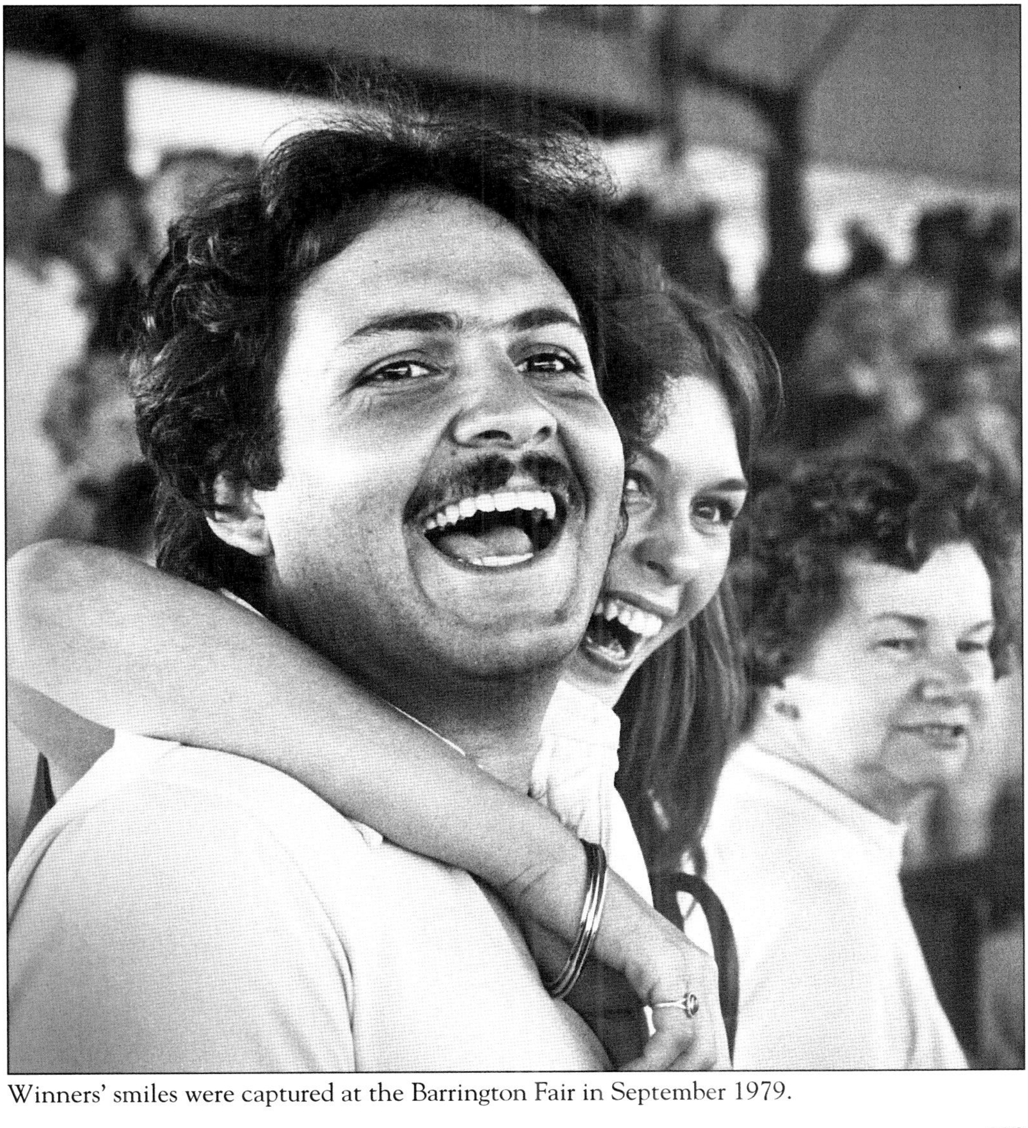

Winners' smiles were captured at the Barrington Fair in September 1979.

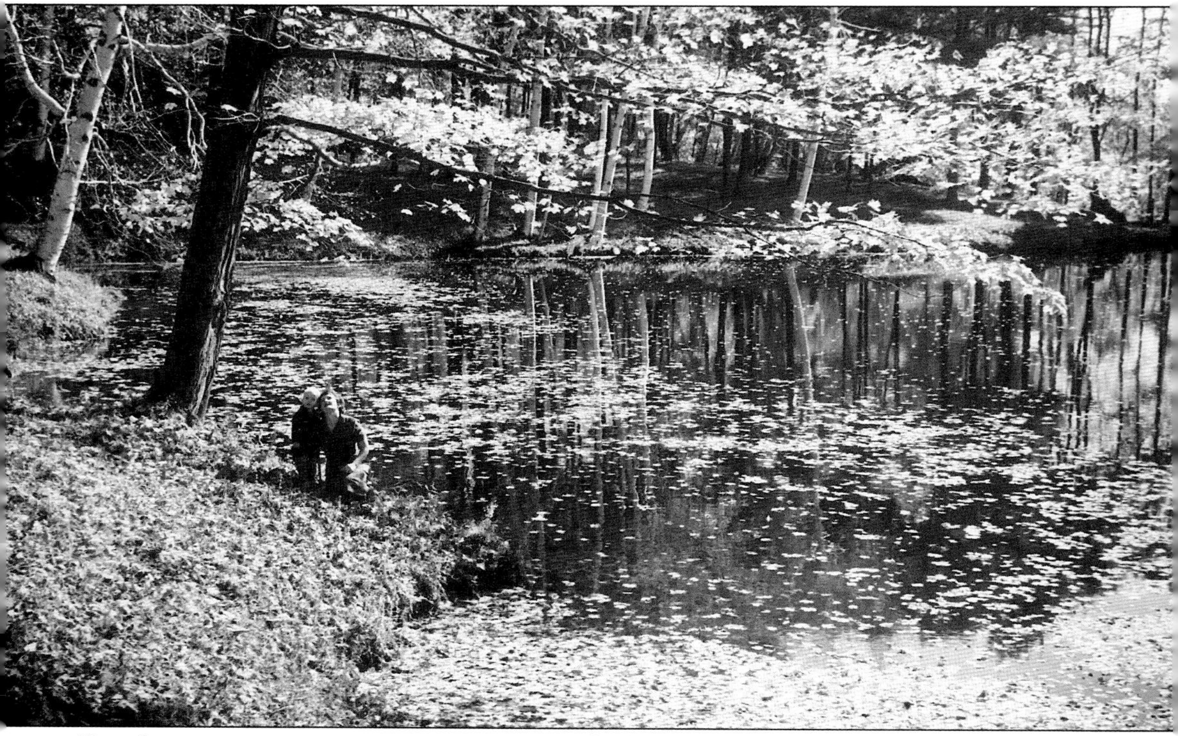

Togetherness suggests uncommon proximity, whether it takes place at a leaf-covered pond in autumn, above, or on a hot summer's day at the lake.

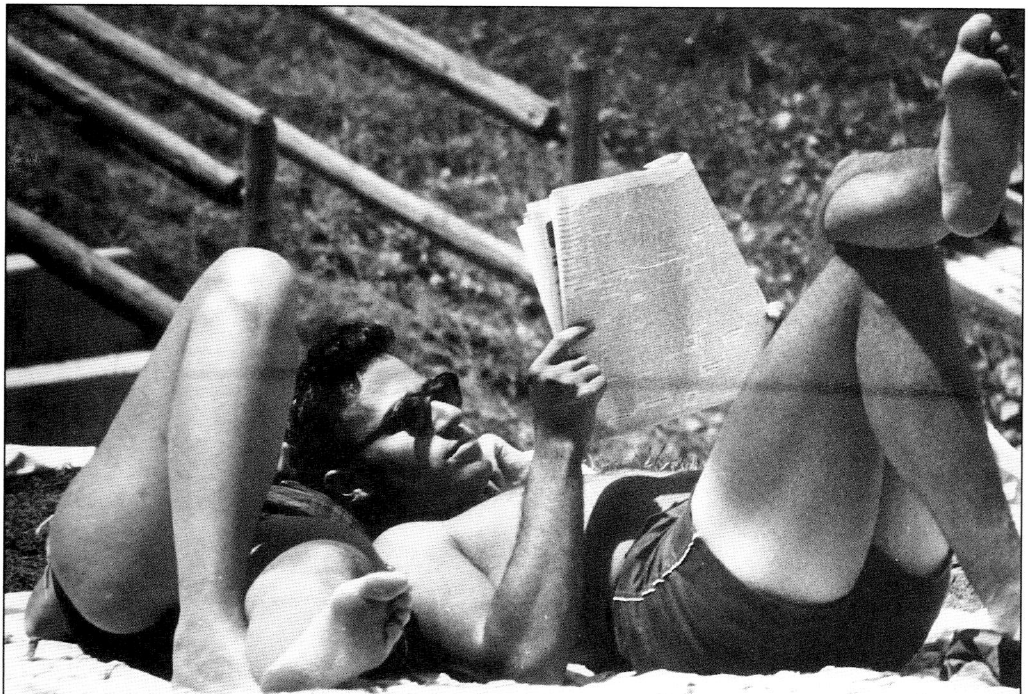

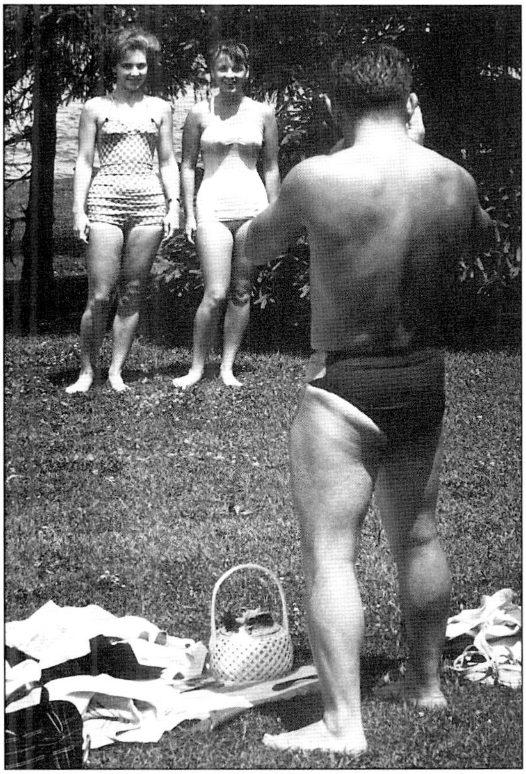

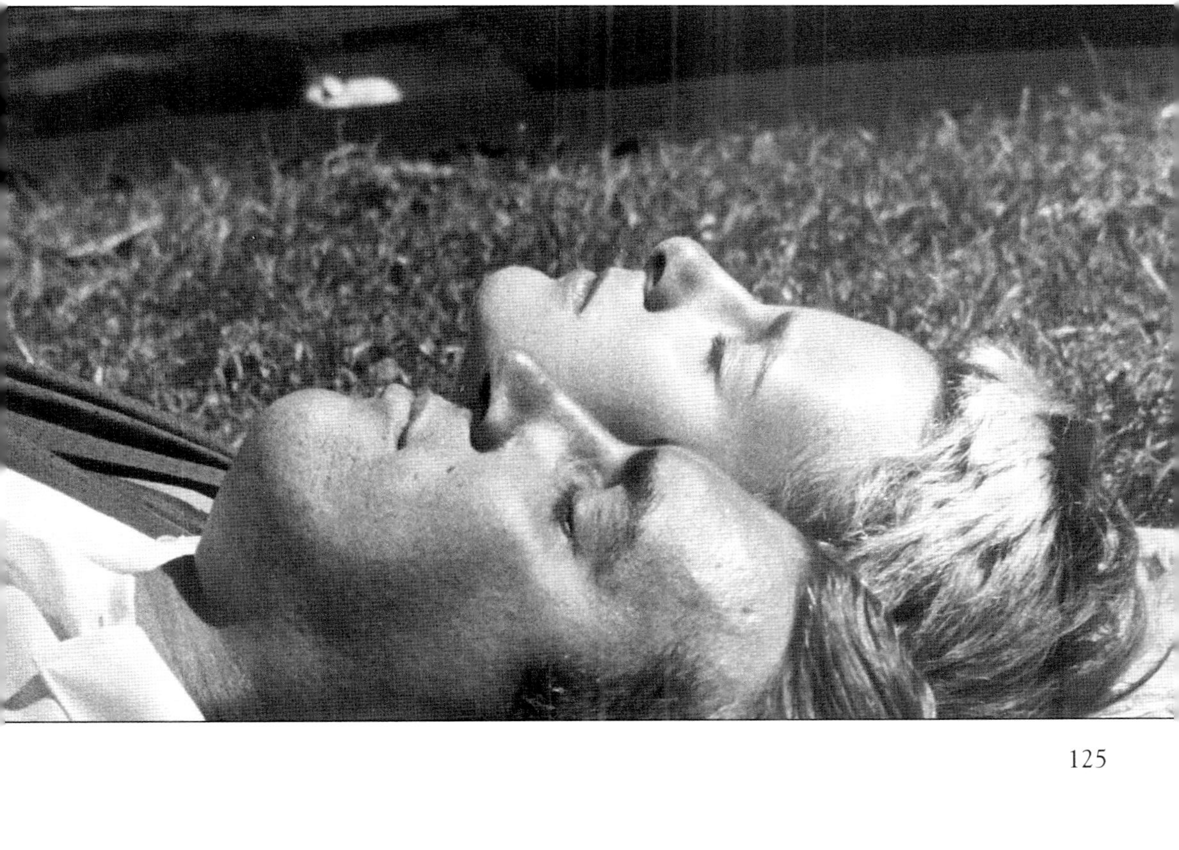

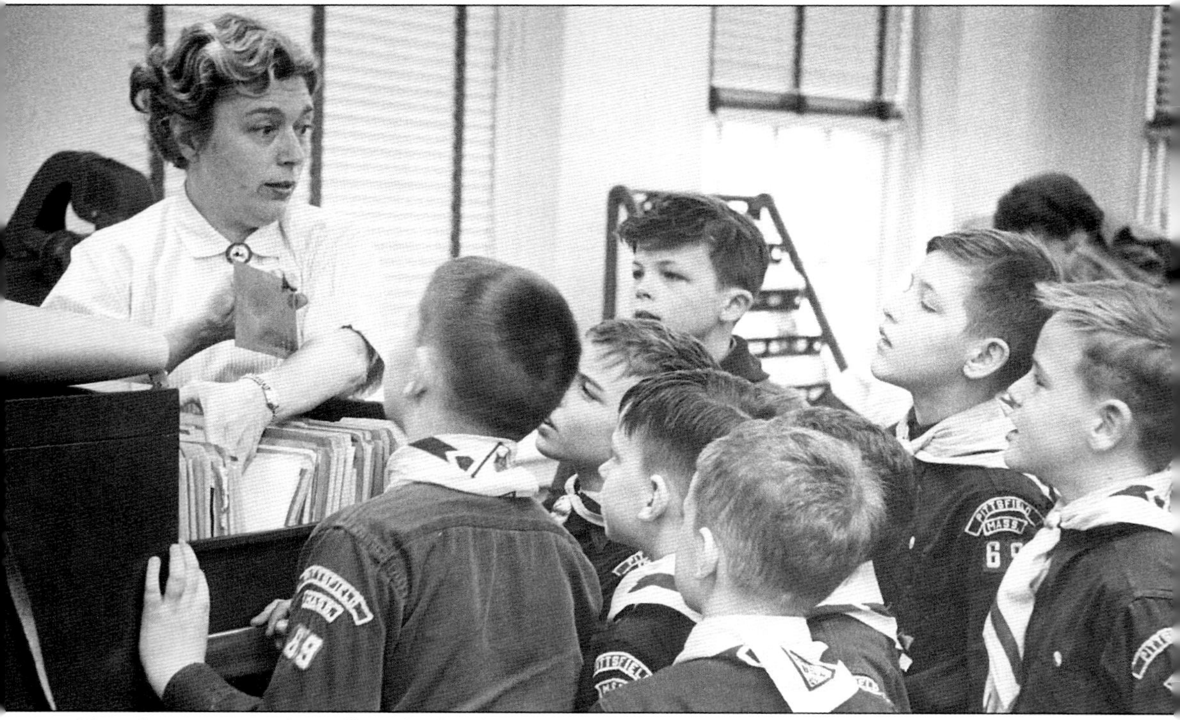

Togetherness can also reflect the herding instinct, as seen among these Boy Scouts on a tour of the *Berkshire Eagle* offices in February 1957, with writer Lee Leahy as their guide.

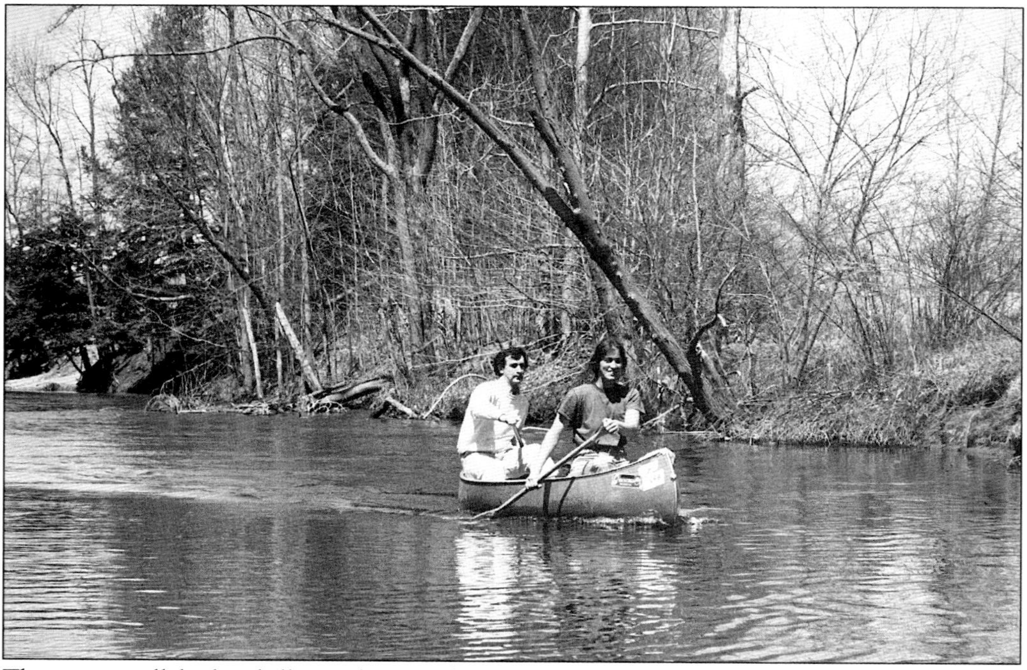

The water still looks chilly in this April 1978 picture of a couple enjoying an early canoe excursion.

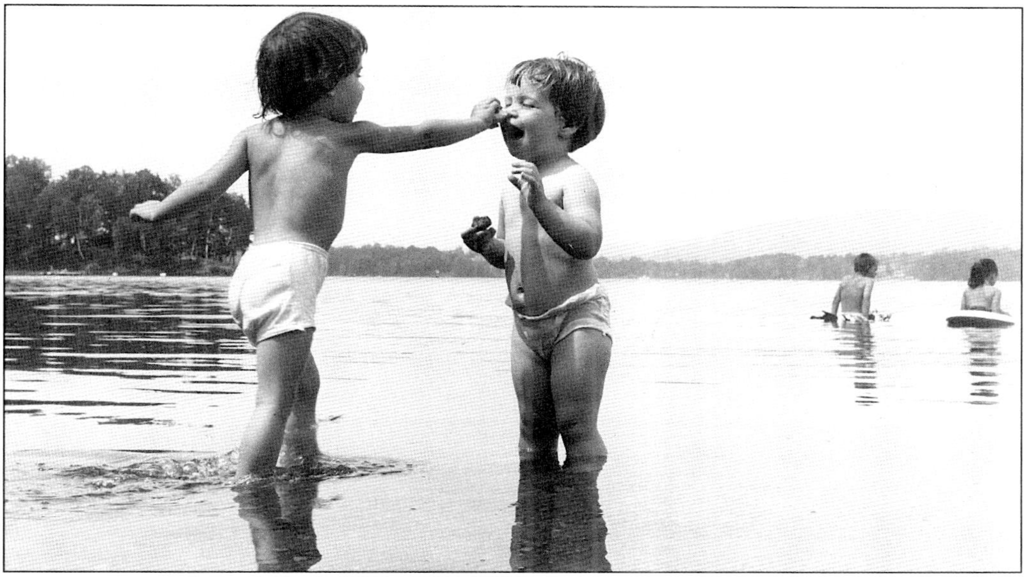

"Take that" has to be the title of this expressive 1957 scene of very young bathers in shallow waters of Pontoosuc Lake.

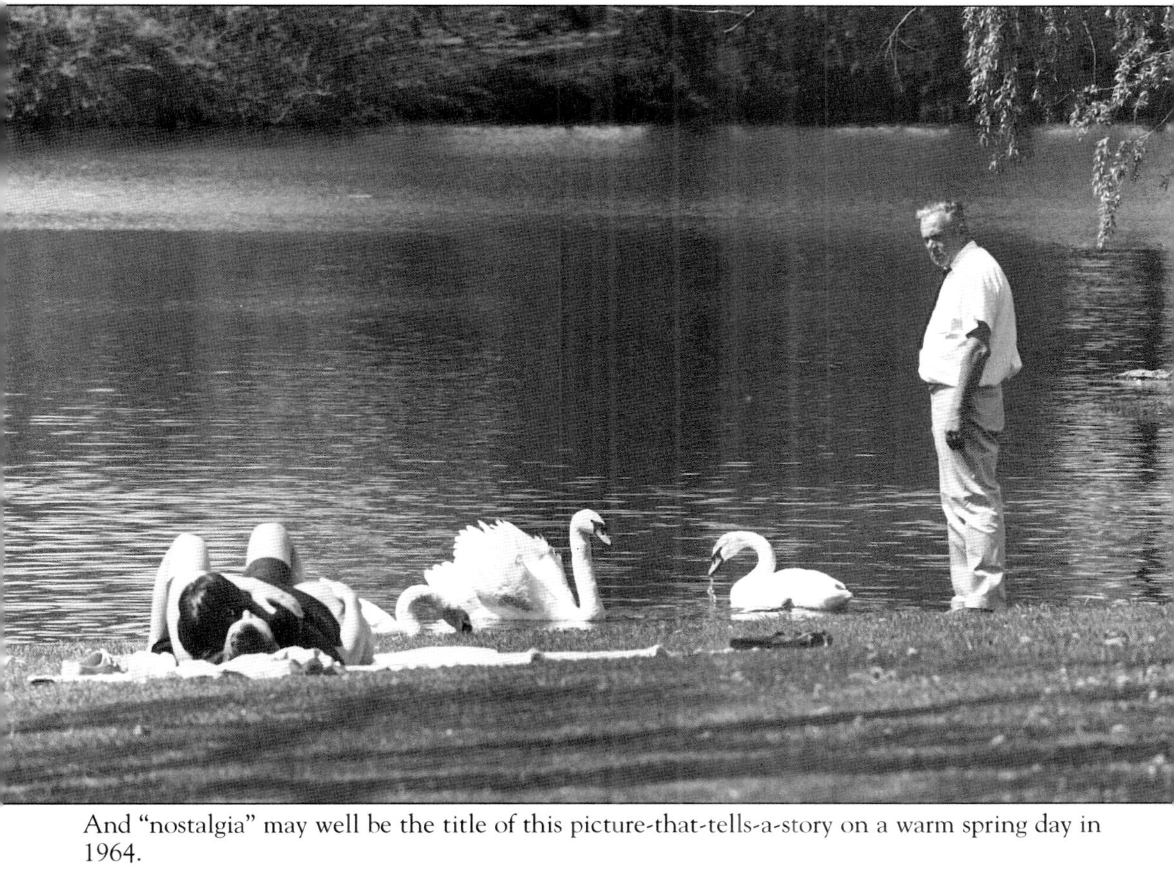

And "nostalgia" may well be the title of this picture-that-tells-a-story on a warm spring day in 1964.

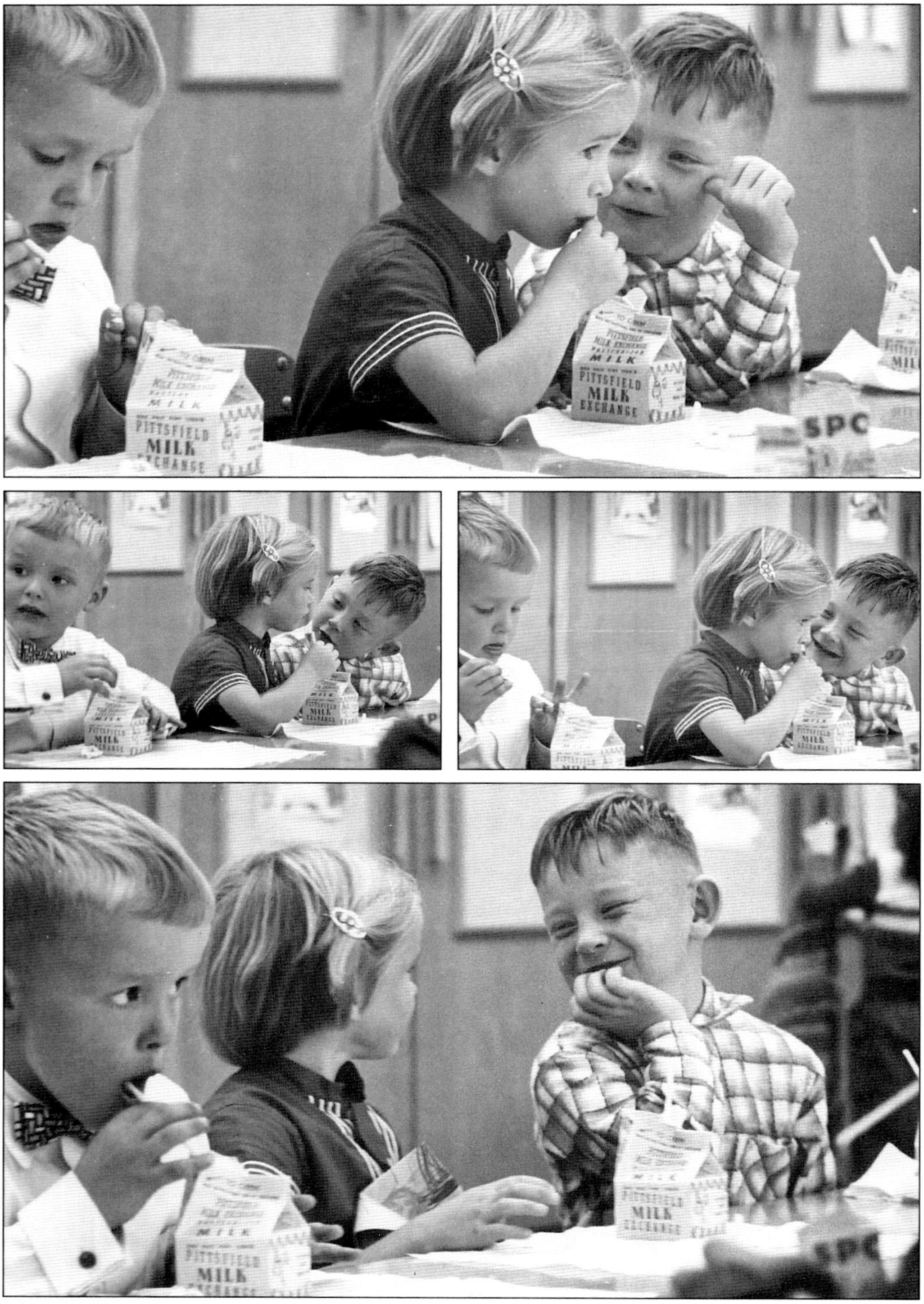

This "kindergarten comedy" at the Allendale School in October 1955 involved Pamela Read and Tommy Gardner.